WINNING
7-CARD STUD

WINNING
7-CARD STUD

TRANSFORMING HOME GAME
CHUMPS INTO CASINO KILLERS

Ashley Adams

LYLE STUART
Kensington Publishing Corp.
www.kensingtonbooks.com

LYLE STUART BOOKS are published by

Kensington Publishing Corp.
850 Third Avenue
New York, NY 10022

All Kensington titles, imprints, and distributed lines are available at special quantity discounts for bulk purchases for sales promotions, premiums, fund-raising, educational, or institutional use. Special book excerpts or customized printings can also be created to fit specific needs. For details, write or phone the office of the Kensington special sales manager: Kensington Publishing Corp., 850 Third Avenue, New York, NY 10022, attn: Special Sales Department; phone 1-800-221-2647.

Lyle Stuart is a trademark of Kensington Publishing Corp.

First printing: November 2003

10 9 8 7 6 5 4 3 2

Designed by Leonard Telesca

Printed in the United States of America

ISBN 0-8184-0635-6

To Deborah Fishbein Adams,
the best hand I've ever been dealt.

Contents

Preface

I couldn't believe it! I stood at the cashier and counted to myself, "900, 1,000, 1,100." I continued quietly, "1,200, 1,300, 1,400, 1,500, 1,600 . . . " I paused when I was done and said to myself, "Oh, my God! I have $2,300!"

As it turned out, when I subtracted the $300 I used to buy in to the $5/10 limit game at Foxwoods Casino twelve hours earlier, and when I added in the stray bills and chips I found in my pocket, I was ahead $2,085 after twelve hours of play. This was not a fortune, to be sure. But for me, a very conservative poker player, having played casino poker for only two years at the time, it seemed like a miracle of good luck.

There was no miracle of course. Sure, there was a good bit of luck that went with the win, but it was also the product of playing consistently excellent poker for twelve hours against poor opposition.

It was about 6:00 A.M. Sunday morning. I went home shortly thereafter, exhausted but exhilarated. When I added this win to my poker bank account that I had been keeping for about two years, I had nearly $7,000. Not bad for someone who, just two years prior, had been happy booking a $40 win in his $1/2 home game.

Admittedly, this was an extraordinary experience. In fact, as it turned out, this was more than I would ever win again in a session of $5/10 poker (though I have won more at high stakes sessions). To be honest, there have been many sessions of only double-digit wins and quite a few with losses as well. But overall, after thousands of hours of play, I have won many thousands of dollars playing poker. It has allowed me to pay for poker trips to many places while having a great time along the way.

I am a consistent winner at 7-Card Stud games from $1–$5 to $15/30. Frankly, I've learned that it's not all that hard to win once you figure out a few basic concepts and learn to patiently and diligently apply them.

I've learned skills that have helped me win in the casino poker game. I'd like to share them with you. And, yes, I believe that I know full well the mistakes and traps that typical players tend to fall into when they play—because *I've made them!* Thanks to these winning and losing experiences, I'm confident that I'll be able to help you make money and avoid the pitfalls that await you in your local casino or public card room.

Through it all, I've noticed that many players who played poker in high school or college, who enjoy poker in their kitchen and as a relaxing and entertaining activity, and who do well at it, are often reluctant to sit down in a casino poker game. They're intimidated, maybe afraid, and certainly confused by the speed and the strategy of this different form of poker. Some have jumped in anyway, gotten hurt, and then vowed never to go back. Most have just stayed away, figuring that it's better to keep to the safer and more secure waters of their home game or not to play poker at all.

This doesn't have to be the case. If one takes a simple, incremental approach to casino poker, the casual player can make it as much fun as his home game or the game he played in high school or college. It can also become a moneymaking hobby.

Winning 7-Card Stud is an attempt to help two types of players: the casual home game player who wants to play 7-Card Stud in a casino and the casino Hold'Em player who wants to play 7-Card Stud. I provide simple instructions, interesting anecdotes, and many examples of solid play. This step-by-step approach, written simply and with many examples, will show you how to start out, how to think, how to learn, how to play, and how to win at 7-Card Stud in a casino.

A Word About Poker

Poker is a wonderful game. It can combine an intellectual exercise with a great social experience. Becoming an excellent player involves a great deal of strategic thinking. But, chiefly, it is much more than that. Poker is about winning money from other people. The better you are, the more you win and the more other people lose; that is the essence of the game.

I have learned how to play well. In so doing I have learned how to take advantage and exploit the weaknesses of other players. This book is an attempt to share what I have learned with you. I want to teach you how to get better. And that means showing you how to win money at the expense of other players who aren't as good as you.

Some might find this notion of exploiting other poker players to be distasteful—perhaps even immoral. I don't think that it is. Everyone who sits down at a poker table does so with the knowledge that they may lose all of the money that they have in front of them. If they freely choose to play with me, the money they put up to play is fair game. In fact, it would be unethical for me *not* to try as hard I could to win their money. (See *Softplay* in the Glossary of this book.)

But if you do think there is something morally or ethically wrong about winning real money from other people, then serious poker, and thereby this book, is probably not for you. (Though it still might make a great *gift!*)

Acknowledgments

I have had considerable help in this project, both in the formation of my ideas and in the development of the book. I owe my initial interest in poker to my late grandfather, Max Levine, who taught me how to play. He was also responsible for teaching me self-confidence and self-control, the most important tools of a winning poker player.

My play developed from kitchen table to casino felt thanks to the ideas of two authors—Herbert Yardley and Edwin Silberstang—and was greatly improved because of the writings of David Sklansky, Mason Malmuth, Mike Caro, Lee Jones, and Lou Kreiger.

This book would never have been written in this final form were it not for the initiative and tenacity of my agent, Gregory Dinkin. Lou Kreiger offered valuable encouragement and direction that I relied upon to turn my initial "brain dump" into a published book.

Many people have contributed to this effort by reading my initial draft and offering comments and suggestions. Many thanks to Jan Fisher (who runs great poker cruises by the way), Linda Johnson, Eric Johnson (a terrific home game player), Jamie Culbertson, Lee Adams, Mike Fadel, Andy Latto, Tim Kunin, Carol Pozefsky, and Herb Adams.

I owe a special thanks to Andy Glazer, an extraordinary writer and poker player himself, who took the time to offer me many suggestions that I shamelessly used in editing my initial manuscript.

Doyle Brunson is truly a living legend. If my writing provides 1 percent of the contribution he and SuperSystem have made, I will consider myself fortunate. His insights were most useful and helped shape the final manuscript.

I remain especially grateful to two writing teachers, without whose instruction I would have remained a near illiterate: Helen Adler of Bethlehem Central High School and Ben DeMott of Amherst College.

Thank you to thepokerforum.com, an Internet site for the advancement of poker. Some of the ideas in this book were first expressed in articles written for them.

I am especially grateful to my poker-playing friends in Boston, especially Jim Hexter, who accompanied me on many late-night jaunts to our favorite games in New England.

I owe a special thanks to the whirling vortex of ideas, which are the Internet discussion groups Recreational. Gambling. Poker (RGP) and TwoPlusTwo. Were it not for these forums, I doubt that I would have had sufficient confidence in my own ideas, shaped as they were in the crucible of peer review, to share them with the public in printed form.

Finally, thanks to Bob Lada for his statistical help.

WINNING
7-CARD STUD

CHAPTER 1

7-Card Stud Basics

Introduction

Poker players pick up poker books for many different reasons and with many different levels of poker-playing experience. Some of you may never have played poker before. Others have played on your kitchen table for small change but never played for serious money. Still others, I'm sure, have ventured down to a nearby casino or card room or to an online poker room—perhaps many times.

All of you share one common interest. You want to play better and win more money playing 7-Card Stud. But each of you starts with a different level of poker knowledge and experience. The information in this book will help you master this great game no matter what you bring to the table.

There are six chapters to this book, including this introductory one. Each chapter covers a general stage in your poker education, includes several sections, and covers a specific topic.

The chapters progress incrementally from basic poker information to more advanced concepts for winning play. This chapter, for example, shows someone who has never played poker before exactly how poker is played—including how it is played in a casino. Chapter 2 includes a number of basic concepts you'll need to know to play thoughtfully. It also includes a very conservative betting strategy for use when you are first starting out. There are specific playing instructions for each betting round suggested for beating the typical lower-limit casino game (with stakes from $1/2 to $6/12). Chapter 3 provides some more advanced poker concepts and instructs you in those poker-playing skills necessary to both increase your winning margin in the lower-limit games and to beat better players who may be in the somewhat higher-limit games. Chapter 4 provides you with more advanced concepts and some ideas for how to approach games that are different from the typical ones you are likely to find. Chapter 5 provides you with a general strategy for playing in 7-Card Stud tournaments. Chapter 6 provides some more advanced concepts for you to use to take your game to an advanced level. At the end of the book you will find a poker quiz to test what you've learned, a bibliography of books and computer software for your references, and a glossary of poker terms.

I suggest that every reader, from beginner to advanced, read the book all the way through—from basic to advanced strategy. If you are an experienced poker player you can treat this first chapter as a refresher course. This will give you the best overview of how to play the game. Then you can go back and concentrate on those chapters and those sections that address your particular concerns.

Poker Words and Phrases

This book uses certain words, phrases, and shorthand that can be very confusing to a non–poker player. The Glossary in the back provides their meaning. I will explain terms thoroughly as they are brought up in the text. But I'd also like to give you a brief lesson on some common poker expressions so you can follow the text more easily.

Action means the betting action made by the poker player: bet, check, call, raise, or fold. All of these actions are both nouns and verbs. A *bet* is the making of a wager and that wager itself. A *check* is the passing of the action to the next player without making a bet. To *call* a bet or *see* a bet is to put an amount of money equal to the bet into the pot. That amount of money is referred to as a call. A *raise* is an increase in the bet.

Rounds of betting are referred to as streets. *Third Street* is the first round of betting when you have three cards; *Fourth Street* is the second round of betting when you have four cards; and so forth. *Seventh Street*, the last round of betting when you have all of your cards, is also known as *the River*. If a player says, "I called him all the way to the River," he means that he called his opponent's bets on every round of betting until the last card.

Poker is played for money—known as *stakes*. Most card rooms and casinos in the United States usually play *Limit Poker*. That means that there is a limit on how much money any player can bet at any one time. There are generally two types of limit poker games that you're likely to encounter: *Spread Limit* and *Fixed Limit*.

Spread Limit means that the amount that can be bet on any betting round must be within a certain range. A Spread Limit $1–$5 game, for example, would allow bets of anywhere from $1 to $5 on any round of betting. I explain this in more detail in the section on betting limits later in this chapter.

Fixed Limit means that the exact size of the bet is fixed at a precise amount. If the game has a $5 fixed limit that means that all bets in the game must be no more and no less than $5. You can bet $5, raise $5, and reraise by $5. But you can't make a $7 bet or a $3 bet.

Typically, there are two levels (also known as *tiers*) of bets in a Fixed Limit game. There is the fixed limit for the early Streets and a higher fixed limit for the later Streets. The higher limit applies on Fifth, Sixth, and Seventh Street. It is usually double the lower limit. If, for example, the game is $5/10 then players may bet exactly $5 and raise or reraise by exactly $5 on Third Street and Fourth Street. But any bets made on Fifth, Sixth, or Seventh Street must be $10. (There are some limited exceptions that I'll cover later in the text.)

I refer to cards with either their numeral or their initial. Hence a *J* is a Jack and an *A* is an Ace. A 4♣ is a 4 of Clubs. Unexposed cards, known as *hole cards* are referred to with parentheses. So if you had three Aces on the deal, I would write (A-A) A. Where the hole cards are held by other players (and thereby unseen) I will use a "?"; for example (?-?) K refers to your opponent's hand with a King exposed on Third Street.

The *Board* refers to the cards that are face up, also known as *up cards*. To be "high on board" means to have the high hand showing. A *scary board* means that your up cards look very strong, with many high cards or all of one suit perhaps.

3-Flushes and *3-Straights* mean three cards to a Flush and three cards to a Straight, respectively. However, if I write that someone is *showing* a 3-Flush, I mean that he has three *exposed* suited cards. *Connectors* are cards in sequence. *Suited* means of the same suit. *Suited Connectors* are cards of the same suit that are in sequence, like the 8 and 9 of Hearts.

A *blank* is a card that doesn't help your hand in any way. I sometimes refer to it as an *x*. So if a player has a K-K-x-x exposed on Sixth Street, that means that she has a pair of Kings and two cards that don't help her and are thereby inconsequential. If I write that a player with a 4-Flush got a blank that means that he got a nonsuited card that didn't give him a Flush or help his hand in any other way.

Seats at a poker table are referred to by number in relation to where they are relative to the house dealer, going clockwise. A player in the One Seat is sitting in the first seat to the dealer's left; the Four Seat is the fourth to the left of the dealer, directly across from the dealer on the typical casino poker table. The Eight Seat is seated all the way around the table, on the dealer's immediate right.

Players are referred to either by their seat number or their exposed cards. "The One Seat with a King-10 showing was raised by the Pair of Aces," means that the player in the One Seat, who had a King and a 10 showing, was raised by the player who had a Pair of Aces showing.

I will often describe the play of a particular hand. Some terms that I'll use may not be self-explanatory to those of you who haven't spent much time in a card room. When I refer to *action,* as in "It was the King's action and he checked," I am referring to the betting action. I mean that it was the person holding the exposed King's turn to bet. Similarly, I often refer generally to the betting of other players by describing their betting action collectively. For example if I write, "The 2♣ bet and everyone folded to me," I am referring to the action of the players who acted after the 2♣. They all folded and then it was my turn.

That should be enough to get you started. Again, if you have any questions about what a word means, refer to the Glossary at the end of the book.

One final note on this subject. Situations that I describe in this book will become clearer after you have faced similar situations in a casino. For that reason I suggest that in addition to reading this book before you play in a casino, use it as a reference as your poker career develops.

Why Play 7-Card Stud?

The two most popular forms of poker played in card rooms today are 7-Card Stud and Texas Hold'Em. There are other games, too, but for the most part if you play in a casino in the United States today, you're likely to play either Texas Hold'Em or 7-Card Stud.

Texas Hold'Em is played with just two down cards dealt to each player and five mutual cards dealt in the middle for everyone to use. The best combination of the two hole cards and the five mutual cards wins. Many strategy books are available on Hold'Em for beginning, intermediate, and advanced players. I recommend a few of them in the Bibliography. But the strategy and the play of that game are very different from 7-Card Stud.

I suggest that whether or not you already play Texas Hold 'Em or some other casino poker game, learn 7-Card Stud. I'm not suggesting that you give up Texas Hold'Em if that's what you enjoy playing—far from it. I play Texas Hold 'Em myself and enjoy it; they both have their place in this vast poker world. But learning another game, especially the game of 7-Card Stud—which is played by millions—can only help you in the long run.

Here's how. Winning at poker often depends on finding "good" games. Good games, from the perspective of a poker player, means games with players who don't play as well as you do. Because you can play better than they, you can win money from them. That's why they're good games. I'll explain later in this book how you find these good games. But leave it to say that if you can play only Texas Hold 'Em well then you won't be able to take advantage of the many good 7-Card Stud games you will frequently see in casinos today.

Expectation: How Much Can You Make at 7-Card Stud?

Poker is a game of skill. But it's not just an interesting mental exercise and competitive endeavor. It is also a game played for money. If you are skilled and play against less skilled poker players you will eventually win their money. Fortunately for you, many people who play 7-Card Stud in a casino do not play very well. Some treat it purely as a game of luck. They play their cards as roulette players play numbers, leaving everything up to chance. Others who know that there is skill involved in the game either do not know how to play better or do not apply what they know rigorously enough to play well.

This is a good thing for you. In fact, your ability to make money depends on players like this in your game. Your profit will be based largely on your ability to play better than your opponents.

Those who learn the strategy that I have laid out in this book and who apply it patiently and diligently *can* earn money from this hobby. How much money depends on many factors including how well you learn the game and how bad your opponents are. Even so, I've observed enough casino poker to give you some sense of the potential profitability in the game.

Based on my observations, I think that players who diligently apply the very conservative strategy that I present in chapter 2 will be able to earn at least one small bet an hour in the typical lower-limit games in casinos today. If they master and effectively apply the more advanced concepts that I present in later chapters they will do better—perhaps earning as much as one to two big bets an hour. These earnings presume the availability of games with a fair number of bad players and without a prohibitively high rake. (I discuss both the rake and how to find good games in later chapters.)

How long should it take you before you can start to win money? People learn at different rates. There's no way to be sure when any person will master what I've written. That being said, I estimate that on average you'll need to play about 200 hours to really learn the game—that is playing and thinking about what I have written. During those *first* 200 hours, though you may win or break even, you need to be prepared to lose money—probably on the order of about a small bet an hour. I don't think you run the risk of losing much more than that, if you start out playing very carefully as I outline. But, given the vagaries of chance and the fact that you are starting at the bottom of a tough learning curve, if you start out by playing $5–$10 you may have to invest as much as $1,000 in your poker education, even with this very conservative method, before you can really expect to be an overall winner at the $5–$10 level.

I should also add that I've seen a few players, who began with the straightforward strategy that I provide in this book, win right away. One of them actually grinds out a $15,000 living at $1–$5 7-Card Stud, using a strategy almost identical to the one I lay out in the following chapters. He's beating the $1–$5 game for slightly less than $10 an hour—and that's even after taking into consideration the relatively larger rake of that game, tips for drinks, and tips for the dealer, known as "tokes."

Basic Rules of the Game

Ignorance Is Expensive

Many players who pick up a poker book skip over all of the introductory material thinking they know that stuff already. Let me ask you to read this true story first if you are so tempted. It will show you that just by knowing all of the basic rules of poker, you will have an advantage over some players in a card room. If you think that everyone who plays for money in a casino knows at least the most basic rules, you are wrong, as this story illustrates.

I was playing $15/30 7-Card Stud at Mohegan Sun Casino in Uncasville, Connecticut—near Norwich—in the central part of the state. It was the biggest 7-Card Stud game going at the time. There were eight players, including me, at the table. I was in the Eight Seat, the seat to the immediate right of the dealer. This hand turned into a contest between the Two Seat and the Four Seat. They each started the hand with about $500 in front of them.

The guy in the Seven Seat was low on board with a 2♦. He bet $5. I folded. The One Seat folded. The Two Seat, a tough regular player named Barry, showing a 5♦, called the $5. Everyone else folded except for the guy in the Four Seat, a visitor from New York City named Ali. He had the Q♣ showing and raised to $15. The Seven Seat who started the betting with his 2♦ folded. The 5♦ called the raise. The hand was now heads up with just Barry in the Two Seat and Ali in the Four Seat.

On the next round, Fourth Street, Barry got an 8♥ to go with his 5♦. Ali got the J♣ to go with his Q♣. He was high on board and bet $15. At this point the hand looked like this:

> Barry: (?-?) 8♥-5♦
> Ali: (?-?) J♣-Q♣

The next card, Fifth Street, didn't seem to help Barry. He got a 4♥ to go along with his 5♦ and 8♥. Ali, who had a Queen and Jack♣, got a K♥. He bet. Barry raised him. Ali called the raise.

Fifth Street looked like this:

$$\text{Barry:} \quad \text{(?-?) } 8♥\text{-}5♦\text{-}4♥$$
$$\text{Ali:} \quad \text{(?-?) } Q♣\text{-}J♣\text{-}K♥$$

On the next card, Sixth Street, Barry paired his 5 and Ali got the 9♣. So their hands looked like this:

$$\text{Barry:} \quad \text{(?-?) } 8♥\text{-}5♦\text{-}4♥\text{-}5♣$$
$$\text{Ali:} \quad \text{(?-?) } Q♣\text{-}J♣\text{-}K♥\text{-}9♣$$

Barry, with his exposed pair of 5s, bet $30. Ali, with his 3♣ looked at his hole cards (drawing attention to how carefully he looked at them); he paused and then he made some odd noises, "aaaaaauuhhhhhhhhhh??????????."

He looked again, carefully and deliberately, as if he was really having a difficult time deciding what to do. Finally, he raised the bet to $60. Barry fired in a reraise to $90. Ali went through the same awful acting routine he did on the prior bet, only he took more time and added a "uuuuuuuuuuuuuuuu-uaaaaaaaaaaaaaaaa?????????" to his remarks before reraising to $120. Barry raised him again. Ali just called.

The dealer dealt the last card down to each player. Barry didn't look at it and instantly bet $30. Ali called immediately.

The showdown was as follows:

Barry had two 5s in the hole with his exposed pair of 5s, giving him four 5s! Ali, with the exposed 9-J-Q♣ and the King of Diamonds, turned over the 10 and K♣ for a *Straight Flush!*

$$\text{Barry:} \quad 5\text{-}5\text{-}5\text{-}5\text{-}x\text{-}x\text{-}x$$
$$\text{Ali:} \quad K♣\text{-}Q♣\text{-}J♣\text{-}10♣\text{-}9♣\text{-}x\text{-}x$$

Ali was, of course, awarded the pot with his unbeatable Straight Flush. As the mountainous pot was being pushed to him, we at the table looked at each other incredulously. Finally, we all blurted out and asked Ali, "Why'd you stop raising? You had an unbeatable hand? You could have gotten in $200 more in raises before either of you were all in?"

Before he could answer, Barry piped in, "Well, I'm glad you just called me because I would have gone down to the felt with my four 5s" [meaning he would have continued to raise and reraise until he was out of chips].

Hearing this, Ali smiled a bit sheepishly and said, "To be honest with you all, I wasn't sure that a Straight Flush beat Four of a Kind!"

Some of us who played that hand are still shaking our heads in disbelief. Our greatest fantasy would be to have someone have Four of a Kind against our Straight Flush. And yet, here was someone in that perfect situation who blew it. We couldn't believe that anyone playing for so much money wouldn't know something as basic as the ranking of the hands. Though he won the pot, had he known the basic hand rankings that I learned at the knee of my grandfather when I was six years old, he may have won hundreds of dollars more.

You will surely make mistakes at the poker table. We all do. You will call with hands you should have folded and, unfortunately, you will even occasionally fold hands that you should have called with. This happens to even the best of players. But if this one-in-a-million opportunity ever presents itself to *you*, I want to make sure you can take full advantage of it. So make absolutely certain that you know the basic rules of the game that I present next.

How to Play

Most readers already know the basic rules for playing 7-Card Stud. You have probably played it in high school, college, or even in a regular home game. Perhaps you've even played casino poker and just want to become better at it. Even so, let's start with the absolute basics. If you know them already, consider this a refresher course in beginning poker.

7-Card Stud poker is a game played with a standard 52-card deck, without the Joker. Card rank from lowest to highest: 2-3-4-5-6-7-8-9-10-J-Q-K-A. Aces can also be low to make a Straight. Cards are referred to by their ranks and then suit. The 5♦ is called "the five of Diamonds"; 2s are sometimes called "deuces"; 3s are sometimes called "treys."

The game can be played by two or more players, though games with more than eight are not standard. In a casino, with few exceptions, a full game of 7-Card Stud has eight players.

Players are dealt seven cards. They receive three cards initially, two face down and one face up. They then receive four more cards, one at a time on four successive deals: three up cards and one down card. There is a round of betting after they receive their first three cards, and then a betting round after they receive each of their next four cards. When the last betting round is concluded the remaining players expose their hands. The player with the highest five-card poker hand is awarded the pot—the amount of money that has been bet during the hand.

Home game players frequently ask what happens if there aren't enough cards for all eight players to receive seven cards. That is a very unlikely event in a casino because players frequently fold before they have seven cards. If there are not enough cards left in the deck at the conclusion of Sixth Street to ensure that every remaining player gets a final card, however, then one final card is dealt face up in the middle of the table for all the players to use as their Seventh Street card.

A listing of all nine basic categories of poker hands, from the strongest to the weakest, follows.

Straight Flush

Five cards in sequence, all of the same suit. For example: 8♦-7♦-6♦-5♦-4♦. Among Straight Flushes, the higher the highest card in sequence the better the hand. For example J-10-9-8-7 of Hearts would beat the 8-7-6-5-4 of Spades. The suit of the Straight Flush has no bearing on the rank of the hand.

Four of a Kind (a.k.a. Quads)

Four cards of the same rank and one unmatched card. For example 8♥-8♦-8♠-8♣-6♣. This hand would be called "Four 8s" or "Quad 8s." The higher the Quads, the higher the hand. Four 8s would beat four 6s.

Full House (a.k.a. Full, Full Boat, or Boat)

Three cards of the same rank and a pair of a different rank. For example K♥-K♠-K♦-7♥-7♠. This hand would be called "Kings Full" or "Kings Full of 7s." Full Houses are ranked by the rank of the three cards. 9♥-9♦-9♠-2♣-2♦ would beat 8♥-8♦-8♣-K♠-K♦.

Flush

Five cards of the same suit. K♥-6♥-5♥-3♥-2♥. This would be called "King High Flush." Flushes are ranked by their highest card. K♦-6♦-5♦-3♦-2♦ beats the Q♠-10♠-9♠-7♠-6♠.

Straight

Five cards in sequence of mixed suits. 9♥-8♠-7♠-6♦-5♣. This would be known as "Nine High Straight." Straights are ranked by their highest card. J♥-10♣-9♦-8♦-7♠ beats 8♠-7♦-6♥-5♦-4♠.

Three of a Kind (a.k.a. Trips or Triplets)

Three cards of the same rank with two unmatched cards. A♥-A♦-A♠-7♦-5♥. This would be called "Three Aces" or "Trip Aces." Three of a Kind are ranked by the size of the Three of a Kind. 5♦-5♠-5♣-2♣-3♦ beats 3♥-3♠-3♦-K♦-A♠.

Two Pair

Two cards of one rank, two cards of another rank, and one unmatched card. For example 7♦-7♣-6♠-6♣-K♥. This would be called "Two Pair, 7s and 6s" or "7s Up". This hand is ranked by the higher pair. J♦-J♣-3♦-3♠-K♥ beats 10♠-10♦-8♠-8♣-A♥. If there is a tie in the rank of the higher pair, the rank of the lower pair decides which hand is better. J♦-J♣-10♠-10♣-2♥ beats J♦-J♥-9♣-9♦-A♠. If both ranks are identical then the fifth card, known as a Kicker, breaks the tie. J♦-J♣-10♠-10♣-A♥ beats J♠-J♥-10♦-10♣-K♥.

Pair

Two cards of the same rank and three unmatched cards. A♦-A♥-10♦-8♣-3♠. This is called "Two Aces" or "A Pair of Aces." If two hands have a pair of the same rank, the highest card among the remaining three unmatched cards determines the superior hand. A♦-A♣-10♦-8♠-3♦ beats A♥-A♠-9♣-8♦-7♠.

High Card

Five unmatched cards. K♦-10♦-8♣-7♠-3♣, known as "King High." The hand with the highest card of the highest rank wins. K♦-10♦-8♣-7♠-3♣ beats Q♥-J♥-10♠-7♣-3♥. If there is a tie in the card of the highest rank, the second highest ranking card is determinative, and so forth.

How Casino Games Differ from Home Games

Yes, 7-Card Stud is still 7-Card Stud. However, casino poker differs from home game poker in some significant ways. Let me explain how.

When you walk into a poker room you don't just take the first open seat you see. You must first go to the person in front of the poker board, which lists all the games. This person, sometimes called "the Brush," will ask you which game you want to play. You should tell him whether you are there to play 7-Card Stud, Texas Hold'Em, or some other game that is being spread. And you should tell him the stakes you want to play.

The Brush will check the board to see what is available, and either send you over to your table (or tables if there is more than one game with an open seat) or tell you that there are no open seats. If there are no seats, the Brush will put you on a list for the game. Some casinos have large displays with the waiting list for each of the games. Others have just a small hand-held list. Either way, the list is made on a first come, first served basis. Some places allow you to phone in your name, before you arrive at the casino, to put your name on the list. This is often a good idea when the poker room is crowded, so you can "wait" while you're driving down. There's usually a limit of an hour or so that your name can remain on a list before it's taken off if you don't show up.

In a casino you don't play with cash, you play with chips. These chips may be purchased from a cashier, usually located right in the poker room. In some casinos you can also buy your chips from the dealer at the table or from chip runners who come to your table and can exchange your cash for chips.

Another difference between a public poker room and a private game is in how players raise the bet. In a home game, and in the movies, players often raise in two motions. When you're playing with your buddies at home, if someone has bet and the betting action is to you, you might say, "I call the bet" shoving out the necessary amount of chips, "and I raise it" at which point you shove out another stack of chips. This gives some drama to your raise and may, in your way of thinking, serve to intimidate other players. In a casino, this two-motion raise, called a *string raise*, is not allowed.

When you want to raise in a casino, you must either say, "raise" before you put any chips into the pot, or you must put the full amount of the bet and the raise into the pot in one motion. This rule keeps sharp players from seeing how other players react to the initial call and then deciding, based on their reaction, whether or not to raise. In any case, it is a rule that other players may call you on. So if you want to raise, the simplest thing to do is to just say "raise" before you start to put money into the pot. Then, no matter how much you start to put in the pot with your initial motion, you can adjust the amount with as many motions as it takes to get the total amount of the bet and raise correct.

Here's another difference between playing at home and playing in a public card room. Home players typically toss their bets into the middle of the table—not so with casino players.

Instead, you place your bet in front of you, where it remains until all of the betting action of that round is completed, at which point the dealer moves everyone's bet into the main pot. Throwing chips into the middle of the table is called "splashing the pot" and is strongly discouraged. The dealer needs to ensure that the amount being bet is correct. Some players, looking for an edge, may attempt to cheat by throwing in a bet that isn't the full amount. Facing a $5 bet, these cheaters may throw in four $1 chips, say "call," and hope that no one will notice they have only thrown in $4. This can't happen if each player places the full amount of the bet in front of them.

Similarly, when the betting is over, if you are fortunate enough to have won, resist the temptation to grab the pot and rake it toward you as you would in a home game. Once again, the dealer has the job of awarding all pots. Patiently wait for her to do so.

It is customary to tip the dealer in a public card room. In the lower- and medium-stakes games this is customarily done when a player wins a medium to large pot. Of course, how much you tip is completely up to you, but remember that dealers rely on these tips for their income much as waitresses in a restaurant do. A tip of $.50 or $1 is typical.

There are other differences between home game and casino poker. Casino players tend to fold many more of their starting hands than home game players do. In a home game, it may be customary for everyone to call the first bet. Nearly everyone may tend to stay in until they have at least five cards. And it is probably not unusual to have a few hands where everyone stays in until the last card is dealt. In the public card room this rarely happens.

Bad though your casino opponents may be, they will be folding much more often than your home game buddies. Sometimes it will be just you and one other opponent betting and calling. It's not unusual at all, especially in the somewhat higher stakes games of $10/20 and $15/30, for the hand to be decided right on Third Street or Fourth Street, with one player raising and every other player folding before they even get a fourth card.

Casino games tend to move more quickly than home games. The professional dealer deals faster than even the most experienced home game dealer. Players, having gotten used to playing only certain types of hands, will fold, call, or raise much more quickly than in a home game. This can, admittedly, be a little intimidating at first. They may seem incredibly skilled and adept, while you feel like a fumbling idiot still trying to figure out how to play your hand, and while everyone else has acted long ago and is staring at you.

Don't be intimidated. Just because they act more quickly and handle their chips and cards more adroitly than you doesn't mean they are in any way better. You will soon grow accustomed to the different style of a casino poker game. And, as you learn the proper strategy of play you will soon see that most of these players are really not very good at all.

Casino poker is also different from most friendly home games in one significant financial respect: in a casino there is a charge for playing. This charge is paid by the player in one of two ways. Players either pay a *rake*—an amount the casino collects out of the pot—or *time*—an amount paid by each payer to the dealer every thirty minutes. Most games $15/30 and lower have a rake.

A rake is usually a percentage of the pot with a maximum amount that can be taken. For example, the rake in most East Coast 7-Card Stud games is 10 percent of the pot with a maximum of $4 that can be collected in any hand. This is usually listed as 10 percent $4 Max. Some casinos have $3 maximums, others $5 maximums, while others charge no more than a 5 percent rake. You need to check where you play.

Time charges are generally for the higher stakes games of $20/40 and up. Typically, there is a $7 per half-hour charge for $20/40. It goes up from there.

Betting Limits

You've already learned that in a casino games are played either spread limit or fixed limit. *Spread Limit* means that the bettor may bet or raise any amount, between the established ranges of bets, during any of the rounds of betting. For example, if the game is $1–$5 7-Card Stud, the player may bet or raise any amount from $1 to $5 during the betting action.

There are some exceptions to this. On Third Street the low card showing *must* initiate the betting action. If, for example, the game is the popular game of $1–$5 and the lowest card showing is a 4♣, then the 4♣ must begin the betting with a forced bet of $1. Since many of the lower-limit, spread limit games like $1–$5 and $1–$3 have no ante, the forced bet becomes the only money in the pot before the betting begins.

This forced bet may either be called or raised by as little as $1 or as much as $5. In most casinos you may only raise *to* $5 but in other places, you may raise by the full $5 and make the bet $6. Check with your card room to find out what your rules are.

On Fourth Street, the betting round with two up cards, the initial bettor may bet as little as $1 or as much as $5. He, in turn may be raised by as much as $5 or as little as the initial bet. You cannot, for example, have a $5 initial bet raised $1. All raises must be for at least as much as the bet they are raising. Similarly so with reraises.

Fifth Street, Sixth Street, and Seventh Street (also known as the River) may be similarly bet and raised.

There are some exceptions to these rules. In most casinos, when there are only two players left in the pot, they may raise each other without limit. So Player A can raise, Player B can reraise, Player A can re-reraise, Player B can re-re-reraise, and so forth until either player runs out of chips or decides to call. Some casinos restrict this unlimited reraising if there are more than two players in the pot when the round begins. So if Player A bets, Player B raises, and Player C folds, these casinos only allow Player A to raise and Player B to reraise. They don't allow any additional raises. Check with your local card room to learn your set of rules.

Most 7-Card Stud games are spread Fixed Limit. This means that the amount by which you may bet or raise is fixed for each betting round. You have no discretion in how much to raise or bet. This fixed limit increases in the later betting rounds. Typically, the limits double after Fourth Street.

For example, if you are playing $5/10, on Third Street, you have the option of checking, betting $5, raising by $5, or folding. Similarly on Fourth Street you may bet or raise $5. On Fifth Street, however, the limits double. You may bet or raise by $10. No more and no less: $10 exactly. The bet may eventually become larger than $10 with raising and reraising. But the amount of each bet, raise or reraise, must itself be $10. Player A may bet $10, player B may raise by $10 making it $20, Player C may reraise making it $30, and Player D may reraise again making it $40, but no player could bet or raise by more than $10 at one time.

There are two exceptions to this.

On Third Street there is a forced bet—some fraction of the lower tier of betting. So if the game is $5/10 the forced bet is typically $2. The forced bet is made by the lowest card showing when the initial up cards are dealt. If there is a tie in rank (let's say one player has the 2♠ and another the 2♦), it goes by suits, in descending order: Spades, Hearts, Diamonds, Clubs. If, for example, you have the 2♥ dealt up to you and someone else has the 2♣, the betting initiates with the 2♣.

That initial forced bet, meant to sweeten the pot by adding it to the antes before anyone may bet for value, is usually $1 in a $3/6 game, $2 in a $5/10 game, $2 in a $6/12 game, $3 in a $10/20 game, and $5 in a $15/30 game. It may be completed to the full lower tier. So if you are playing $5/10, the bring-in begins with a $2 bet. That $2 may be completed to $5 and that $5 may be raised by $5.

One other note here is that the initial bring-in bet has the option of initiating the betting for the full amount. If, for example, in a $5/10 game you have the lowest up card showing with the Deuce♦ dealt up and a Pair of Queens dealt down. You may want to initiate the betting with the full bet and bet $5 instead of just the required $2. Even so, this is rarely done. Typically players just toss in the bring-in bet without even looking at their down cards.

The second exception takes place on Fourth Street when the second up card is dealt. If an exposed pair is dealt, the betting or raising may be by *either* the lower limit *or* the higher limit, at the discretion of the bettor or raiser. Once the higher limit has been bet or raised, however, the lower limit may not be used.

So, by way of example, in a $15/30 game, on Fourth Street if someone has a pair of exposed 8s and elects to come out with only a bet of $15, the next player can call the $15, raise by $15, or raise by $30 (or fold of course). If she raises by $30 the next player has slightly more limited options. He may call the full $45 (the initial $15 bet plus this $30 raise) or he may raise by $30. He does not have the option of raising by $15 (and, of course, he may also fold).

Fifth Street, Sixth Street, and Seventh Street are limited to only the higher limit, as are Sixth Street and Seventh Street.

Here's an example of how this plays out. Let's say the game is $3/6. The up cards are the following: 8♥, 4♣, 3♦, J♥, 10♣, 5♦, 8♠, and 2♠. The 2♠ is forced to bring in the betting for $1 (she had the option of betting the full $3 if she wished). The 8♥ folds, the 4 folds, the 3 calls the $1 bet, the Jack completes the bet to $3, the 10 folds, the 5 folds, the 8♠ raises by $3 to $6, the 2 folds, the 3 folds, and the Jack calls the raise.

The J♥ and the 8♠ are the only remaining players. The fourth card is dealt. The Jack gets another Jack and the 8 gets an Ace. The hand looks like this:

(?-?) J♥-J♠
(?-?) 8♠-A♥

The exposed Pair of Jacks has the option of betting either $3 or $6. He elects to bet $3. The 8♠-A♥ raises by $6 to $9. The Jacks reraise by $6 to $15. The 8♠-A♥ just calls.

On Fifth Street both catch blanks. The Jacks bet $6 and the Ace calls.

Neither hand improves on Sixth Street. The Jacks bet $6 and the Ace calls.

On the River, the hands look like this:

(?-?) J♥-J♠-6♥-9♦ (?)
(?-?) 8♠-A♥-3♣-9♣ (?)

The Jacks bet $6, the Ace raises, the Jacks reraise, the Ace reraises, and the Jack calls. They turn over their hands and reveal:

(J♦-K♦) J♥-J♠-6♥-9♦ (K♠) for a Jacks Full and
(A♦-8♣) 8♠-A♥-3♣-9♣ (A♠) for Aces Full.

The Aces Full wins the pot.

Sample Hand of 7-Card Stud

Here's an example of a hand of 7-Card Stud poker. The seats are numbered from seat 1 to 8, beginning to the left of the dealer. For the sake of simplicity you will be in the Eight Seat.

Seat 4: (?-?) 8♣	Seat 5: (?-?) 5♥
Seat 3: (?-?) 2♣	Seat 6: (?-?) K♠
Seat 2: (?-?) 6♥	Seat 7: (?-?) J♥
Seat 1: (?-?) 5♦	Seat 8: (9♣-9♦) 4♠

On Third Street, the first three cards, you have a Pair of 9s. It is a *wired* pair, meaning that both 9s are dealt face down. This is also known as a *concealed pair* or a *pair in the hole*.

The player with the 2♣, in Seat 3, has the lowest up card and would start the betting in this example. Each player then acts in turn, going clockwise around the table. As I have diagrammed it, players go from lowest number to highest. So after the 2♣ bets, the betting action—meaning the decision to bet, call or raise—moves to Seat 4 who has the 8♣. This player may either call the bet by putting an amount of money equal to the initial bet, raise the bet by putting in the amount of the bet plus an additional amount of money, or fold. If the player folds she turns over her exposed cards and is out of the hand. She may not participate in it in any way thereafter.

For the sake of this example let's say that the 2♣ makes the required bet of $3 in this game (I'll explain forced bets and betting limits later). The 8♣ and the 5♥ fold. This means they are out of the hand. They will get no more cards and will not participate in any more betting. The K♣ is next to act—that is, he is next to decide whether to call, raise, or fold. Let's say he raises the bet by $7, putting in $10 (the addition of the initial $3 bet and his raise). The betting action moves to the J♥ who, in our made-up example, calls the $10 by putting in $10 of his own. You are next. You have a Pair of 9s. You decide to call—putting in $10. The 5 and the 6 also fold. The action returns to the 2♣, who started it all with his initial forced bet of $3. He may either call the $10 bet by putting in $7 more, he may fold as others have done, or he may raise if he chooses. He folds. That ends the betting on Third Street. Three of you remain in the hand and will receive your next card.

Just so you can start to get a feel for poker terminology, let me express what just happened on Third Street, the first round of betting, as a casino poker player would.

> The 2♣ brought in the bet for $3. It was folded to the King who raised to $10. The Jack called and it was $10 to you. You called with your wired 9s. It was folded around to the Deuce who also folds.

The next round of betting is Fourth Street when you receive your second up card (and fourth card overall). In this example the K♣ received a 3♣, the J♥ received a 10♥, and you received a 9♠, giving you three 9s (also known as Trip 9s). Here is how the hand looked at the beginning of Fourth Street:

Seat 6: (?-?) K♠-3♣
Seat 7: (?-?) J♥-10♥
Seat 8: (9♣-9♦) 4♣-9♠

The betting on Fourth Street and all subsequent rounds begins with the highest hand showing. Unlike Third Street, there is no forced action. The first player to act does not have to bet. He may check—meaning he passes the option of starting the betting to the next player in turn. The option to check continues until a player decides to bet or until every player still in the hand checks. If no one chooses to initiate the betting, the hand continues with another card being dealt. That is called *being checked around*.

Once a player bets, however, subsequent players must either call, raise, or fold. Players may only check if there has been no bet made during that round. If a bet has been made and a player elects not to call that bet they must fold. They turn their up cards face down and push them toward the dealer. The dealer takes these discards and puts them with the other discards into what is known as the *muck*. A player who folds her hand does not participate in the rest of the hand in any way. This is called being *out*.

In this example the King-3 is high on board. That means he has the highest poker hand showing. He has the option of betting or checking. He decides to bet. Since this is a Fixed Limit $10/20 game he must bet $10. He bets $10. (Note: If he had an exposed pair he would be allowed the option of betting either the lower or the higher amount.) The Jack-10 folds. He is out of the hand. The action has moved to you. It is now your turn. You have three 9s, also known as Trip 9s. Keep in mind, however, that since two of your 9s are face down your opponent cannot see the true strength of your hand. He sees only your up cards. You raise by putting in $20 (his $10 bet and your $10 raise). He calls your raise by putting in $10. This ends the betting on this round.

The hand progresses to the next round of betting, after you are dealt your third up cards. This is called Fifth Street. In this example you receive the 4♦. This gave you a Full House. Your opponent receives the Q♥.

> He now has: (?-?) K♥-3♦-Q♥
> You now have: (9♣-9♥) 4♥-9♠-4♦

In this example you are the high hand showing with your exposed pair of 4s. The action is to you. You may bet or check. In the typical casino game and in this example the betting limits double on this street, from $10 to $20. So you bet $20. Your opponent calls.

The subsequent round of betting is Sixth Street, when you have four up cards. You receive the A♥, your opponent receives the Q♦.

He now has: (?-?) K♥-3♦-Q♥-Q♦
You now have: (9♣-9♥) 4♥-9♠-4♦-A♥

Your opponent is now high on board—meaning he has the high hand showing. He has the option of checking or betting. He bets $20. The action moves to you. You may either call his $20, raise by $20 to $40, or fold. You raise to $40. He now has the option of calling your $20 raise, raising your raise by $20, or folding. He calls your raise by putting in $20 more.

The last card is dealt. This is the final round of betting, known as Seventh Street or the River. In this example you receive a 5♣.

Your opponent has: (?-?-) K♥-3♣-Q♠-Q♥ (?)
You now have: (9♥-9♣) 4♥-9♠-4♠-A♥ (5♣)

He is high on board. He may check or bet. He checks—meaning he passes his betting option to do. He can do this because no one has yet bet on Seventh Street. You have a Full House—9s full of 4s. You can either bet or check. If you check there will be no more betting as the betting will have been checked around. You will then expose your hands and the higher hand will win the pot. But you have a strong hand and so bet $20.

He can no longer check. He must either call your $20, raise another $20, or fold. Your board is only a pair of 4s. He does not know what else you have and doubts you can beat him. So he decides to call, placing $20 in the pot. This ends the betting.

When the betting is over on the last round, either because it has been checked around or because the bet or raise has been called, there is a *showdown*. The players still involved in the hand must expose their hole cards and reveal their complete hand. The pot is awarded to the highest hand. The highest hand is the best 5-Card poker hand.

In this example, when your opponent turns over his down cards he reveals the K♣-7♣-A♦ as his hole cards. Together with the cards you've already seen he has K♣-7♣-K♥-3♣-Q♠-Q♥-A♦. The best poker hand he can make out of those seven cards is a Pair of Kings and a Pair of Queens, known as Two Pair, Kings over Queens, or just "Kings Up."

You turn over your down cards as well, revealing the two 9s you started with and the last card you got, a 5♣. Your full hand is 9♥-9♣-4♥-9♠-4♠-A♥-5♥. Your best hand is a Full House—9s full of 4s. A Full House beats Two Pair. You win all of the money in the pot.

Antes and Forced Bets

An ante is an amount of money, usually about 10 percent of the small bet, that players must put into the pot before they receive a hand. Nearly all of the Fixed Limit casino games require an ante, but some of the lower spread limit games do not. $5/10 7-Card Stud typically has a $.50 ante. $10/20 typically has a $1 ante. $1–$5 is played both with a $.50 ante and with no ante. $1–$3 generally has no ante.

The bring-in, also known as the *forced bet* or just the *force* is an amount that must be put in the pot by the player with the lowest exposed card on Third Street. In the Spread Limit game it is generally an amount equal to the small bet. In the Fixed Limit game that you're likely to be playing it is usually equal to an amount roughly equal to one-third of the small bet. In $5/10 it is typically $2, in $10/20 it is generally $3, and in $15/30 it is generally $5.

The simple reason for an ante and a bring-in is to give the players something to play for beginning with the first round. If there were no ante and no bring-in, a player betting initially would win absolutely nothing if everyone else folded. So poker is "sweetened" with money that is placed in the pot before any of the players decide whether to check or bet.

Many players new to casino poker view an ante and bring-in as little more than an annoyance. They throw it into the pot at the start of the hand and never give it another thought. But as we'll see later when we address strategy, the size of the ante and bring-in often determines how you will play the hand. For now, all you need to know is that the larger the amount in the pot to start with the more reason there is for the players to fight for it with aggressive betting and raising.

Table Stakes

As stated previously, in a casino you don't play with cash, you play with chips. Some casinos allow you to use cash temporarily during the play of the hand as well (some places allow this only if it's a $100 bill). But the dealer will make sure to convert it immediately, or at the end of the hand, to chips, which are the currency of the realm.

Casino poker is played *Table Stakes*. This means that, unlike a home game, you can't reach into your pocket for more money during the play of the hand. The simple rule is that you can bet only as much as you have in front of you when the hand begins.

So what do you do if someone bets more than you have in front of you? Do you have to fold? No. In casinos, players may enter the pot for as much as they have remaining and continue to receive cards and participate in the showdown. But they are considered *all in*, and may win from other players only the amount that they have already put in the pot.

This is best understood with an example. Imagine you have $22 left after the antes in a $10/20 game. You're last to act. The One Seat bets $10, the Two Seat raises, and the Three Seat reraises. The addition of the raise and the reraise means that the bet is now $30 for you to call. You have Trip Aces. If you had more money you would call the $30 and raise another $10. But you can't because all you have is $22.

You are allowed to put all of your remaining $22 into the pot and call the bet. This is called going all in. That would entitle you to get all of the remaining cards without putting in more money. If you win the hand, however, you win only $22 from each of the players. The second best remaining hand would win the side pot of the remaining money.

Let's look at the hand more closely. It is $10/20 Stud. The ante is $1 from each player. Everyone antes and then receives the following hand.

Seat 4: (A-A) A   Seat 5: (?-?) 7
Seat 3: (?-?) K   Seat 6: (?-?) 2
Seat 2: (?-?) 6   Seat 7: (?-?) 6
Seat 1: (?-?) J   Seat 8: (?-?) 9

The pot is $8 with the antes. You have $22 remaining.

The Six Seat makes the forced bet of $3.

The Seven Seat folds, the Eight Seat folds, the One Seat completes the bet to $10, the Two Seat raises to $20, the Three Seat raises to $30.

You call for the $22 you have left. The dealer makes a side pot of $8. He puts all of your $22 in the main pot with all of the antes, the bring-in, and all bets up until that point, except for the $8 of the Three Seat. It is the $8 that you couldn't call because you only had $22 out of the $30.

After you make your $22 call and the side pot is created, the Six Seat folds and the betting comes back to the One Seat. She calls the bet and the dealer puts $8 of hers into the side pot and the rest, the $12 remaining from the $20 raise she called, into the main pot. Similarly, the Two Seat calls the $10 raise to her, $2 of which goes into the main pot and $8 goes into the side pot. Remember, the main pot contains only $22 from each player because that was all the money you had when you went all in.

The other players similarly bet Fourth Street, Fifth Street, Sixth Street, and the River. All of their money goes into the side pot.

At the showdown, you have Aces Full and win the main pot that has $8 in antes, the $3 bring-in, and $22 from each of the other three players and from you for a total pot of $99. The next best player wins all the money in the side pot. You don't compete for that money because you were all in for just the $22 you had left.

Let me add one strategy tip for you to consider. In fixed limit games such as these you never want to put yourself in a position where you might have to go all in. You lose the opportunity to take full advantage of the great hand you might have—as you did in this example hand. Always make sure that you have enough money on the table to bet and raise if the situation calls for it.

Casino "Players"

Casino poker differs in other ways from a typical home game. They have many regular *players*. Some may be professionals, earning either their primary income or a nice supplementary income from the game. You will rarely see them in the lower- and medium-stakes games that you'll be playing in however. Even so, many other people whom you *are* likely to be playing against may have some of the habits and mannerisms that seem to the new visitor to the casino to be a sign that they are experts or professionals.

Most of these opponents, at your lower-limit tables, are the "wannabes." They wannabe like the professionals and experts. Every hobby, sport, or group has them. You know the type. They dress, act, and talk—to the best of their abilities—like the professionals or experts in their field whom they see and admire. These poker wannabes may wear sunglasses, a baseball cap, and maybe a slick silk jacket with a poker room logo. They are the insiders who have the lingo and mannerisms down—even if they can't play a lick.

Because they are often insecure about their poker-playing abilities, many of them seem to enjoy putting down and correcting the play of other players. They're often more concerned about maintaining their image as a knowledgeable player than in maximizing their profit from the game by keeping the unknowledgeable player uninformed about good poker play. Instead of letting their opponents make whatever mistakes they are inclined to make, they obnoxiously share all their unsolicited opinions about proper play with the whole table, correcting what they see as mistakes in strategy, berating bad players, and, in short, showing off all that they think they know about this game.

Indirectly, of course, this hurts the game. Some bad players actually learn to play better when their mistakes are pointed out. Other new players are scared off or intimidated by this. Hell, they thought this was just a fun game of chance like Bingo. Now that they're being scolded, berated, and educated about how bad they are, they think that they might as well to go back to the Keno lounge or take up Cribbage.

These loudmouths are frequently regular players. They may come down every day (if they're retired or unemployed) or once a week or so. So they know other players there, as well as the staff. They have spent a lot of time sitting at the poker table, so they often handle the chips with great dexterity; they've had a lot of practice shuffling and twirling their chips, tossing them into the pot, stacking them, and the like.

This intimidates many new players. They don't want to do the wrong thing and embarrass themselves in front of these smooth "experts."

You should neither be intimidated by these players nor be concerned, one iota, with how they view your play. Don't fall into the easy trap of changing anything you do in the interest of fitting in, appealing to them, or looking like you're a good player. It doesn't matter. It is a distraction.

And think about this. If they were really the poker experts they sometimes appear to be (at least to themselves) then why aren't they playing the higher stakes games where they could be making serious money? Why are they playing for peanuts with you?

No, don't worry about impressing them, or anyone else at the table. Focus on playing a good solid game. And before long, you'll be doing all sorts of fancy stacking tricks with *their* chips!

Different Casino Rules

Casinos do not all have identical rules. You should know the many differences among them before you sit down. And you should read their rulebook before you play your first casino poker game. Not all places have one, but many do. If they don't have one, don't be discouraged. Speak with the floor person or the poker room manager to make sure you understand any differences between your expectations and their rules. Here is a list of questions to ask and have answered before you play your first hand.

What is the rake for each game and how is it collected?

The rake is the amount the casino takes out of the pot. As we'll see in later chapters, how much they take and when in the hand they take it affects your strategy. If it is too high you may not be able to win no matter how good you are.

Do you allow check-raising?

I deal with check-raising later in this text. Most public card rooms allow it. But some do not. You need to know whether you can do this before the situation arises when you want to.

Can I keep cash on the table?

In all public card rooms poker players play with poker chips. Some poker rooms allow you to use cash as well. Others prohibit it. You don't want to be caught in a situation where you are barred from using cash you would like to use.

Where do players exchange their cash for chips?

Some rooms have chip runners who do this for you, some allow dealers to convert your cash, and some allow you to do this only with a cashier. If you can't buy chips from the dealer or chip runner, you may want to have more chips on the table when you first sit down so you don't have to get up, leave the game, and stand in line to convert more cash to chips.

How long can I be away from the table before I am kicked out of the game?

Some casinos have special rules that may limit you to five minutes away from the table in certain circumstances before you lose your seat. Other casinos may allow you to be away for as long as two hours. You wouldn't want to lose a seat at a good table because you didn't know the rule.

Do they have a "Third Man Walking" rule?

This means that if two players are away from the game, the third person must return in five minutes or have her chips picked up. (See previous.)

Do the dealers keep their tips or pool them?

If dealers keep their tips, you can personally reward a good dealer as you would a good waitress. If the dealers pool their tips, there's less incentive to tip a good dealer.

Are there any premiums paid for high hands?

Some casinos give out jackets, hats, and even cash when players get certain hands like Straight Flushes. If you're playing where they do this, you might want to play more loosely in certain situations to try for that special hand. It's normally a mistake to do this—but since other players may be doing it, you should know the practice where you're playing.

Is there a bad beat jackpot? If so, how exactly does it work?

Bad beat jackpots are special cash pools, usually funded with $1 or so from every hand played, and awarded to a player who loses with an outstanding hand like Four of a Kind. Just like the premiums, though it rarely pays for you to adjust your strategy to try for these jackpots, other players may be adjusting their play. So it helps to know if they exist.

Do they offer comps, promotions, or other bonuses to players based on their time playing?

Some poker rooms offer free meals, rooms, food, and the like to seated players. Other places credit players with points based on their level of play, which may be accumulated and used to purchase such items as food and lodging. Find out about this and make sure you do what needs to be done to earn points or money while you are playing.

That should be enough to get you started. Make sure you understand the answers. As you play you will think of other questions, no doubt, so it's important that you ask them. Don't be afraid of poker room managers. Their job is to make you comfortable so you'll want to play. My experience has been that these managers are some of the nicest and friendliest people in the poker business. So take advantage of their good nature and their eagerness to make you happy.

One last word on poker rules. You will find, as you play, that there are some players who seem to be experts on every rule in the book. They combine this knowledge with a familiarity with the employees of the poker room and other players to intimidate new players. Some of them use their knowledge of the finer points of the rulebook to gain an advantage. Sometimes they will try to intimidate new players by arguing with them or hectoring them over certain plays.

Don't be bullied by these jerks. If the dealer seems to be buffaloed into making a decision you either don't agree with or just don't understand, calmly ask for the floor person or the poker room manager. Ask them to explain the situation to you. Continue to ask questions until you are satisfied that you at least understand why a certain decision has been made. You may not agree with it. But don't be afraid to ask as many questions as necessary to get a firm understanding of the explanation.

Summary. Ask questions and learn the rules before you play poker in a casino for money.

First Time in a Casino

I know that many players are nervous about playing in a casino. It can be somewhat intimidating at first. Let me tell you about my first experiences. You'll see that it wasn't easy for me either. The good news is that I overcame the initial bumps and bruises I received during my first couple of visits and went on to become a very successful poker player. Perhaps by learning what I did wrong you can avoid some of these potential pitfalls.

My friend Jim and I drove down from Boston to Foxwoods Casino in Ledyard, Connecticut. It was 1994. The poker room had been open for about a year, but we had just found out about it recently during a home game. We were very excited about this place, having heard reports about the many games and high limits that they had. But neither of us had ever been to a poker room before, let alone played in one. Our poker had been limited to the kitchen or living room table, with a $2 limit, and with a typical win or loss ranging from $20 to $50.

Coincidentally, our discovery of Foxwoods' poker room came at the same time our interest in playing poker had already been reinvigorated. I had recently read a new book about poker strategy. "Read" is probably too inactive a word to describe my relationship with this text. I absorbed this book, reading it and rereading it many times. I took it with me to work, read it while I ate, and even brought it with me into the bathtub. In fact, I read the book so many times and so closely that I made a list of about twenty-five errors in syntax, grammar, and spelling that I proudly sent on to the publisher, who gave me a 15 percent discount on all future purchases.

I discussed the book and the strategies it laid out with my friend Jim, who had also read it. I tried them out at a home game (successfully). Another friend also read it and the three of us would talk about it over lunch, after poker games, and on the phone. This was long before I discovered that great online poker discussion group Rec.Gambling.Poker (RGP). So this was the limit of my poker universe.

As we drove down, this first time, to Foxwoods, my friend Jim and I were both hungry for all of the action we had heard about. I announced, cautiously and fearfully, that I wasn't going to play this time down—though I was eager to. I said I wanted to get the lay of the land first. The truth was I was terrified of playing in a casino.

Even so, I brought $100—double my normal stake for our $1/2 home game—just in case.

Jim and I had been playing in home games for about twenty years each by then. You know the kind of game: Dealer's Choice, $1–$2 limits or so, maybe no check-raising in some of them. We played standard games like 7-Card Stud, Draw, and Texas Hold'Em, but we also mixed it up with many variations such as High Low with a declare, "Push," "Replace," buy, twist, and three-card poker. We didn't allow wild cards, but just about every other variation was okay.

We were both winning players in our home games. We each fancied ourselves to be pretty damn good—having won a little money from the game over the years. Neither one of us kept careful records, but we both knew, intuitively, that we were ahead.

The wins were normally around the $20 range, with an occasional $50 win to brag about. To win or lose $100 or more in a session was a rarity.

I thought that I understood casino poker because I had just devoured this great book. Everything was laid out so clearly and precisely. I knew I could follow the instructions in a casino and win. I decided that I'd start my play at $5/10 Texas Hold'Em, so well described by this poker author. And then, by following the rules he laid down, and with my hard work and natural card sense and ability, I would naturally rise through the ranks, making money along the way to build my stake, until before long I'd be playing No Limit Texas Hold'Em as described in two other poker books I had recently read: *Big Deal* by Tony

Holden and *The Biggest Game in Town* by Al Alvarez. I figured it might take me a year or two before I raised the $20K I would need to really have the bankroll I wanted to play in the World Series of Poker at Binions Casino in Las Vegas. But I was smart and I was patient, so I could wait.

Now, keep in mind, I was no college kid or wide-eyed poker *newbie* (new poker player). I was a thirty-seven-year-old, married father of two and well-seasoned veteran union organizer and negotiator. I owned my second house, and had years of life lessons under my belt. Even so, inspired by a single poker text, what now appears as a pathetic and silly dream of poker glory seemed very much within my grasp. I wonder how many others have shared this dream, if only briefly. And it was with these green-colored glasses that I drove into the Foxwoods Resort Casino parking lot that Saturday night in 1994.

Foxwoods is a grand site, made grander by its unique setting in the beautiful Connecticut woods. Foxwoods seems to rise literally out of nothing. I've always said that it reminds me of Oz or Shangri-la!

A strange impulse hit me when I got out of the car. I felt like running to the casino. I had enough self-control to force my legs to resist that urge, but it wasn't easy. I was in such a state of anxiety and eagerness.

I managed to control myself and walk to the casino. When I entered, the tidal wave of sounds and visual stimuli literally stopped me in my tracks. But this momentary pause of amazement would not deter me from my serious mission of playing poker. We quickly found the poker room, which was downstairs then, and again we were stopped in our tracks by what we saw.

The poker room was a more subdued kind of a whirlwind. There weren't the flashing lights and sounds of the slot machines or the shouts from the crap table. Instead, we were dazzled by dozens of action centers, the sign-up area where a few people were milling about waiting to get assigned to their table, and the cashier with lines of people waiting to cash in or buy chips. People were being called to games over the loud PA system.

And then there were the poker tables, more than fifty of them, all jammed together, with dealers slightly elevated and in uniform dealing out hand after hand and occasionally announcing or encouraging the action at the table.

I felt like a hungry man at an elaborate buffet. What would I try first?

It didn't take us long to figure out where to sign up for a game. And there we were, with an inquisitive woman standing with a magic marker in front of a board with dozens of games, "What'll it be, boys?" she queried, like some barmaid in a saloon. "What'll it be?"

Frankly, I was terrified. I was now more convinced than ever that I shouldn't play during this first time. As eager as I was to dive in, my excitement and eagerness short-circuited my desire to play. I still wanted to but I was paralyzed with the fear of the unknown.

My friend was not similarly discouraged. He signed up for $1–$5 7-Card Stud, the lowest game in the house. There were also: $3/6, $6/12, $10/20, $20/40, $30/60, and even a table of $100/200 going! And that was just *Stud!* For Texas Hold'Em they had $3/6, $6/12, $10/20, and $20/40. Later that night they got a higher-stake game going, maybe $75/150. They also had three tables of Omaha High-Low (Hi-Lo) 8 or Better, two of $5/10, and one of $10/20. The joint was jumping!

It seemed like poker paradise. My friend and I, clearly the two best players in our home game, were practically drooling. Everything seemed possible. Everything was accessible! Millions of dollars in chips were just a few feet and a few winning hands away from us. We quickly learned that appearances could be deceiving.

After about a fifteen-minute wait, Jim and I went to an open seat at a $1–$5 table. Since I wasn't playing, I checked out the lineup. Frankly, I was a little surprised. I had expected a bunch of happy-go-lucky folks who really weren't too serious about the game. I figured we'd be the most serious of all the players— having read a book on the subject and all.

Not so! Everyone at the table seemed very serious and extremely focused on the game. No one was drinking, few were smiling, and fewer were laughing. Most had on stern, "I mean business" expressions.

My friend, thinking himself sharp, bought in for the minimum of $30. His idea was to start small, go all in when necessary, and build his stack. Unfortunately, the other players at his table had a different idea. I think he went through six or seven buy-ins before we decided to leave.

I, on the other hand, broke even for the night. Getting four hours of lessons about how the poker room worked was free for me. I learned about the rake, about paying time, about free drinks, about getting food at the table, about tipping, about switching seats, and about switching games once you're seated. I learned everything I thought I would need to know in order to turn my next visit into a winning experience. My fear, unwarranted and embarrassing though it was, had kept me safe—at least for the time being. Of course, I didn't learn anything about how to play.

I came down the following weekend. I sat down at a $6/12 Texas Hold'Em game (there was no $5/10 back then), having decided that this game had the lowest rake as a percentage of the pot that I could get in this casino. Anything higher and the house collected time ($5 for a half hour at $10/20). I didn't want to pay $10 an hour while I learned the game, so the 10 percent, $4 maximum seemed better to me.

Armed with the solid guidance of one poker book and what I knew to be my excellent "card sense," I sat down to take my shot. I followed the author's advice and bought in for 100 times the small bet: $600.

Things started out okay. I was a little nervous about appearing foolish. There was the problem of looking at my cards, for example. On my first hand, I picked up the cards as I always did in my home game, drew them to my lap as I looked at them, and was immediately told by the dealer to keep the cards above the table.

All of the other players seemed to have a really polished and professional way of lifting their cards up to view them, but without actually taking them off the table. I didn't think I could master that. So, after I was chastised, I strained my neck awk-

wardly. It took me about three humiliating hours before I realized that I could see them fine by just lifting up the corners with
my right thumb and index finger, while protecting them from
others with my left hand.

In addition, the other players handled their chips with great
dexterity, stacking them effortlessly and seeming to flick them
from their stack. It took me a while to get used to that—as well as
the quick mental arithmetic needed to figure out change from a
$6 raise of a $6 blind with five-dollar chips. I was always asking,
"So how much is that to me?" and "What do I put in to raise?"

I was, to say the least, intimidated by what seemed to be a
table of professionals and strong amateurs. To show that I wasn't
afraid or intimidated and to buttress my table image, I raised
every time I entered the pot. Of course, that wasn't exactly the
advice in my book, which encouraged *selective* aggression, but it
was close enough at the time for me to think that it made sense
under the circumstances.

My overly aggressive style paid off at first. I actually won a
pot or two when everyone else folded to my raise (or reraise). I
literally thought to myself, "This is easy!"

My confidence was shattered as I lost a couple of contested
pots with pitiful holdings that I had tried to bluff my way to victory. I started to think only about how much I was down and
how much I needed to win to get even. I started to play very
weakly, folding to any opposition, even if I had initiated the betting. The other players surely noticed this and started playing
more aggressively against me. I lost and lost and lost until after
about four or five hours I was down $475.

I tried to analyze my play, as I had read I was supposed to
do. But my head was spinning. I just couldn't get my arms
around that number "475." It was about five times my largest
loss up until then.

Since then, I've been back to that casino a few hundred
times. I've played in dozens of other casinos and card rooms
across the United States and Europe. But I never forgot how un-
prepared I was, that first time, for playing with strangers in a
place unlike my comfortable home game.

I realized later that my discomfort, though understandable, need not have affected my play. Had I just anticipated the differences I was about to face, as you will now be able to do, I would have been much better able to concentrate on following a winning strategy of play. Instead, I was distracted, confused, and befuddled.

Let me give you a list of "Do's" and "Don'ts" about playing in a casino—especially about playing early on in your career.

DO'S AND DON'TS FOR YOUR FIRST CASINO POKER GAME

Do's	Dont's
Do take fifteen to thirty minutes when you arrive at a casino to consider your game and what your plan of action will be.	Don't expect to win the first time you sit down.
	Don't be intimidated by others or change your play to enhance your image.
Do think about how you are playing more than whether you are up or down.	Don't be distracted by the mannerisms of other players.
Do stick to your strategy regardless of whether you are winning or losing.	Don't assume that other players are good because they are regulars and talk a lot.
Do evaluate your session immediately after you have finished playing for the evening.	Don't assume that you will be able to win just because you have read a book.
Do stop playing when you have lost more than you can handle psychologically.	Don't rush into playing when you first arrive in a casino.
	Don't continue to play when you are distracted about how much you are down (or up).

That completes your introduction to poker. If you knew it all already I hope it served as a nice refresher course. If you didn't know before, you should now be ready to learn how to play strategically so you can win against the opponents you are likely to face in the lower-stakes casino 7-Card Stud games.

CHAPTER 2

A Winning Basic Strategy

Introduction

Chapter 1 provided the basic rules and concepts of poker. Additionally, you learned how casino poker is played and how it's different from your typical home game. But there are two more steps you must take before you're ready for taking on a casino 7-Card Stud game: You need to understand some strategic concepts that will help you handle the pressures of playing in a casino. And you need to have specific, concrete instruction on what cards to play and how to play them. I will provide you with both in this chapter.

Starting Strategy

When you first play poker for money you want to be able to learn a lot about the game without getting hurt. Eventually, when you have gained experience, confidence, and skill, you will be able to build on this learner's strategy and develop a more complete poker game. But, at first, you want to keep things simple and safe.

Let me use an analogy from another sport. If you want to learn to ski you don't start by having your instructor tutor you on how to go down the black diamond slopes. That could be deadly. And even if you did manage to make it down the mountain alive, the experience would probably be so awful, with so many falls and bruises, that you would be unlikely to get back on skis again.

As every ski instructor will tell you, the way to begin is on the bunny slope, using the snowplow stance. It's not as elegant or as advanced as learning to do parallel turns, as the experts do, and you surely won't win any Grand Slalom or Downhill competitions. But learning the snowplow is the basis for all more advanced skiing. Though it is slow, it is safe and effective. Once you can confidently use it to go down the bunny slope you can move on to the intermediate and then the expert slopes.

It's the same in poker. You want to survive your first experiences at casino poker with minimum risk. This basic strategy will allow you to do that. And, it is the basis on which all more advanced strategy is based. When you master this you can build on it, then move on to more advanced strategy, until you are ready to try the expert level of high stakes poker.

So first we learn our basic strategy.

How Good Players Make Money: Loose and Tight Players

Before we start in with the specifics on how you will play your cards, I want you to understand how it is that a good player can make money from bad players in poker. To understand this best, imagine a game like poker, but without the betting. We'll call it *Lucker*. There are two players. Each player puts in $10 to start. They are then dealt only one card face down. Each player looks at it then turns it face up. The highest card wins the pot. If there is a tie, the pot is divided between them.

There's no place for skill in Lucker. The players make absolutely no decisions on whether to bet. Accordingly, every player will, over time, do as well as every other player. You are dealt your card. You turn it over. The high hand wins the pot. No betting, no thinking, no skill at all. Frankly, it doesn't sound like it would be a lot of fun.

Now imagine that you change the game a little. You don't put any money in at first. First, you're each dealt a card face down. But before you turn it face up you can do one of two things. You can either put a bet of $10 in the pot or you can fold. That's it. Either put in $10 or get out of the hand.

Let's say that you know your opponent very well. You used to play Lucker with her. She liked that game and she plays this new game the same way. After she looks at her cards she always puts in $10 no matter what she has.

Here's a game where a good player can make money from a bad player. If you knew that your opponent would always put in $10, you could win money by only playing the cards that were more likely to win. You'll only bet with the better hands. She'll bet with every hand. Sure, sometimes when you are playing one of your better cards she'll have a good card too and will win. But most of the time, since she plays everything and you play only high-quality cards, you'll win. Eventually you'll have all of her money.

This is an extreme version of lower-limit poker—those casino 7-Card Stud games of $1/2 up to $6/12, including the spread limit games of $1–$3, $1–$5 and $2–$10. Many players in these games play just like your imaginary Lucker opponent. They are known as *loose*. They call too much with substandard hands. In 7-Card Stud they don't think about whether the three cards they start with are likely to become a winning hand. They just like to play. And so they do, calling bets too frequently.

Most of these loose players are unlikely to initiate a bet or make a raise. Remember, they liked Lucker, when you just put your money in automatically as required. They don't push their good hands or fold their bad hands. This is known as being *passive*. This type of poker player, who really enjoys the game of Lucker is known at the poker table as *loose-passive*. There's another name for them, too. They're known as *calling stations* because they call so much. They are your ideal opponent. I designed the following basic strategy for playing against this type of player.

A skillful player can take advantage of them by playing more conservatively—or *tight* as it's called in poker. You will be staying in only with those hands that have a high likelihood of becoming winning hands at the showdown. You'll be playing like the player in the imaginary example who only plays high-quality starting hands against his Lucker opponent.

But in poker, just playing tight isn't enough. In poker, players decide whether to initiate the bet. It isn't automatic. If you want to win money from loose-passive calling stations, you must take the initiative and be aggressive at the poker table, betting and raising when you have high-quality hands. You want to get more money from your loose opponent when you hold the advantage. You must push the betting action. You do this by betting and by raising. This is known as being *aggressive*.

Simply put, against the loose players that you are likely to face in these lower stakes games you want to be tight and aggressive, known familiarly as *tight-aggressive*. That's the style of play that I recommend.

When you are playing poker at the proverbial "bunny slope" of lower stakes games you want to follow my recommendations explicitly. Snowplow only. Do not try the more advanced skiing on the Black Diamond course yet. As your skills and experience increase you will be able to mix up your play somewhat to take advantage of the different types of opponents you are likely to face. But even then, the fundamental element of your play will be this tight-aggressive style.

Game Selection: Finding the Bunny Slope

To win in the long run, you need to play better poker than the people you are playing against. Seems obvious enough, right? So you learn whatever you can about the game to become better. Again, an obvious point.

What is often not as obvious is that there are two ways to become better than your opponents. One is to improve your skills. You can assiduously study, learn about the game, and practice. If you are at least somewhat intelligent, observant, and very disciplined, this can help improve your game. It is only one half of the equation of making you better than your opponents, however. The other half (the easier half in fact) is to play against players who play worse than you do. You become better by playing against bad players.

So find bad players! In one sense that is counterintuitive for the competitive person. We are trained, and our instincts pull us to want strong opponents as we seek to get better. In fact, this is generally how we improve in other competitive endeavors. If we want to play better tennis we play against better tennis players. If we want to be a great musician, we look for other fine musicians to play with. Name the sport, hobby, or avocation. Just about everything else you might do is improved by doing it with those who have done it longer and are better at it than we are. Not so poker!

We want weak opponents in poker. We want beginners, losers, has-beens, and also-rans. Specifically, we want players who are playing because they love to gamble, just want to have fun, or even need to lose. Although this raises ethical issues I suppose, the best people we could find ourselves playing against are compulsive, losing gamblers.

This is because we play poker to win. Sure, we might want to go up against a world-class player now and again just for the glory of it. But we want to do it when there are plenty of lousy players around to make the game good. We don't want to have a regular diet of heads-up poker against someone who is better than we are because it will cost us money. Better to spend our money on poker lessons.

I've run some simulations on an excellent computer software program: Turbo 7-Card Stud by Wilson Software. I corroborated my theory (and those of many others) that you need bad players to play against if you want to win at casino poker. I set up a sample $5/10 7-Card Stud game with eight "strong player" simulations. I ran it for 500,000 hands (or about 20,000 hours of steady play at 25 hands an hour). If you're a full-time player, by the way, that's about ten years' worth of play. If you're like me and play closer to 400 hours a year then it's about a lifetime of play.

With the 5 percent, $3 maximum rake, typically taken out of

each pot by the casino as the cost of operating the game was considered, *all* the players lost money. Every last one of them! Then I changed the program. I threw in a solid mediocre player. You know what happened? They still all lost money; similarly so with two solid, mediocre players (though not as much money to be sure).

However, when *one* bad, loose calling station was thrown in, or three solid mediocre players were thrown into the mix, the remaining strong players *won* money. And, despite some players' anecdotal evidence to the contrary, the more bad loose players in the mix, the more the strong players won. The highest winnings were for the lucky son of a gun who played against seven bad, loose players.

So I repeat my premise. To win at poker you need to be better than your opponents. Anthony Holden, in the poker classic *Big Deal*, lamented the fate of Eric Drache. Holden noted that Drache, a truly great poker player, was perhaps the eighth-best poker player in the world. Unfortunately, he had the bad judgment of wanting to only play against the seven other better players.

How do you find these bad games? Surely the casino isn't going to tell you, the casual player, where the fish are. So you must learn to spot these good games on your own. Actually, it's pretty simple.

Bad players call too much, raise too little, and call too much. And, lest I forget, they call too much! All you need to do is watch a few hands and count the number of people who stay in beyond Third Street. If there are generally four of them or more, it's probably a very good game. Similarly, if there are three or more people at the showdown you've probably spotted a good place to park yourself for a while. If players seldom raise each other, so much the better.

Let me be clear. Just because the game is tight, with nearly everyone folding for the bring-in and few hands going to showdown, doesn't mean it isn't beatable. In fact, for the skilled player these games may be more profitable than the loose ones. For you, however, someone who is attempting to master this basic strategy as you learn how to become a better poker player, you should start with the loose passive games.

Conversely, stay away from the tough games. They're relatively easy to spot, too. There will be fewer hands reaching the River; fewer with showdowns, rarely more than two players seeing Fifth Street. And you'll see many raises and reraises. Few if any bring-ins go around without being completed.

Other signs might steer you in the right direction. Look for games where people seem to be enjoying themselves. If there are a lot of dour faces, folded arms, scowls, or just expressions of intense concentration, there probably isn't a lot of loose money to be had. If people are laughing it up, loud, drinking some, sending off Keno slips, talking about the simulcasts race on the TV screen, and generally having a ball, however, *that's* an invitation for you to join in the fun.

There's also a fringe benefit to playing in games like this: even if you don't end up making money, you will have a better time playing poker when you are laughing with people who are enjoying themselves. Just be careful that you don't fall into the habit of making loose calls and gratuitous raises just to be one of the gang. Add to the merriment and spirit of the table with words rather than deeds and you'll be just fine.

Other games can be profitable, too. Loose and aggressive games (a lot of raising) can be great, but you need to have a much larger bankroll with which to withstand the swings in the games. For a beginning player, this can be very difficult because you get nervous that you'll run through all of the money you have allotted to play poker.

Tight games, with opponents folding to little pressure, can also be very profitable, but they require a level of aggression and confidence that the beginning player may not possess. Better for now to stick to the games in which there are few raises and many calls. That's where you'll be most comfortable and make the most money.

Games change, though. A game that starts out great, with lots of players who call too much and raise too little, can go bad after these bad players leave or their money dries up. Good players who have been waiting for a seat in such a game may replace them. If the game changes and you find yourself witnessing heads-up play most of the time, it's time for you to leave as well.

Do not be concerned with how other players react to your leaving the table. You want to get into the best game, *period!* If you sit down to a table, notice that the players are very tight, then see a seat open up at the next table over where the players seem very loose, don't be shy. Ask for a table change right away. Don't worry about what the players may say about your leaving so quickly. Ignore them. You're going to keep your eye on the money, not on your popularity.

One final note. I used to think that a sign of a good game were young faces at the table. My opinion has changed. With the advent of Internet poker, I've found that many young players play extremely well. They have been able to accumulate the experience of playing in thousands of hands much more quickly than when it took a trip to a casino to find a serious poker game. And as far as the generalities about other demographic groups of players—well, I'll leave them to someone more observant and brave than I. As a practical matter, there's no need to make these generalities, since you should be able to tell within a short while of observing play how loose or tight any player is.

Here are some warning signs of games you should avoid.

- People looking at their opponents' cards intensely
- Serious expressions
- Small pots with heads-up action
- Few showdowns
- Raises and reraises
- Short stacks
- Notebooks labeled "Wins/losses, Vegas, AC, CT 2002"

Here are some green lights that should signal that the game is good.

- Laughing, happy faces
- Lots of people in the pot
- Calls, calls, and more calls
- Loads of chips, preferably unstacked, on the table
- Keno slips and racetrack forms
- Big cups for carrying quarters to slot machines
- Lots of half-filled beer bottles

Summary—Table Selection. Find the table with the largest number of bad players you can. Don't worry how you look by changing tables until you find the one you want.

Seat Selection

When you find the best poker game and decide to sit down in it, you also want to try and find the best seat in that game. Some seats are better than others at the poker table. Not because they are lucky but because of where they are relative to other players. Your task is to sit in the best seat at the best table.

What's the best seat? There is some disagreement on this point, but my opinion is that the best seat is the one with the loose players and the very aggressive players to your right. Mike Caro, a well-known poker author and theorist, has pointed out that money moves clockwise around the table. I agree with him. You want to be in a position to have the money move from the loose player (with a large stack) to you before other players can intervene with their poker action. You want first crack at their stash! So you want to take the seat immediately to the left of this type of player.

For example, with a loose moneybags on your right, you can raise with your good hands after he calls (with what is likely to be an inferior hand). This raise will often prevent other players from competing against you for this bad player's money. You'd prefer not to give your good opponents a chance to make this move on you.

You also want to see what an aggressive player will do before you have to act. Having him on your right is the best way to do this.

What you want to avoid, at this level of basic play at least, is having a loose aggressive player who plays a lot of hands on your immediate left. You will be calling or raising before you see what he is going to do. You may end up calling or raising pots you wouldn't play for another player's raise. So try to get these persons to act before you do, if you can.

There's another matter to bear in mind. You might spot another player like you. He plays very tightly as well. You might be tempted to want him on your right, so you'll know to stay out of the pot once he enters it, but this isn't necessary. You really don't mind if he's on your left, acting after you. Why? Because he, like you, will play very, very few hands. Even though he will have a positional advantage over you, it will seldom come into play because you and he will seldom be in the same hand.

As you become more advanced, you will be able to take advantage of aggressive players, loose players, and maniacs who sit to your left as well. You will be able to take advantage of their predictable behavior by adjusting your own. But for now, when your bag of tricks is deliberately limited, try to keep those loose, aggressive players to your right.

Ideally, when you come to play, there will be a choice of seats at the table you want. This makes it easy. When the floor person asks you which one you want, just pick the one that meets the criteria that I've just laid out.

Unfortunately, all too often, there is only one seat available. You don't have a choice. What do you do then?

Simply take the seat and ask the dealer to move to the next open seat. They often have buttons that say "seat change" on them. When a seat becomes available you have first option for moving. If it's a better seat, giving you a positional advantage over a person with a lot of chips for example, you can then take it. If it isn't a better seat you can always decline it and save your seat change for a time when you think it will be to your advantage.

One final note. You may not want everyone at the table to think that you're changing your seat to get an advantageous position over them. You don't want to alert the other players to the fact that seating position really makes a strategic difference. It may help for you to think of some other excuse to move. I want my opponents to think of me as someone who isn't thinking about strategy. So I might say that I want a better view of the TV, or I'm having trouble seeing the cards, or I think my seat is just unlucky.

Summary—Game and Seat Selection

- Sit at the loosest/most passive table you can find.
- Sit with the aggressive/loose players with large stacks to your right.
- Don't be afraid to change seats or tables when you think it will be advantageous.

Science of Hitting and Advantage of Quitting

Here is one last concept for you to consider before learning the nitty-gritty of how to play your 7-Card Stud poker hand. I want you to understand the basic premise for the tight-aggressive poker style that I recommend; it is an analogy to another competitive sport.

Ted Williams, perhaps the greatest pure hitter ever to play baseball, wrote a book about his craft, *The Science of Hitting.* In it he tried to guide the reader toward a better understanding of how a good hitter becomes a great hitter. He began with a fundamental concept that applies to poker as well. In a nutshell, Williams's concept is this: *Wait for your pitch!*

Even the greatest hitters will not have an average much over .400. So why try to bat 1.000 and hit every single ball that is thrown? Swing only at those pitches that are likely to produce hits, avoiding those pitches that, though in the strike zone, are least hittable. To be a truly successful hitter, you must wait until the pitcher throws pitches in this favorable hitting zone.

In Williams's eyes, the job of the hitter is first to discern which part of the hitting zone the ball is entering. Then is to exercise the self discipline to refrain from swinging at the unfavorable pitches, and finally to make the most of the good pitches with a powerful and consistent swing.

The same theory applies to poker. *Wait for your cards!*

We must learn which cards have the greatest chance of becoming winning hands in 7-Card Stud. We must develop the discipline to throw away the bad cards. And we must learn to be aggressive when we have the cards that are favored to win.

This seems obvious. And yet, how counterintuitive this is for the eager competitor—of which I count myself. We want to succeed *all* the time. We become even more keenly competitive when we think we're behind and about to be beaten. Those of us with good competitive instincts are trained to *not* give up. And so, motivated by this desire, we stay with weak hands, trying to turn them into winners. This, however, is a recipe for poker bankruptcy.

You've probably heard the old saying, "Winners never quit and quitters never win." Well, in poker, the opposite is true. Learning a basic strategy for 7-Card Stud is all about quitting! Not all the time obviously, but regularly, and especially when you are behind. The winners are the ones who *do* quit (when they should); the losers are the ones who never quit.

Let me give you an example. You are playing in a game of $5/10 7-Card Stud. You are dealt (J-2) J. The player to your left has the forced bet with a Deuce; the next player, with an Ace, calls; the next player who also has a Jack folds; the next player, with a Queen, raises; the next player, with a King, reraises; the other players fold. It's your action. What do you do?

Well, since you started this fight with your raise, shouldn't you finish it by capping this pot with another raise? No, of course not! Your only action here should be to fold—as quickly as you can. You are probably woefully behind two and maybe three other players. Your odds of improving and overtaking the Queen, who based on her action is probably a Pair of Queens;

the King, who probably has a Pair of Kings, and maybe even the Ace (if he's waiting in the weeds with a Pair of Aces) are practically nil—certainly not worth a call.

So your best action is to quit right there. But, you may plead, if you quit how can you win? The answer is simple, though it may not be obvious. By quitting when you are behind, you save the money it would take to see the hand to its conclusion. This money you save from the losing hands you don't play is just as good as the money you win from the winning hands. Put another way, poker is not about winning the most hands. It is about winning as much as possible when you win, and losing as little as possible when you lose.

There is more to the art of quitting than just learning how to quit the hand, however. You also need to know when to quit the game. There are times when you should pack it all up, admit you lost for the night, and go home a loser! My basic 7-Card Stud strategy addresses that too.

A good example is in order. Imagine the same game. Unfortunately, you didn't quit. You played the hand all the way to the end and lost. The guy with the King had his pair, as did the Queen and the Ace. You stayed until the River when you hit Two Pair on Fifth Street and lost a bundle to Aces up. Thereafter, you got bad cards for thirty minutes and folded every hand. Being a good player, however, you observed your opponents carefully during that bad run of cards.

You observed that four of the players were very tight. This was obvious. They folded just about every single hand they were dealt. They also practiced all of the good habits you had learned recently. They were observant of other players. They weren't distracted by the football game playing on the TV. None of them were filling out Keno cards or reading the Racing Form. When they were in hands they were aggressive. They were tough to figure out. Nor were they timid, picking off a couple of bluffs on the River a couple of times.

You noticed something else. Many of the players seemed to know one another, the dealers, and the floor people. In fact, when you thought about it, you remember some of them from the last time you were in the card room about a month ago. You also noticed a couple of them were signed up to play in the $20/40 game. In other words, these weren't the typical bad low- and middle-limit players you had expected to be playing against.

So what should you do? Should you stick it out against these strong players to prove that you're in their league? No. You should *quit the game!*

Well, you don't have to stand right up, take your chips off the table, and cash out. But stop playing for a while. Go for a walk. Have a cup of coffee at the snack bar. Go outside for some fresh air. Maybe, when you get back, the good players will have gone and been replaced by bad players. Then you can sit down and resume your play. But give yourself a chance to think while you're away from the action. Think about where you stack up against the opposition. Are they as good as you, or better? If so, then why slug it out against them? You're not going to make money playing against better players. So don't try.

A good poker player must assess his own skill and abilities, especially relative to other players. And then he must also have the temerity to walk away from his betters. This is not easy to do. Poker players tend to have a lot of pride; they don't like to lose face or admit weakness. But if you are going to win money at the poker table over the long haul, you must be able to put your wallet ahead of your ego.

There's a classic poker saying that addresses this situation perfectly. "There's a fish at every poker table. And if you can't spot him, it's *you!*"

Basic Strategy for 7-Card Stud

This section tells you exactly how to play the cards you're dealt in 7-Card Stud. It will take you from your first three cards to your final hand, instructing you at every street in between. This strategy is meant to be a place for you to confidently begin your casino-playing career. I will build on this in later chapters.

Third Street: First Three Cards

When you start playing in a casino, with very few exceptions, you will fold every starting hand you are dealt unless it is:

- A Pair
- Three of the same suit
- Three to a Straight
- Three cards, 10 or greater
- Three of a Kind

You will not play these cards all of the time either.

Playing Premium Pairs

First of all, you should play *Premium Pairs*—a pair of 10s or higher. They are excellent. They are significantly better than Middle or Low Pairs. If you get them you want to raise to drive out other players and thin the field. Ideally, you want one caller against your Premium Pair. But you are happy if you win the hand right there. You don't want many players hanging around with lower pairs or unmatched cards. If they do because you didn't raise, they may very well catch up to you on the next card and end up beating you.

Avoid the temptation of the casual poker player who wants to call and not raise the bring-in bet in the hope of seducing more players into the hand. That's called *slowplaying* and is a big mistake with Premium Pairs. You will lose money over time with this strategy because the players you have sucked in to the pot may end up beating you when they improve their hands.

Say, for example, in a $5/10 game you have a pair of Jacks and you just call the bring-in bet of $2 instead of raising to $5. Three or four other players come in after you because it is so cheap. Had you raised they would have folded. A guy with a

Queen and an Ace comes in and someone with (3-6) 6 calls too. Why not, they figure; it's only $2. Well the Queen pairs and the (3-6) 6 catches another 6 and you don't improve. Now where are you?

You see, Premium Pairs play better against very few opponents because they are not likely to improve to huge hands. They are a favorite over one other player, but they are not a favorite to win against three or more players drawing to Flushes or Straights. Against a full field of opponents they are not likely to win the hand.

Again, don't fall into the trap of slowplaying big Premium Pairs. Don't call. If you have a pair of 10s or better, raise!

Now let's say there is a raise ahead of you—in other words a person raises before it is your turn. For example, the bring-in bets $2, a Queen raises to $5, and you have a split pair of Kings—meaning one King is in the hole and the other is exposed. You should reraise here, raising the Queen's raise to $5 by another $5. You want to make it $10 if people want to call! If the other players fold, good! Ideally you only want that Queen to call you. If, as you suspect, that player who raised with the exposed Queen has a Pair of Queens then you are a favorite over her. But what if the Queen folds? Don't worry about that. At this level it is very unusual for a player with a Premium Pair to fold after raising. Players at this level aren't that tight. But if the Queen folds, good. You've won $11. Better that than losing the hand to someone who draws another card to beat you.

Here are two examples of what I mean.

Seat 4: 9	Seat 5: 9
Seat 3: K	Seat 6: 5
Seat 2: 7	Seat 7: 3
Seat 1: 2	Seat 8, You: (Q-6) Q

The 2 brings in the bet. The King calls. All others fold. What should you do? *Raise.* There's no question about it. True, the King may have a Pair of Kings. But if he did, why didn't he raise? Maybe he's slowplaying. But you can't worry about that.

Similarly, any of the other players could have Trips or a higher pair in the hole. But with your Premium Pair you need to be aggressive and get those with lower pairs or just high cards to either fold or pay money if they want to improve. Raise here!

Let's look at another example,

Seat 4: Q	Seat 5: 5
Seat 3, You: (J-K) K	Seat 6: Q
Seat 2: 7	Seat 7: 6
Seat 1: 2	Seat 8: 3

You should raise here. And, if any card raises you should reraise.

Summary. Raise with a Premium Pair. If another player raises in front of you and you have a higher pair than his up card, reraise!

Don't get carried away with this. Though you should raise and reraise with the best Premium Pair at the table to limit the field, if you're likely to be second best to another player at this point, get out immediately.

Sometimes you don't really know where you're at initially. Make sure to look around. Is your pair higher than all of the other up cards? Let's say you have a pair of Jacks. Is there a Queen or a King or an Ace yet to act. In other words, do you see any cards higher than a Jack that haven't yet bet. If one of these cards is exposed then you may have the second best Premium Pair. Others may have a pair that is higher than yours. If this is the case, you might just want to call in this situation and see what they do.

But what if they show strength by betting before the action gets to you? Simply put, fold if you think you aren't the best pair. Keep in mind that there is no prize for the second best hand in poker. So if you're dealt a pair of Kings but an Ace raises in front of you, you should usually fold. True, she may be bluffing. But, generally speaking, players at this level usually have the hands that their betting indicates that they have on Third Street. Not always of course. But usually. Do you really want to pay for Third Street, Fourth Street, Fifth Street, Sixth Street, and the River to find out?

Here's a specific example of what I mean. It's taken from a game I actually played.

Seat 4: 2	Seat 5: A
Seat 3, You: (K-9) K	Seat 6: 6
Seat 2: 7	Seat 7: 8
Seat 1: Q	Seat 8: 7

The 2 brought it in for $3 in this $10/20 game. The Ace made it $10. Everyone else folded to me. I had a split Pair of Kings with a 9. I had a good hand with a Pair of Kings. But it was only a good hand in the abstract. In reality, against what was most probably a pair of Aces, I had a terrible hand. And so I mucked it.

If you're somewhat experienced at poker you might argue that I conceded too easily. You could point out that he might have been bluffing. I may have thrown away the best hand. And that's true. I might have.

But until you have developed excellent skills at reading other players, when playing in the typical loose and passive games I'm describing, give your opponents credit for having what they are representing. Fold your Premium Pair if you believe you are against a bigger Premium Pair. You will save money.

There's another consideration on Third Street when you have a Premium Pair that should cause you to slow down. Is your pair *dead*? By dead I mean that one or two of the cards of the same rank are already exposed. If, for example, you have a pair of 10s and see a 10 in front of other players, then your 10s have a much worse chance of improving to Trip 10s. There are only four 10s in the deck. If another player has one of them, your chances of getting one on later streets has been greatly reduced. If both 10s are exposed elsewhere then you have no chance whatsoever of getting a third ten. This means your 10s are dead.

If one of your Premium Pair is out, you probably should just call and not raise. If they are both dead you should fold, especially if there are higher cards out. Similarly, if there were two or more higher cards out ahead of you, consider calling.

So, for example, look at the following:

Seat 4, You: (J-3) J   Seat 5: K
Seat 3: 10   Seat 6: A
Seat 2: 3(♣)   Seat 7: 9
Seat 1: J   Seat 8: 3

The 3♣ brings in the bet, the 10 folds, and it's up to you. Well, do you want to raise here? No, probably not. One of your Jacks is out. Two of your 3s are out. There is a King and an Ace yet to act after you. At best, you might call the bring-in and fold if anyone raises. In fact, if this were a game with aggressive players who were likely to raise, you would be better off folding.

You also don't want to call with your Premium Pair if you gauge it to be second best or worse and another player raises. Let's say that a King, in front of you, raises and you believed he had a Pair of Kings. If you had a pair of 2s would you call that raise? No. How about if you had a Pair of Queens? Now that may seem like a more likely call. Queens are much closer to Kings in value than are Deuces. But that doesn't really matter. In a poker showdown, whether you lose by a little or a lot, you still lose all the money you've bet. So what difference does it make if you have Queens or 2s? You're still second best to the Kings. So fold!

A simple rule that you should follow is this. If on Third Street the betting action of your opponent and his up card indicate that his pair is higher than your pair, concede. Let's look at an example.

Seat 4: 2♣   Seat 5: 6
Seat 3: K   Seat 6: 7
Seat 2: 7   Seat 7, You: (6-J) J
Seat 1: 9   Seat 8: 2♦

The 2♣ brings it in this $10/20 game for $3. The 6 and 7 fold. You call the $3 with your Jack. The 2♦, 9, and 7 fold. The King raises. Now it's to you. What do you do?

Fold here.

Yes, it's true that you already have $3 in the pot. And you'd like to call. But toward what end? Are you going to call all of his bets to the River, thinking he's on a bluff? Maybe. But that's an expensive game to play ... especially when it's unusual for players at this level to bluff in this situation. Don't go down that Black Diamond course just yet. Unless you know that this player is likely to complete this bet as a bluff (which few players do at this level) your only play is to fold.

Summary. Don't raise; only call if your Premium Pair is not higher than up cards that have yet to act. Call or fold if your pair is dead. Fold your Premium Pair if you believe you are against a higher Premium Pair.

Other Pairs

Smaller pairs are much worse than Premium Pairs. You wouldn't be too far wrong if you just never played any pair smaller than 10s on the first three cards. But if you want to maximize your wins at these small stakes 7-Card Stud games, there are profitable ways to play the small pairs, if you are prepared to get rid of them on later rounds if they don't improve.

Kickers

One thing that makes those small pairs better is a high third card called a *kicker*. Let's say, for example, that you have a pair of 5s with an Ace kicker. A Queen in front of you raises. A Jack calls the raise and it is to you. In a game with many loose players you can call the raise. Why? Though you are probably against a Pair of Queens and a Pair of Jacks, you have a shot at getting Aces Up, which is the next best hand to Three of a Kind (Trips). You are drawing to what will likely be the best hand. In general, you can draw to a low pair with an Ace or a King kicker if none of the Aces, Kings, or your low pair card is out.

Summary. If your low pair and Ace or King kicker are fully live, you can call one full bet.

Wired Pairs

A *wired* pair, a pair that is concealed in the hole, is worth more than a split pair—a pair with one of the pair exposed. This is because when you have a wired pair you can make Trips without your opponents suspecting it. They will therefore be more likely to call your bets if you hit your Trips, giving you more money when you win the pot.

Consider this hand. You have a pair of 8s in the hole and a 3 exposed. You are the low card showing and bring in the betting in this $5/10 game for $2. Two players fold. The third, with a Queen exposed, raises. One player calls the raise and it's up to you. If none of your 8s are out, go ahead and call the raise. You're playing for that third 8. If you hit it, no one but you will know that you've made Trips. So they are much more likely to call your bets, putting more money in your pocket when you win the hand.

And, don't forget, since you brought in the bet for $2 it is costing you only $3 to call the raise. Don't take this too far, however. Don't play a low or medium pair, even if it is wired, for two bets or more. If there is a raise and a reraise before the action gets to you, even if your pair is wired, fold.

Summary. If you have a wired low or medium pair, you can call a full bet. But fold for two bets.

Position

Players make their bets in a certain order. Those players who get to make their bets later in the order usually have an advantage over players earlier in the order. Think of it like an auction. Imagine you are bidding on something you want. Everyone at the auction gets one bid. You bid in order. Where would you like to be in that order, first or last? Last of course. You'd get to see what everybody else bid before you would have to decide.

The advantage of good position in poker can't be overemphasized. All too often, however, it's overlooked—especially in 7-Card Stud. That's because in 7-Card Stud, unlike Texas Hold'Em, your betting position may change for each round of betting.

In Hold'Em the betting starts to the left of the dealer on every round of betting. If the dealer is to your immediate right then you know that you will be in very early betting position for each round. This is a big disadvantage. You can play many fewer hands in early position that in late position. (That's why in Hold'Em the position of dealer changes on every hand—to make sure that over an entire round of poker hands no matter where you sit at the table no one has an advantage or disadvantage.)

In Stud, however, the betting starts with the player showing the highest poker hand (except on Third Street). This may change on each betting round as the exposed hands change. You may be high on board on Fourth Street, but then be last to act on Fifth Street, because someone else's board improved.

You will have an advantage over most of your opponents by thinking about position when you decide which action to take. Remember, in general you are in a better position if you are last to act. It is generally advantageous to see how your opponent acts before you have to decide what action to take with your cards.

Consider the following example. You have a split pair of 5s with a Queen kicker. This is truly a borderline hand—one that you will usually fold. You don't have an Ace or a King kicker, you have a low pair, and your pair is split so your opponent is likely to fold if you make Trip 5s.

However, in this hand the bring-in bet is to your immediate left. He has a 2 and brings in the betting for $2. As it turns out, in this hand, four players call the $2—a Jack, a 6, a 4 and a 7.

(This is typically a game with a bunch of loose-passive players.) Everyone else folds until it is up to you with your pair of 5s and Queen kicker. You don't want to fold this hand!

Your position, being the last to act, allows you to call the $2 without risking that a player after you will raise. Though your hand is a little weaker than your normal starting requirements, you can see a Fourth Street card by calling only the bring-in bet.

Were you're first to act, on the other hand, with the bring-in to your right instead of to your left, you would probably have to fold this hand because you wouldn't want to have someone, or maybe more than one person, raise the pot after your call. Let's look at a hand to see how this works.

Seat 4, You: 6	Seat 5: 3
Seat 3: 9	Seat 6: 6
Seat 2: A	Seat 7: K
Seat 1: (5-Q) 5	Seat 8: A

The 3 brings it in. The first 6 calls, the second 6 folds, the King folds, the first Ace calls, the 9 folds, the second A calls. What do you do? Call this hand.

This is a good example of how your position has helped you determine that a call makes sense, though a Pair of 5s with a Queen kicker is normally not a calling hand with an Ace or a King out. In this example, because of your position, you can see that there is no risk of getting raised because no one is left to act after you. Compare that position to the same cards, but the following changes:

Seat 4: 3	Seat 5, You: (5-Q) 5
Seat 3: A	Seat 6: 6
Seat 2: 9	Seat 7: K
Seat 1: 6	Seat 8: A

Here, you should probably fold. What's different? You are first to act. The bring-in 3 acts right before you. This means that you must decide whether to call the bring-in bet, raise it, or fold before you know the betting action others will take. It makes a difference. Maybe the King will raise. If he does then you've got to fold. Maybe everyone will fold except for the King? You wouldn't want to go heads up against him with your low pair and weaker kicker. In short, lacking necessary information (that you would have gotten had you been in later position), you should fold this hand.

Summary. You can play low pairs. But make sure that you have good position or a good kicker to go with them.

3-Straights: Three Cards in Sequence

First of all, you wouldn't be too far wrong if you never played three cards to a Straight. Why would you throw money in early if you have a 3-Straight? There are too many problems. For one, even if you catch a Fourth Street card in sequence you may not make your Straight. And even if you do, you may lose against a higher Straight, a Flush, or a Full House. In fact, when you are first starting out, toss away 3-Straights unless they are three high cards like 10-Jack-Queen.

You want 3-Straights that are most likely to produce open-ended 4-Straights. An open-ended 4-Straight is a four-card sequence that can make a Straight with one card at either end. An open-ended 4-Straight is 5-6-7-8. It can become a Straight with either the 4 or the 9. However, 5-7-8-9 is not. It would be a *gut shot* 4-Straight because you can only make the straight by catching the perfect card "in the gut" (also known as a *Bellybuster* for similar reasons). It can only become a Straight by catching the 6. Therefore, 10-Jack-Queen is much better than 10-Jack-King. That's because open-ended 4-Straights are always better than close-ended 4-Straights or gut shot Straights that have four cards in sequence except for one gap, like 5-6-8-9. With an open-ended Straight like 9-10-Jack-Queen there are 8 cards that make a Straight—four Kings plus four 8s. But with a close-ended Straight, like 9-Jack-Queen-King or Ace-K-Q-J, only 4 cards, in this case four 10s, make your hand.

You are more likely to have an open-ended 4-Straight if you start with an open-ended 3-Straight. Hence, 4-5-6 is twice as likely as 4-6-7 or 3-5-6 to make 4-5-6-7 or 3-4-5-6.

Again, you wouldn't be too far wrong if you just didn't play for Straights. That being said there is some profit in them, especially if the players at your table are especially bad and will always call you even when you've obviously made a Straight. You don't want to play for Straights if you're at a table with very conservative players who fold every time they sense you're strong. We'll deal with this more when we talk about table selection. But for now, let's look at the minimum standards for playing 3-Straights.

First, only play three sequential cards, like 8-9-10 or 4-5-6. *Don't* play three cards with one or two gaps in them like 4-5-7 or 2-4-5. (The one exception to this rule is if your table is very, very loose. By that I mean that nearly everyone calls the first bet. If you have six or seven people who tend to stay in the hand on Third Street then you can call a bet too with a 3-Straight and see another card, but only if the missing card and the other Straight cards are completely live. So if you have 8-9-J and there are no 7s, Qs, or especially 10s that are in front of other players, you can play this hand against loose opponents.)

Second, only play these sequential cards if the next cards in sequence are completely live. For example, if you have 5-6-7 you play only if you don't see any 8s or 4s dealt to other players.

Third, play only if the secondary sequential cards are very live. For example, if you have 5-6-7 you play only if there are no 8s or 4s showing and no more than one 3 or 9.

After Third Street do not play Straights at all if you don't make four sequential cards. Do *not* play your 5-6-7 if you don't catch an 8 or a 4. Even if you catch a 3 or a 9, dump these hands for a bet. (Again, I would make one very limited exception in a very loose game. If you have five or more callers on Fourth Street and your cards are still completely live, you can call a bet.)

Also dump your 3-Straights if there is more than one full bet on Third Street. If, for example, you have 7-8-9 and the guy to your left raises and another player reraises, fold, regardless of the other up cards. You're not going to pay $10 to see your next card. If your cards are live and it's only $5, go ahead and play. For $10, don't.

High 3-Straights are better than low 3-Straights for two reasons. The first is obvious. If you make your Straight, a high Straight will beat a lower Straight. And, if you start with a high 3-Straight you have a chance to pair one of your high cards on Fourth Street and then have a Premium Pair. (Remember, a Premium Pair is a pair of 10s or higher.) Premium Pairs are very playable on Fourth Street. Low pairs are not. So by starting with a high 3-Straight, you have two ways to improve your hand.

Summary. Only play 3-Straights if the cards that make your Straight are live; higher Straights are better to play than lower Straights.

3-Flushes: Three Cards of the Same Suit

3-Flushes are better than 3-Straights. If you make a Flush you will beat every Straight. How do you know whether or not to play your 3-Flush?

Ideally, your suit is completely live; no cards of your suit are out elsewhere. But you can also take a card off if there is one of your suit out—even if two are out if one of your cards is a high card like an Ace or a King. But if more than two of your suit are out on the deal, don't even pay the bring-in to see another card. The odds are too long against you drawing the Flush.

There is an advantage to your 3-Flush if one or more of your cards are premium cards: 10 or higher. If you start with a suited 2-4-9, for example, your hand really has no future unless you catch another suited card. But if you start with A-K-9, you can improve with either another suited card or another Ace or King. This makes high 3-Flushes more playable than low 3-Flushes. But don't fall in love with this hand. If you don't catch another suited card or hit a Premium Pair, the hand is pretty worthless and should be folded for a bet on Fourth Street.

In addition, you should fold your 3-Flush on Third Street if there is more than one raise. If the pot has been raised and reraised, fold.

Another consideration for both Flushes and Straights is how many players are going to be in the pot to see the next card. When you're trying to make a Flush or a Straight you want lots of people in the pot with you. That's because you want the eventual pot you win to be large to justify the relatively small chance that you'll make that Flush or Straight.

Put another way, hands that need to draw cards to make a Flush or a Straight (known familiarly as *Flush draws* or *Straight draws*) don't play well short-handed. You don't want just one other opponent in the pot with you as you try to make your Flush or Straight. So if the betting action makes it seem likely that it will heads up (just you and another player), you should generally fold these drawing hands.

Here's an example. The player to your immediate left is dealt the 2♣, the lowest cards showing, and thereby has to start the betting for $2 in this hypothetical $5/10 game. Each player folds until it gets to the player to your right. He has an Ace showing. You have the 4♥, 8♥, 9♥. He raises to $5. It's now your option. What do you do?

You should fold here. If you call and the 2♣ folds for the raise, it's just going to be you against that other player with an Ace. You'll be drawing for the Flush. You won't win enough of the time to justify calling a pot that will be small. The only possible exception to this is if you have two or three high cards of the same suit that are higher than the card of the raiser. Then you might call the raise, hoping to pair one of your high cards. If you do, play the hand as a Premium Pair.

Summary. If you have a Premium Pair, raise. If you have a small Pair, fold unless you can call for just the bring-in, unless it is wired or unless your third card is an Ace or a King. And your pair must be live. If you have a 3-Straight either fold, call for the bring-in if your Straight cards are very live, or call for no more than one bet if your Straight cards are high and live. If you have three to a Flush, call for up to one raise if there aren't three or more of your suit out and if it looks like you'll be up against at least two players.

Three of a Kind

What if you have Three of a Kind? Don't worry too much about this; it happens rarely. But if you are dealt Trips, play them aggressively at a table with people who generally call the initial raise, but slowly if the players are very *tight* (tend to fold a lot). Similarly, if a number of players have already called the bet before it gets to you, go ahead and raise with Trips. At this level, players who have thrown in one bet or even the partial bring-in bet are unlikely to fold for your late raise. They'll tend to call for the one additional raise.

Summary. Play fast if you're with loose players likely to call; slow play if you think they will all fold if you raise.

STARTING HAND SUMMARY

Playable hands in loose-passive game on Third Street (first three cards):

- Three of a Kind
- Pair
- Three to a Flush
- Three to a Straight

Play the High Pair aggressively.
Play the Low Pair sparingly and with a big kicker or in good
    position.
Only play the 3-Flush if there aren't more than two of your
    suit out.
Play the 3-Straight only sparingly, if at all. High 3-Straights
    are better than low 3-Straights. "Gapped" 3-Straights
    aren't worth playing.
Take your position into consideration when making your
    play.

Fourth Street: The Second Up Card

You're going to start by learning to play very conservatively (tight). As your skills improve and you can better gauge the relative strengths and weaknesses of your fellow players, you can loosen up some to suit the situation. But for now, we're going to concentrate on playing tight.

If another player pairs his or her *door card* (first up card), you should fold unless you've made a higher *set* (Three of a Kind). Say, for example, that you are dealt a split Pair of Aces (one Ace in the hole and one face up). You raise and get called by someone with a Jack up. The Jack then gets another Jack and you get a blank. He then bets. If there are no other Jacks that have been folded you should fold to this raise. Odds are that he has Trip Jacks. Even if you have made Aces up (a Pair of Aces and another pair), you are probably badly behind and likely to be buried if you play this hand to completion. The exception to this is if you have already seen a Jack folded. If that's the case, you could consider a raise here, especially if you have Two Pair. The reason is threefold: to see whether he raises you back (in which case he probably has Trips), to get him to fold (if he only has a pair of Jacks), or to get him to call with an inferior hand.

What should you do if you pair your up card and make Trips on Fourth Street? You have the option of betting the lower amount or the higher amount. I suggest that, generally, you bet the higher amount. If you bet the lower amount, better players may think you have the Trips anyway and fold. They'll be good enough to suspect your low bet with a pair showing means that you *want* them to call. And this will convince them to fold. The bad players will call you regardless of what you really have. So bet them strongly, hope for a call or two, and build the pot.

If you are playing a Premium Pair and you make Two Pair, bet and raise if you figure to have the top Two Pair. If someone else pairs a door card, fold to her bet or check if you are in the lead, with the expectation that she will bet and you will fold.

I can't stress enough the power of a paired door card. Most of the time this means that your opponent has Trips. You don't want to hang around hoping he's bluffing or hoping to get lucky and outdraw him. Especially at this level, when you are learning a basic strategy, don't bet against what your opponents are representing in the early rounds of betting. They usually have what they appear to have.

Now, if you have not made Two Pair or Trips, you should still bet your Premium Pair unless you see evidence that it isn't in the lead. You can't fail to bet just because your opponent *may* have you beaten. That's a frequent mistake of losing casino players.

If a person hasn't paired his door card, and if the betting action hasn't gotten very aggressive by the time it's your turn to act, go ahead and put in a raise. If you don't see anyone else obviously improve by catching a pair or a card higher than your Premium Pair, you should surely lead the betting.

Let's say you have a pair of Queens or Jacks and you are high on Fourth Street. You should bet. If, on the other hand, a player with a 6 who just got a King bets in front of you and it is up to you, you should just call. See what develops on Fifth Street.

If you are drawing to a Flush or Straight, fold your hand if you don't improve. Improvements may be in the form of pairing one of your cards. But be careful. You need to make a Premium Pair to continue. For example, if you're starting with suited 6-9-Q and you get a 6, this hand should be dumped. But if you pair the Queen and it doesn't look like anyone has a higher pair, bet this hand.

Your hand might develop in different directions at the same time. On Fifth Street you might get another heart; on Sixth Street you might make Two Pair or Trips. But you want to have the high pair to play on.

Summary—Fourth Street

- If you are the best hand on Fourth Street, play aggressively.
- Fold if someone else has a paired door card.
- If you are drawing to a Straight or Flush, either improve or fold.

Fifth Street

Fifth Street is the trickiest round to play. Poor players become committed to their hands by then and feel they have to play on to protect the money they've already put into the pot. You are not going to play that way. The money you have already bet is no longer yours. Each round involves an independent decision.

The stakes double on Fifth Street. If you have a low or middle pair and someone bets, fold. Figure that the bettor has a higher hand than yours. Similarly, two low pair should generally be folded if you believe your hand is second best or if your cards are not very live. You probably lose more with two low pair than with any other hand. It's enough to suck you in but it's usually not enough to win. So if you've seen a couple of cards of the rank of your Two Pair, get out now.

Seat 4, You: (4-8) 4   Seat 5: Q

Seat 3: J   Seat 6: 5

Seat 2: 6   Seat 7: 4

Seat 1: 8   Seat 8: 5

Let's say the game is $5–$10. You started the betting with $2 as the bring-in with a (4-8) 4. Everyone called you. On Fourth Street you got an 8. All of the other players checked to you. You bet with your Two Pair. One player, who caught a 10 to go with his Jack, called.

You: (4-8) 4-8   Him: (x-x) J-10

On Fifth Street, he got a Jack and you got a 10.

You: (4-8) 4-8-10   Him: (x-x) J-10-J

He bet. You should fold. Your hand is probably second best and unlikely to improve since two of the four cards that will give you a Full House are gone. The pot is heads up, just you and another player. This means that even if you did pull the long shot, you wouldn't win a huge pot. So it doesn't make sense for you to chase here. So *fold*.

You may argue with me here. You may say that there's no way to know that he has your 8s and 4s beaten. After all, you may point out, all that you see is a pair of Jacks. And you're correct. That's all I see. So, frankly, that's all I really know. I don't know that he is in the lead. I don't know that he has better than your hand.

But 7-Card Stud is not usually a game about knowing. It is a game about deducing. You are seeing his up cards, remembering cards that have been folded, remembering his betting action, and *deducing* what he is *likely* to have. That's one important part to winning at 7-Stud. Deduction.

The deduction alone is not sufficient though. Many players get very good at figuring out what their opponents are likely to have. But they lack the ability to make correct betting decisions based on that information. You need to do both to be a winning 7-Card Stud player.

In this instance, you are deducing that your opponent has a better hand than yours. You remember that he called your bet on Third Street and then again on Fourth Street. So you figure that he probably started out with at least a pair. Maybe a Pair of Jacks (though if he had a pair of Jacks why didn't he raise?). But more likely some small or medium pair in the hole. When he pairs his Jacks he has *probably* made Jacks Up—a Pair of Jacks and a pair of something else. Again, you're not 100 percent certain, but you can deduce it. So you should fold.

Broken Straights (hands that start out as Straights but don't get there) on Fifth Street are tempting but should also be dumped. If I have 4-5-6-8-x and there is a bet to me on Fifth Street I am out of there.

If your Premium Pair still hasn't improved, bet if you figure to be the best hand. Bet if you read someone for a Flush draw. If there are higher cards out, however, and you figure you are probably second best, now is the time to fold to a bet.

For example, let's say that you raised on Third Street with a pair of Jacks and were called by two players. Player A catches another heart to go with her up card and the other player catches a King to go with his 10. You bet on Fourth Street and the King folds and the player with the hearts also calls. Now, on Fifth Street you catch a blank and the hearts catch a blank. Do not check! Even though you have only a pair you must bet here to prevent your opponent from getting another card without calling your bet. That's called a *free card*. And if you figure that you have the better hand, make your opponent pay to see another card.

Yes, she may have Two Pair or even Trips. But what is likely is that she is going for a Flush or has a lower pair and is looking for Trips or her second pair. Don't allow her to get a card that will help her without paying for the privilege by calling a bet. So you bet.

Now if your opponent did catch a Flush card on Fifth Street, you would have a difficult decision. Should you check and see if she bets or should you bet and see if she folds, calls, or raises? Your ability to make deductions is tested again here. Did she seem to be on a Flush draw? Were there a number of cards of her suit that folded already? Does she play 3-Flushes from the start? Is she capable of raising on Fifth Street without a Flush? If you check, will she bet if she has caught her Flush? Might she bet even if she hasn't caught it as a bluff?

All things being equal, my advice is—on Fifth Street—to bet when your opponent has three suited up cards. True, she may already have a Flush. But if you check you are just giving a player with four suited cards a free chance at that fifth card. That for me is much more of a mistake than betting into a potential Flush. If she raises you back, you can always fold.

Let's look at the same scenario but instead of the heart hand getting a heart, it catches a blank and the King gets another King. If the King bets you are definitely gone. Even if he doesn't have Trips, he has a higher pair than your pair. So you are a dog—maybe a huge dog. Save your money for another hand. Don't think about the money you have already put in the pot. It is irrelevant.

Let's look at another case. Imagine you bet on Third Street with a Pair of Jacks and were raised by someone with a 5. A third player called the two raises with a 10 and you called. On Fourth Street you all caught blanks. You bet again, the 5 called, and the 10 folded. On Fifth Street, your opponent caught an Ace. She bet. What do you do?

Unless this player is a maniac I would be strongly tempted to fold. I'd have to think, "What is this player likely to have?" If she started with a pair of 5s and a blank, would she have re-raised me on Third Street? Maybe, but not unless she had a very big kicker, probably an Ace. So if she is betting now I'm going to give her, most of the time, Aces up. She may even have Trips if she raised with a pair of Aces in the hole. Of course, she may be bluffing. And if the action were four-way or more until that point so the pot was very big I might decide that I was getting sufficient pot odds (see Odds and Ends, chapter 6, for an explanation of pot odds) to justify a call. But if it had been heads up from Fourth Street I would probably see myself as too likely to be a dog to justify throwing any more money into the pot.

There are a few things that you should watch for to prepare for situations like this. If your opponent looks at his down card when he gets the second or the third up card, you can pretty much rule him off of the Flush. He is likely to have *one* of his suit in the hole, not two. If he started with three suited cards, he'd be much more likely to remember that fact. Of course he may be doing it deliberately, to fake you out—but you should be able to figure out whether your opponent is tricky enough to do this.

The decision is different if he improves. If he pairs his door card you are out of there. If he pairs his Fourth Street card, you should sometimes call. The decision to call depends on a few factors and is somewhat complicated. Here's what I consider.

If I have a pair higher than his paired Fourth Street card I call him. For example:

He: (x-x) 10-9-9   Me: (J-6) J-5-2

My Pair of Jacks is higher than his 9s. I would call here. I figure that he might very well have Two Pair—maybe 10s and 9s or maybe some other hidden pair and 9s. Even so, my Pair of Jacks is only a slight underdog even if he does have Two Pair. So I'm going to call.

I would also tend to call if I had a kicker higher than his Pair—and if my kicker was at least a King or an Ace. For example:

He: (x-x) 10-9-9   Me: (6-A) 6-8-Q

I'd call his Pair of 9s here as well. I have a good chance of getting an Ace or even a Queen to give me a higher Two Pair.

Remember, my cards need to be live. It also helps if his cards are not especially live. In the example just given, it would be especially good if I'd seen a 9 and a 10 folded by other players.

But let's say the situation was different. If, for example, I didn't have the Ace or the Queen but still had just the pair of 6s.

He: (x-x) 10-9-9   Me: (6-10) 6-8-2

I'd fold here to his bet. That's because, without the Ace or the Queen I'm unlikely to make a pair higher than his exposed Pair of 9s. If I make another Pair it's more likely to be by getting another 8 or another 2. (Notice that he has an exposed 10. And remember, he called a bet on Third Street and Fourth Street before he caught his Pair of 9s. So he's likely to have two 10s, meaning that there's very little chance I'll get another 10. And even if I did, with his likely 10s and 9s he'd beat me even if I made 10s and 6s.)

Other factors might make me call a bet from a player with a paired Fourth Street card, even if I had only one Pair. If the pot were especially large at this point because there had been many callers on Third or Fourth Street, I'd be more likely to call. If I estimated that my opponent was the type of player who played very loosely early on and might not have Two Pair, I'd be more likely to call. Finally, if I thought she was a player who folds too often on Sixth or Seventh Street if her opponent bets, I would call, thinking that I might be able to out play her on these streets.

Small pairs on Fourth Street and Fifth Street are played pretty straightforwardly. If your cards are live and you have a small pair with a big kicker, you should call on these streets unless your opponent catches something scary. For example, if he catches a pair higher than your kicker, fold; if he catches three to a Flush or three to a Straight and you had put him on a draw to either of those hands, fold. Also, if the hands remain multi-way, consider folding. A small pair with a big kicker doesn't play well multi-way. You can lose too many ways even if you improve to Two Pair. But if it's heads up, your cards are live, and your single opponent doesn't catch anything scary, you can call.

Now is the time to fold your Flush and Straight draws if the cards that you need are not still very much alive. If, for example, you have seen five or more of your Flush cards hit other players, you should fold with your 4-Flush. If you are on a Straight draw and have seen more than three of the primary cards that make your Straight, you should fold. There are exceptions to these rules, but until you are an experienced casino player (500 or more hours), play close to this strategy and save your money for better opportunities.

Summary

- If you are the best hand, play aggressively.
- If you are on a draw and your cards are very live, call.
- If you are on a draw and your cards are not very live, fold.

Sixth Street

In general if you called on Fifth Street you are going to call on Sixth Street. There are exceptions however. If your opponent's board makes you think they've improved, you might fold. You have to use your power of deduction. If you have what you gauge to be the lead hand, continue to bet—to require the drawing hands to put up money if they want to see their next cards.

If you have a drawing hand, the pot is probably sufficiently large to warrant calling another bet. But again, you need to pay attention to the cards that are out. If you see all of the cards that you need to catch to make your hand falling on your opponents' board, get out of there. Similarly, if you are catching cards that you think your opponent needs to make her hand, be more aggressive.

Let's look at some examples of hands on Sixth Street that should be folded.

Suppose that on the deal you received (J-8) J.

The cards out were 8, 6, 5, 9, 2, (J-8) J, 9, 10.

You raised the 2 bring-in and were called by the 10, who is a very tight player, and the Deuce who is a very loose player and was the bring-in. Everyone else folded.

On Fourth Street the 10 caught a suited Ace; you caught a 5 to go with your Jacks. He checked. You bet. He called. The 2, catching an offsuit K, called.

On Fifth Street the Ace-10 caught another 10, the 2-K caught a Q, and you caught a 4. The pair of 10s checked, the Deuce checked, and you checked.

On Sixth Street this is what you see.

2, K, Q, 7 (7 and Deuce suited)
(J-8) J, 5, 4, 3
10, A, 10, 6 (10, A, 6 are suited)

Now the pair of 10s bet. The Deuce calls. It's your move. What should you do? Fold here.

Sure, the 3-Flush may be bluffing, and the Deuce may be a fool for calling with no more than a pair or maybe a 4-Flush. Sure you might be the best hand, since you only see a pair of 10s. And you could improve to Trips or Jacks up on the River. But there are so many ways that you may be beaten now—and therefore drawing dead—that a call isn't justified.

What do I mean by "drawing dead"? That means that even if you make the hand you are drawing for, a hand that someone currently holds may still beat you. Even if you make your Trip

Jacks, someone could have a Flush. You should fold if you strongly suspect that you are drawing dead.

Summary. In general, on Sixth Street, if someone looks like they may well have a hand that you can't beat even if you hit your hand on the River, you should fold to a bet. On the other hand, if you estimate that you are in the lead, you should bet. And if you are on a draw, and are likely to be the best hand if you hit, you should call.

Seventh Street (a.k.a. the River)

The strategy for Seventh Street is to bet if you think you are the best hand, check if you're not sure where you stand, and call on the end with nearly any hand that has even a slim prospect of being the best hand. If you've made your Flush on the end, bet unless you're pretty sure you're against a higher Flush or a Full House. It's true that someone might raise you with a Full House you didn't see. That's okay. You'll make more money in the long run by getting that last bet in and getting called by lesser hands. On the other hand, if you have Kings Up and you're against a Flush draw, check if you're up first. Why bet? He'll raise if he made his hand and probably fold if he didn't. So you don't make any extra money by betting.

On the other hand, if you have a Pair of Jacks that never improved and a guy who was drawing for a Flush bets, call even if you feel pretty sure but not certain that he made the Flush. Since this final bet is so small compared with the size of the pot, it makes sense to call.

Similarly, sometimes you should bet on the River if the pot is large, even if you haven't made your hand. If the pot is $100 at the end, your bet of $10 has to win only 1 in 10 times for you to break even. So if you decide that there is a better than 1 chance in 10 that your opponent will fold to your bet, you should make this play.

Admittedly, this kind of estimating is far from an exact science. After all, how do you really know that there is a better than 1 chance in 10 that your opponent will fold to your bet?

You don't. But 7-Card Stud is a game of estimation, not certainty. Think about how sure you are. If you're undecided—on the fence so to speak—then that would be about a 50-50 chance— 5 times in 10. If you're almost certain maybe it's a 90 percent probability. That's 9 chances in 10. If you think you don't have more than a very small chance—but there is some small chance after all—well maybe that's a 1 in 10 possibility.

Most of the time we make these decisions intuitively. But it helps sometimes to think about them precisely, even if you can't come up with the math every time you're making a decision.

It's easy to learn some lessons too well. Before you started playing poker in a casino, you played very loosely. You didn't think of poker as a game of skill much back then. So you'd throw your chips into the middle of the table like everyone else and hope to win. That was showdown poker. You won; you lost; you drank some beer and you had a good time. (Come to think of it, not such a bad time after all.)

But you've since learned that things are different in a casino. In fact, every book you've picked up stresses the same thing— that is—play only quality starting hands, exercise discipline, fold, fold, fold, and folding.

If you are like most recreational players, you didn't get much beyond the first chapter of those books. So folding was the only lesson you took with you. *That* you remembered. To win in a casino you must play tightly.

To some extent, that's a good message. It is probably the biggest difference between playing in a loosey-goosey home game and playing in a casino. If you can't learn to throw away 75 percent or more of your starting hands, you probably can't win.

The problem arises when a player extends this lesson mindlessly to all rounds of betting. The inexperienced or losing player usually errs on the side of looseness early in the hand; however, this same player may very well err on the side of tightness late in the hand. Simply put, players often fold too readily on the River.

Consider the following scenario. You are dealt a split Pair of 8s with a Queen kicker. The bring-in starts the betting with $2 and four players call the bring-in to you. You think about raising to drive out other players, then remember that players are unlikely to fold for one full bet if they have already put in part of the bet. You decide correctly to call since none of your 8s or Qs are out.

On the next hand you get a 10. You check. The player, with a 7 Up, starts the betting with $5. He has a 7 and a 2 of Hearts showing. One other player calls as do you.

The 7-2 2-Flush gets an unsuited 5. You get a King and the third player gets a Deuce. You think about checking but you hate to give a free heart to the 7-2. You decide to bet with your pair of 8s and your 10, K, and Q. The 2-Flush calls you; the other player folds.

On Sixth Street you get an unhelpful 7. Your opponent gets an 8. You check and he checks after you.

Now it is the River. You haven't improved. You have nothing but your bare pair of 8s. Your opponent bets. What do you do?

Many players, especially those who have just become casino 7-Card Stud players, will fold in this situation. Here's their reasoning. They think that their opponent probably made the Flush. But even if he didn't he's bound to have a hand that can beat a lousy Pair of 8s. They think about all of the hands their opponent could have: Two Pair, Trips, a higher pair in the hole—even a well-hidden Straight.

And you know what? They're probably right. Their opponent probably has them beaten. But, without question, unless you know your opponent *never* bluffs, you should call. Let's look more closely at the decision the player has.

The bet is $10. The pot is around $80. So you are getting 8:1 pot odds for your call.

Should you call? How sure are you that he has a better hand? Well you are at least more sure than not, right? You are at least more than 50 percent sure because if you were less than 50 percent, you'd think that he probably was bluffing. Even if you're leaning in the direction of folding, however, think about how sure you really are. Are you 60 percent sure? 70 percent sure? It's hard to put a number on it, I know. But do your best.

Keep in mind, that if you had to pause to think about what to do, it's probably pretty close to a 50-50 decision. That's why you had to pause. Otherwise, if it were a more clear cut decision you would make it quickly. There's at least a good chance that you're not sure or you wouldn't have paused.

Now, do the math. (I know it seems absurd in a way—how do you quantify these things? But do your best.) If you think he's twice as likely to have you beat than to be on a stone cold bluff, that's 66.6 percent sure (66.6 to 33.3 or, simplified 2 to 1). If that's born out statistically, 66.6 percent of the time you will be correct and 33.3 percent of the time you will be wrong. Two to one.

Now let's look at the pot along with that frequency of right and wrong calls. Your fold will save you $20 (two times the $10 bet you save each time you are right). But when you are wrong that one time you will fold with the winning hand. Then you will lose the $80 in the pot that you *would* have won had you stayed in. So, folding with a pot that large is clearly a mistake even if you're pretty sure your opponent was bluffing.

But what if you're really, really sure that he was bluffing? Let's say you were four times as sure that he was bluffing as not bluffing. That would mean that 80 percent of the time you'd be right and he'd be bluffing and 20 percent of the time you'd be wrong and he wouldn't be bluffing. Then you're *really* sure. You were *four* times more sure that he had a hand than that he was bluffing

Eighty percent of the time he had the hand and only 20 percent of the time he was bluffing. Do the math now. That's easy; 80:20 is the same as 4:1, right? So 4 times you will be right and 1 time you will be wrong. Four times you will save $10 by folding and one time you will miss out on the $80 pot that you would have won if you called. So you either save $40 or you lose $80. Did you make the right call by folding? No.

Just how sure did you have to be? Well the pot is $80 and

your bet is $10. You do the math. You have to be right eight times for every one time you are wrong. In other words, if you are about 87 percent sure, then you break even! And in poker, with unknown or little known opponents, you are rarely, if *ever* that sure of what they are doing.

So a call makes sense. In fact, some players will tell you that you should raise. Raise? "What, are you crazy?" you think. "Until a few minutes ago I was thinking I should fold. Why would I even consider raising with my lousy Pair of 8s," you ask.

The reason you might raise would be if you were playing against a player who plays too tightly on the River. You would have to have observed her for a while to reach this conclusion. But if you've been observant you may have noticed that she folds when she thinks she's beaten, even on the River. If you think there is even a small (but not minuscule) possibility that your opponent might fold for your raise, the raise makes sense.

Think about it. If you had a busted 4-Flush (a 4-Flush that never became a Flush), and only a Pair of 10s, and bet on the last card after your opponent checked, and then she check-raised *you*, what would you do? Any chance you might think, "Oh, my God. All I've got is a lousy Pair of 10s. And she's raised. She *must* have me beaten." And you might fold. Right? Well, so might your opponent.

But how sure would you have to be that your opponent would fold here for this raise to make sense? Well it's the same simple math that is getting you to call more on the River.

The pot, after your opponent's bet, is $90. Your raise would cost $20. She will call only if she can beat you. What are the chances she has you beat?

If she calls you less than four times out of five, you win money. Four times you wasted your $20 raise, for a total cost of $80. One time you bluffed her out of the pot and won $90. So your raising strategy nets you $10 every five times you do it.

In these typical lower- and middle-limit games you will seldom be in situations where you feel certain that your opponents will fold if you check-raise them. Most of the players I play with are very loose, will call with just about anything on the River, and are more likely to check on the end even with hands like a pair of 10s. But, as you can see, unexpected aggression can pay off, especially if you've gauged your opponent correctly as a tight player who is capable of folding on the River.

Curiously, even after many players learn how important it is to call on the River, even if their chances of winning are small, they often fold too much and raise too little. Even when they know that the odds favor calls on the River, they have a very tough time making those calls. Why is that?

Part of the reason is because calling with a hand they think is likely, though not certain to lose, goes against all of the basic notions they have about the difference between good and bad players. Good players can fold bad starting hands. They have self-control. They are aggressive with their hands when they are in the lead and they fold when they are behind. We have learned this not as a general concept but as a mantra. And calling with a likely (though not definite) loser goes against that grain like misused chalk on a chalkboard.

We call players like this, who inappropriately fold under pressure *weak-tight*. They suffer from the timidity of the inexperienced. Armed with some knowledge, and very little experience, they lack the courage to take chances even when the odds are in their favor. They want sure things. Their emotions are still too closely tied to the outcome of each hand.

They know that winning feels good and losing feels lousy, so they avoid losing. Losing a hand is humiliating to them because they do not yet have the deep-rooted confidence that comes from years of winning play. What other players think still matters. Therefore, to avoid looking foolish, they avoid showdowns where they are likely to lose.

It's like the inexperienced fielder in baseball who prays before every pitch, "Please don't hit it to me; please don't hit it to me!" Beginning players—and even many veterans—would rather concede than lose. By that I mean that they would rather pat themselves on the back for being able to fold hands than face the emotional letdown of showing down a loser. It's as if the losing hand was an example of their being bad players. They become afraid to lose, afraid to show weakness to the other players, lest they be thought ill of.

It goes deeper than that, too. Some tight players, who have been able to make some profit at the game, give up even more profit because they are afraid to lose. They are not willing to lose three of four hands even if winning the fourth hand will make money for them in the long run. They don't like the experience of losing a hand, so they wrongly avoid the showdown by folding prematurely.

Just like skiers must learn to fall so that they will fall correctly and avoid injury, so too must good casino poker players learn to lose. You must lose hands, many hands, to be playing optimally. So learn to deal with losing.

Another analogy comes to mind. It's from baseball.

Ever heard of a ball player who has stolen 15 bases in 15 chances? The general public thinks that he must be a great base stealer. A score of 15 for 15 is perfect, isn't it? But in fact any baseball coach will tell you that this player is not playing great. If he is stealing every time he attempts a steal then he is not attempting enough steals. By going 15 for 15 he is probably only attempting a steal when it is a sure thing. And if that is the case, he could probably maximize the bases he steals by attempting steals more often—even though he will be caught some percentage of the time.

You don't want to play poker as if you must win every hand you show down. You will be giving up an enormous amount of potential profit if you do this. Excellent poker is *not* a sure thing. There *is* gamble to the game. If you make or call bets only when you are absolutely certain you have the best hand, or a winning hand, you will doom yourself to folding on the River too often. And as we have seen, that will cut into your profit and your overall winnings.

Now, don't go crazy with this. Don't call when you are absolutely certain you are beaten. But, when the pot is large, the best action on the River is usually a call.

Think about whether you are afraid to lose in poker. If you

are, there may be some good reasons. Perhaps you're not ready to play in a casino for money. Maybe the stakes are too high for your bankroll. Maybe they're just too high for you. That's possible you know. There are many people who can financially afford to play medium or high poker but who can't handle it psychologically. There's no shame in this. For some people it just is. Stick to enjoying your home game if you are one of them. If you've thought about it, and if you're sure that you really do want to play in a casino, there are some things you can do to accommodate your anxiety about losing. When it comes down to the River and you have one of those hands like I've described when you think you'll probably lose, try leaving the game mentally. The betting is over. There's nothing else you can do, so take off! Turn your head away from the action if you must. But *call* the bet first!

Summary

- Call on the River unless you're certain that you are beat.
- Check if you're not sure where you stand.
- Bet your hand on the River if there is even a slight chance your opponent will either fold or call you with a lesser hand.

Strategy Variations for Spread Limit Games

Spread limit means that the size of the bet on each betting round is not fixed at a specific amount but may range between two amounts. $1–$5 spread limit, for example, means that the bettor can bet between $1 and $5 on each bet. There are some restrictions to this, as I'll explain later, but in general it allows more flexibility in betting than in fixed limit betting.

For the most part, very low-limit, spread limit games involve similar strategy to those in the low-limit fixed limit games. There are some exceptions however.

Your strategy needs to be adjusted to compensate for two significant differences between spread limit and fixed limit. In the typical spread limit game, the bring-in bet is often not raised on Third Street. And there tend to be many more multi-way pots in spread limit than in fixed limit. Players at this level are often very timid, checking and calling a lot. This leads to many showdowns with three, four, and even five players.

When the initial bring-in isn't raised in a $1–$5 game, for 20 percent of a full bet you can often call and see Fourth Street very cheaply, fairly confident that you will not be raised. This is a useful ploy when you have starting hands that might develop into powerful hands, but which can only be helped in that direction by very few cards. For example, in a fixed limit $5/10 game you would rarely call the initial $2 forced bet if you held a three-suited 7-8-10 in early position. In a spread limit game, where the bring-in is rarely raised, even if you are in early position, you may call the forced bet of $1 if all your straight cards, especially the 9, are completely live. But you must be prepared to throw the hand away if someone raises the pot or if you don't hit a 9 on Fourth Street.

Similarly, you can play small pairs with a small kicker for just the bring-in. But you must be willing to throw them away for a raise or if you don't catch Trips on Fourth Street. Keep in mind that two small pair is a trap hand. It should not be played for any full bet—though you can call on Fourth Street for $1 in the hope of getting one of the four cards that will give you a Full House on Fifth. For any serious betting, however, you will fold on Fourth Street with your two small pairs.

Another hand that is worth a call of $1 would be three high cards, even if they were not straight cards. A hand like A-K-10, for example, which has only a minuscule chance of making a Straight, is still worthy of making a call for $1 in a $1–$5 game because of the possibility of getting a Premium Pair on Fourth Street. If you don't get it or if someone after you raises the pot, you must fold.

Another variation comes when you have a very powerful hand on Third Street. If you hold a Pair of Aces on Third Street in a spread limit game, you might not raise the full amount unless you know, from your observation of other players, that at least one player will call. You might only raise to $2 or $3 with Aces, to get someone with a lower pair to call, who might fold for the full bet of $5. Note that you don't have this option in a fixed limit game. In a fixed limit game your only options are to call the bring-in or complete the bet to the full amount (or fold of course). In those circumstances, it is nearly always correct not to allow players in for just the bring-in—as nearly everyone will call it and you'll be in a multi-way hand when you want to be playing heads up. But in spread limit the action tends to be fairly weak. Few players raise the full amount on Third Street. So your raise of $1 or $2 may properly thin the field without scaring away everyone. So you get exactly what you want with a small raise—by getting one or two bad calls and five or six good folds.

Don't confuse how you play Aces (and usually Kings) in spread limit on Third Street with how you play other Premium Pairs. When you raise with 10s, Jacks, and Queens on Third Street, always make the maximum raise. In a $1–$5 spread limit game the maximum raise would be $5. So raise by $5.

You want to limit the field and are willing to win the hand right there rather than go to Fourth Street and beyond. Don't try to suck people in with a $1 or $2 raise when you have anything but Aces or Kings.

In some situations it isn't wrong to just call with your Premium Pair. Here's why. Much of the time you'll be folding this hand on Fourth Street when it doesn't improve and when there are many opponents. So you'll be saving money by not making an unhelpful and unnecessary raise.

A Pair of Jacks, especially without an Ace or King kicker is a dog if there are three or more players chasing Straights and Flushes. Don't lead with it in a way that gets a bunch of callers. If your raise on Third Street didn't have the intended effect of significantly thinning the field, don't stubbornly push this hand on Fourth Street. Instead, think about either thinning the field on Fourth Street or getting out if there is any betting. Be less inclined to be as aggressive as you would be in a typical fixed limit game on Fourth Street with the lower tier of Premium Pairs: 10s, Jacks, and Queens, for example.

When players are less aggressive, looser, and more passive as they frequently are in a typical $1–$5 game, it often pays for you to be similarly so. It seems contradictory, but your response to the bad play of your opponents may be to become more like them in certain ways.

From early position, on Fourth Street, with three or more players left to act, check this hand most of the time, with the expectation that everyone else will check or that there will be a bet to your right that you can raise to limit the field. The loose callers may call for a single bet in this loose spread limit game, but they are unlikely to call for a double raise.

Be thoughtful about this. You have to consider how your additional raise will affect other players. If a player to your right bets and then you raise, you make it two bets for anyone after you if they want to call the bet. People who might have been willing to call a single bet with their marginal hands will often fold for the double bet that you've created with your raise. But if someone has already called a bet and then you raise, they often will call the additional single bet, having already put money in the pot. Therefore, if the initial bettor is on your right, you can make it two bets to limit the field. If the initial bettor is on your left, however, and has been called by a few players, think about folding. Remember, your hand is a dog against many drawing hands.

Other than that, I've found that the strategy for betting, raising, and folding in Spread Limit is similar to fixed limit—although you are often playing against worse players than you find in the lower fixed limits. Don't waste too much effort or money on trying to deceive your opponents with fancy plays. They will often not have a clue about what *they're* doing, let alone what your bets are supposed to mean. Straightforward, solid poker will get the money in the long run.

Summary. In a spread limit game, you can play somewhat more loosely and passively on Third Street, but you must be careful not to overvalue lower Premium Pairs on later streets.

Conclusion

You've now learned the basic mechanics of playing every hand you're likely to receive from Third Street through to the River. You're probably tempted to rush out to the nearest poker room and try them out. Let me suggest that you read, at the very least, the rest of this chapter before you start to indulge your desire to play. The following ten concepts will help keep you safe and thoughtful as you try out your new skills.

Predictability

I've given you a basic strategy to use in the lower stakes casino games. I've made it very clearcut and straightforward. This is on purpose. When you are starting out and learning 7-Card Stud you should use this as your fundamental method of play.

Let me address some seeming contradictions. You have probably heard that in poker, you should not be predictable. This is often correct. There are many reasons for this, but the primary one is that your opponents should not know what cards you hold based on how you bet your hand. If your betting patterns are too mechanical and predictable, the argument goes, your opponents will eventually learn them and be able to gain an advantage over you by knowing what you hold.

This is generally true. You don't want to become a player who is so easy to read that a good player knows exactly what cards you are holding. However, while you are learning how to properly play 7-Stud, I want you to forget about mixing up your play. Forget about it completely.

The natural tendency of the inexperienced casino player is to play too many hands. In short, he doesn't fold enough. He's made the sojourn to the casino. He didn't come to *fold!* Even if he read a book about how to play conservatively, he's still looking for excuses to play. A convenient excuse is the attempt to play unpredictably.

It is certainly correct that you don't want to become a player who is easy to read—meaning you don't want to be completely predictable. However, when you are starting out—while you are really learning how to play 7-Card Stud in a casino—don't worry about being predictable. In fact, it is much more important at this stage in your 7-Card Stud poker career that you learn to follow the basic guidelines I lay out than to mix up your play.

There are two reasons for this. First, most of your opponents in the games you should be in initially will not notice what you are doing anyway. And even if they do notice, they will usually lack the discipline or knowledge to adjust their play correctly. I've played in many of these games where I've folded every three-card poker hand that I was initially dealt for over an hour, then raised with an Ace Up (and Pair of Aces) and been called on every Street until the River by someone with a low pair that never improved. Either he didn't even think about what I was likely to have or, having thought about it, he still determined that calling me all the way to showdown was an acceptable play. Why mix up your play against a guy like this?

True, a good player would have noticed that I was a very tight player and been inclined to fold right away. But enough of these lower-limit players play so poorly that your consistent tight play will get their money.

Keep this in mind as well. Unlike a home game, your opponents change regularly and frequently. Players bust out, move to another table, or move to a different limit. New players, who have never seen you before, replace them. Even if your opponents do pick up, after a while, that you are pretty tight, they may very well be replaced before too long with someone who doesn't know anything about you. It's critical that you exercise great discipline by folding bad hands if you want to win at poker. This point can't be stressed enough, so let me repeat it.

You must exercise great discipline by folding bad hands if you want to win at poker.

There are too many excuses for loose play—weak calls, bad folds, and impulsive raises—you've got to eliminate them for my basic 7-Card Stud strategy. Get in the habit of tight-aggressive play. It's better to learn to play mechanically at first, losing a small amount of profit against the few players who do occasionally adjust to your strong play by not giving you action, than to play subpar in an effort to deceive your opponents, most of whom will not be observing or thinking about what you are doing.

Put another way, it is just too damn tempting to play badly for you to start to think that it can be justified in an effort to "mix up your play." As you learn the patience and diligence to apply this basic strategy well, you will be ready to move on to some of the more advanced concepts explained in the third and fourth chapter of this book, where deception does come into play. But for now, concentrate on playing correctly, even if you think that it makes your hand obvious.

Tells

One of the skills that beginning poker players seem most concerned about is the detection of tells. *Tells* are those behaviors or mannerisms that observant poker players notice in other players, which help to reveal the true strength of their hand. It is portrayed in many movies about poker. On the big screen, the observant and shrewd hero notices that his opponent has a habit of loosening his collar when he has a good hand, twirling his ring when he's bluffing, or listening closely as he separates the two halves of his Oreo cookies when he really has the goods. But that's the movies. In the real world, how does a good poker player actually take advantage of these types of idiosyncrasies at the poker table?

The question reminds me of a conversation I had online with an earnest young player who was trying to master the art of reading tells. He noted his assiduous study of other players, how he looked for hours and hours, trying to spot some giveaway mannerism, tic, or habit that would reveal hidden information about his opponent's hand. He mentioned that he saw many mannerisms but just didn't know which ones meant what. Did the extra blinking mean bluffing? Did it mean a strong hand? Or did it just mean he had too much cigarette smoke in his eyes?

My answer then and my answer now is the same. Don't put much stock in finding these giveaway tells. For the most part, especially in the lower-limit games, they are not worth looking for. In fact, they are usually a distraction. Your energy is better spent noticing and remembering other things, like which cards have been folded, who raised the bet, and what type of player you're up against.

If I am discouraging you from thinking about these kinds of tells, am I saying that it's not important to keep track of what your opponents are doing at the poker table? Certainly not. In fact, I think what they do is a window into their hands. Primarily, however, I'm concerned with what they are *intentionally* doing. And I'm much more interested in having you get the big picture than the small details.

Consider this analogous situation. If you wanted to become an expert at identifying cars you would not begin by staring at each car close up for a long time, memorizing all of the small details of the grill, the tread of the tire, or the small detail work of the chrome finish. You would most probably start instead by learning general patterns of the broad categories of motor vehicles. You'd learn first how to distinguish SUVs from trucks, vans from station wagons, and coupes from sedans. Then, perhaps, you'd advance to distinguishing Chevys from Fords or Toyotas from Chryslers by studying silhouettes of the cars in these major car companies. Only after you mastered that would you advance to more detailed observations about the model of the car.

Similarly, when it comes to reading players, you must first find the broadest and simplest categories into which to put your opponents. Keep it very, very simple and basic.

Start with this. Is your opponent tight or loose? Tight players play very few hands. Loose players call with many hands. Can you figure out what type of player you're up against? That's it, *tight* or *loose*! Does she fold a lot? Does he call a lot? Is he in a lot of hands or out of a lot of hands?

Tight or loose! Now, can you remember it as you play? If you could put every player you play against in a casino into one of those two broad categories you would be way ahead of the game.

Okay, you've mastered loose and tight. You're ready for the next lesson. Figure out if the player you're playing against pretends to have a good hand when he has a weak hand and vice versa. In other words, does he act? Some do; some don't. If you can label players as actors, you can then assume that if they are acting strong they are really weak and vice versa. And, if you have put them into the category of non-actor, then you can assume that when they act strong they are strong; and when they act weak they are weak.

In general, you don't need to know what a specific trait means. Rely on your general impression. If your general impression is that your opponent is strong, then if he is an actor in your book, he probably has a weaker hand than he appears to have. Similarly, if your general impression is that your opponent is weak, then if he is an actor, he probably has a powerhouse.

There are a few tricky players who are very hard to figure out. You really aren't sure if they are acting or not. Many players, especially novices, spend a great deal of time studying and trying to figure out these players. Don't waste your time. Just categorize them as tricky. I'll show you how to deal with tricky players later in the text. Focus on the untricky players. If you can read them you'll be doing fine. Kind of like Ted Williams again. The best hitters in baseball are happy to hit .300. Don't worry about batting 1,000!

Finally, once you've mastered loose and tight and whether they act or not, see if you can put them into the category of bluffer or nonbluffer. That's right, bluffer or non-bluffer. I would guess that about 90 percent of lower-limit players bluff sometimes. But if you can spot the 10 percent who never bluff, you can greatly improve your winnings. See if you can remember it. Knowing that one particular player *never* bluffs is worth a ton of money in the long run.

Finally, let me ask you a question. What is the best way of keeping track of this information? Are you better off just trying to memorize it or are you better off writing it down for future reference? Good, we agree. So write it down!

Keeping a poker journal is very simple. Get a notebook. Any type will do. Carry it with you to the poker table. You *can* make notes during play. But you are liable to get some strange looks. If that doesn't bother you, and it shouldn't, write down notes as you make your observations. You'll be folding a lot of hands so you should have time to write when other people are playing out the hand. If you feel uncomfortable about taking notes during play, jot down what you notice about other players after your session ends or when you take a break.

If you can master these three simple steps of reading other players—loose vs. tight, actor vs. non-actor, bluffer vs. non-bluffer—you are ready to read *Mike Caro's Book of Tells* (also available on video). In it, he demonstrates general behavior that many players exhibit at the poker table that gives away whether they are weak or strong.

For example, many players instinctively look quickly at their stack of chips when they make a good hand. If they bet after doing this, chances are strong that they really have a good hand and you should fold unless you, too, hold a powerhouse. Similarly, many players will stare aggressively at their opponent when they make a bet. This is often an indication that they are really weak but trying to look strong. If you see this you can usually call with your average-type hand.

I won't try to cover any more of Caro's excellent work here. Leave it to say that his work is "must reading" for any poker player who wants to improve his game. It has made me a lot of money. I'm sure that if you can master the three simple steps of reading other players that I have just outlined, Mike's book will be most useful to you as well.

Summary. Categorize people generally as loose or tight and straightforward or tricky before worrying about what all of their personal quirks and idiosyncrasies mean.

Image and Attitude

Many home game players come to a casino with the wrong attitude about winning, money, and playing poker. Their general attitude seems to fall into one of two types.

Either they come ready to prove themselves to the poker world, having been successful at home. They are, as my grandfather would say, "Tyrones" strutting their stuff for all to see. Playing poker, for them, is part of the image they have of themselves as tough guys (or gals).

They may even dress the part with gold around their neck and wrists and fingers, a sexy looking companion on their arm, and maybe a stack of black chips ($100 chips) that they've brought over from the craps pit. They see themselves as "players": people to be reckoned with. They come down to a casino ready to push around and intimidate players with their bets as they do at home. Their first concern is to show how tough they are.

Or . . .

They are humbled by the size and speed of the casino. They fear that they are really outclassed. They hope that they might be able to play carefully and tightly enough not to lose too much while they are figuring things out. They hope they don't make any obvious mistakes that will embarrass them and show the other players in the casino how inexperienced and inept they really are. Their first concern is to avoid humiliation.

These are caricatures to be sure. Even so, I can see in my mind's eye many players who fit these descriptions to a tee. Look at yourself when you first entered a poker room. Into which category did you fall? (I was in category two, by the way.)

The attitudes of these new players are all wrong because they are focused on their image, how they appear to other players. Though the time will eventually come when you can use your image to your advantage, it is a serious mistake to be concerned with it when you first sit down.

Do not worry whether other players think of you as a complete idiot or a macho poker player. There's an old joke about an egotistical guy who goes to a party. He meets someone and starts to talk to her. Of course, being an egotist, he talks about himself. He tells her all about what he does, what he thinks about movies, what sports he plays, and his attitude about politics, the economy, and the environment. He thoroughly covers all of his opinions and insights into everything. And then, running out of gas, he pauses for a breath. He looks at the person who has been politely pretending to listen to all this blather. He pauses. His expression changes to one of concern and interest. And then he says, sincerely, "Enough about me. What about you? What do *you* think of me?"

This guy would be a terrible poker player. Good poker players are the opposite. They focus not on how they appear but on what the other players are doing, what *they* are like, what hands *they* play. Their observations of others help them decide which poker actions to make in different situations. Once they have mastered this they try to imagine how they appear to others, not so they can improve their image but so they can exploit it to make more money.

Similarly, don't worry about whether other players respect your poker play or not. You get no extra money if you win the award of best player at the table. Most players don't notice anything about you anyway. But if you could convince them all that you knew nothing about the game, didn't even know the hand rankings too well, do you think you would make more or less money playing against them?

My experience is that at this lower limit level of play, if opponents think me a fool, they probably call me down more than they should, expecting me to have a bad hand—worse than the one I am representing. And that's what you should want: bad loose calls! Therefore, if you look really clueless when you first sit down at the table, why cover it up?

Summary. Don't worry about looking like an experienced or winning player. If you look like a fool, use it to your advantage.

Dealing with Losses

I was dealt two Aces in the hole and a 10 as my up card. Fourth hand of the night and I got the next best thing to having Three of a Kind. Not only that, but my up card 10 gave me some deceptive value too. See, if I had a really low up card, like a 4, and I raised, some of the sharper players might wonder what I was doing raising with only a 4. They might correctly assume that I had a Premium Pair in the hole—or at least an Ace kicker. So if I caught another Ace they might be very cautious—perhaps even folding if I bet.

Instead, with my 10 up card they would probably think, incorrectly, that I had a pair of 10s. This way, if I caught another Ace, they probably wouldn't be too concerned if I bet—not imagining that I had my secret pair of Aces in the hole. So I was very pleased.

I was sitting to the left of the low card who brought in the bet. I raised to $5 and got three callers. There were no 10s or Aces out. I was sitting pretty.

Next card I got was a Jack It didn't help me but I didn't mind. I now had 10-J as up cards. No other player paired. The high hand had a King and a 6. He sat to my right and bet $5. It was my turn to act. I had to decide whether to call his bet, fold, or raise.

Now I'll tell you—I am not a slow player. I am aggressive just like the book says. So, no deception here, I raised to $10. Let the other players think the Jack gave me Trips or gave me Two Pairs or that I started with a 3-Straight. I really didn't care. I wanted to win the pot right there if I could (fat chance at this loose table) or at least drive out other players who might stick around for only $5. Sure enough, all the other players seated in between me and the guy with the King folded. Now he had to decide what to do.

He raised me back another $5. But that was okay too. I thought I still had the better hand. I had a pair of Aces and I figured him for having only a pair of Kings.

This was one of those times when I had to think about what

he thought I had. I figured he saw me raise with just a 10 and Jack showing and presumed, incorrectly, that I had only a pair or that I had only a 4-Straight. He probably concluded that he should raise with what he figured to be the better hand.

Of course, I couldn't know this with certainty because he didn't show me his hand. But, as I've said before, poker is a game of deduction. And I deduced from all the information I had that I still was in the lead with my Pair of Aces.

I did consider the possibility that he had Kings Up. This hand, though less likely, was also possible. But even if he did have this hand, I figured that I had a good chance of improving to a better hand: Aces Up or even Trips—since the Aces and 10s were completely live. So I called.

The next card I got *was an Ace!* He got a blank. So I had (A-A) 10-J-A and he had K-x-x. I *could not* be behind. No matter what his down cards were, he could not have a better hand than I had. It was a beautiful world.

I was high on board so I bet $10. He raised me. "Good," I thought. "He 's a maniac." I raised him back. He called.

On Sixth Street he got a blank. It matched the suit of one of his up cards but offered him no other apparent help. I got a blank too. But so what. I had a higher hand than anything he could possibly have. I bet. He called.

So here's how it looked at the end of Sixth Street.

Me: (A♠-A♣) 10♠-J♥-A♥-3♦   He: (?-?) K♥-6♣-9♦-2♥

There's $120 in the pot. That's a lot for a $5/10 game at this stage.

Now we're at the River. I don't make my Full House or Four of a Kind. Even so, I figure I'm the winner. I have Trip Aces. Even if he had his Two Pair the odds of him improving to a Full House were roughly 12:1. So I bet $10. He raises me.

"Shit," I think. Did he catch something? Is he just screwing with my head? I realize, I have to call. Even if he has a Flush, Straight, or Full House, I have to think that the chance that he is bluffing is still large enough to make my call into a $130 pot worthwhile.

If you think there's a 50-50 chance that you have the best hand you should call if the pot is giving you even odds. If you think there's a 10 percent chance that your opponent is bluffing, the pot has to give you 10-1 odds for a call to make sense. Here I'm getting 13-1 odds. (I explain odds and probability in more detail in chapter 6 under "Odds and Ends.")

So I make my call. My opponent turns over a King for a Pair of Kings. Then I see the five suited cards for a Flush. I am dumbstruck for a moment. I then say, "Nice hand."

But I am crushed. That hand would have put me up another $75 or so. I would have been ahead for the night. Instead I am in the hole. And all because he played poorly and got lucky. I want to yell at him, tell him he's a moron for raising me when I was in the lead and then calling all of my bets when he was behind. I want to ask him what he thought he was doing getting a *runner runner* (two suited cards in a row) Flush to beat my set of Aces.

I have just suffered what is known in the poker world as a *bad beat*. It is a hand that you played correctly against someone who played incorrectly but that you lost. It is enough to make good players go on *tilt*. What is *tilt*? Did you ever play pinball? Remember what happens if you jostle the pinball machine too much? You cause it to shut down. A big red word appears on the screen when this happens. Tilt. It's the same thing in poker. When some players are jostled or shaken up too much from a bad beat they just go on tilt. Their poker skills completely shut down and they play wildly until they run through their bankroll and self-destruct.

You see, poker is a game about wins and losses. To be successful you have to be able to deal with both. It's important to realize that bad players are often not punished by losing in the short term for playing poorly. If you allow that fact to set you off and upset you then your game will suffer. Many players who might otherwise be winners, end up losing money because they allow themselves to get distracted by situations like the one I've just described.

Bad beats happen regularly at the poker table. They are frustrating. Even though you played the hand better than your opponent, she still won. She got lucky. It seems unfair.

But look at it this way. If poker were only a game of skill, like chess for instance, then the better players would always win. If the better players always won, and the worse players always lost, pretty soon the worse players would stop playing completely. What would be the point?

Poker attracts many gamblers precisely because there is some luck involved. It's the lucky draws that keep them coming back—even if they are overall losers. In an odd sort of way, a good player wants to suffer bad beats every now and again if only to keep the bad player in the game. After all, if bad players never won hands from good players, the bad players would stick to the slot machines and the roulette wheel. And then where would we be!? A winning player, therefore, must be able to withstand the occasional bad beat without losing composure.

Here's what I did after suffering that bad beat. I'm not Superman. I was very upset by the loss. But I knew that I was upset. So I left the table. I took a walk, went to my favorite Chinese restaurant, had some terrific Chinese noodle soup, and took some time to relax and gain some perspective. I didn't return until I had gotten the loss out of my system and could concentrate on the hand in front of me (instead of the hand I had just lost). I played a couple of more hours, with a clear head, and managed to win back the amount I lost on that hand—and then some.

Three weeks later I go to Mohegan Sun. I haven't been there for a while. I've been playing a lot online (and winning a lot). But I want to earn some frequent player points and make sure I still can play with real people.

So I sit down in a $10/20 game. One guy is a regular whom I've played with many times before. He's a solid player and rarely gets out of line. If anything, he tends to underbet his hand and offer too much free advice to newbies. Another woman is a calling station. And there are four players I've never seen.

I go a long time without winning a hand. Maybe it's only

three hours and maybe I've won a couple of small pots. But it *feels* like five hours with nothing. My once prodigious stack of $1,000 has been reduced to about $400. I am, quite simply, getting crushed in this game—this game where I should be *ro-o-oll-ing*!

Finally, I get a good, solid, playable hand . . . wired Aces. It is, by the way, my second favorite hand. My favorite hand is a set of 2s with the bring-in. No one puts you on that hand. Anyway, I get my wired Aces with a 7 up card.

Here's what happens. A player a few to my right has the bring-in. I raise. The guy to my left, who is a royal pain in the ass with all of his arrogant comments about what everyone else has, says, angrily, "What are you doing raising?" He has a King showing and he reraises. Well this is good. I look like the poor schnook to him. Two other players call his raise as do I (don't want to make him think I might actually have something).

On Fourth Street, the King bets and gets two callers. They seem to have blanks though they each have two suited cards showing. I raise. He throws in two bets as if to say that I clearly don't know what I'm doing but he does. (Actually, it was a good play no matter what the reason. If you have a high pair on Fourth Street and there is what might be a 4-Flush, make it as expensive as possible for that player to continue—and hope that they will fold, but insist that they pay a heavy price for trying to draw their Flush.) They each call the double bet, as do I.

On Fifth Street I make a second pair, not with my door card but with the Fourth Street card I've been dealt. The King does not pair up but one of the other players gets a third up card to a Flush.

Now this is a difficult position for many to play. They are concerned that the player who called with a visible 2-Flush might have made the Flush when he got his third suited up card. So they don't bet. (From my perspective, however, it would be a mistake to let the guy with three suited cards and a 4-Flush make the Flush on the next card without paying for it.) So I generally don't check here. And I didn't. I bet. The King calls my bet, after looking at me like I was a cockroach. The

3-Flush checks her down cards and calls. The other player folds.

So now there are three of us. There's the guy to my left whom I've put on a pair of Kings or maybe Kings Up. There's the player with a 3-Flush showing whom I've put on a 4-Flush (because of the rechecked down cards) and maybe a pair (she had a Queen so I gave her credit for at least Queens) and me with Aces Up and presumably the lead.

Sixth Street comes. The King pairs his Fifth Street card, a 10. He shows two 10s, better than my exposed pair of low cards. He bets. The 3-Flush calls. I call.

The River comes. The King checks. The clueless 3-Flush slowly looks at her cards. She bets. She has always appeared to be a very straightforward, though somewhat timid, player. I figure either she has made her Flush or is attempting a bluff. Frankly, I think she probably has the Flush, since she's unlikely to try and bluff two of us at once. But I'm not absolutely certain, so I call. The Kings quickly raise. The 3-Flush calls.

I think for a minute. "Damn," I swear to myself. I realize that even if the visible 3-Flush didn't make a Flush or Trips, the Kings must have filled up? Why else would he be raising an apparent Flush? "12-1 shot and he makes it," I think to myself. So, I conclude, I'm third best. I curse to myself, "Damn these lucky players. This is nuts. I hate this game!" So I muck my loser.

Then it's the showdown. The 3-Flush turns over a Pair of Queens! And the King turns over Kings Up! I folded what would have been the winning hand. A $350 pot and it would have been mine except for my weak play!

I pause. I resist the strong urge to cry out "Waaaaaaaaaah I had the winning hand!"

I slowly gather myself and leave the table. I retreat to my Chinese food palace armed with the latest issue of *Card Player* and a terribly low opinion of myself, the game of poker, and life in general. I can't concentrate enough to read. But at least I'm not at the table compounding my mistake with bad play. I finish my roast chicken and noodles, which is wonderful. In fact, since

I'm still shaken up, and I haven't finished *Card Player* yet, I decide to order another dish. I get a small plate of kimchi. It's wonderfully spicy and aromatic. I drink some tea and pause. Okay, maybe life isn't so bad.

What can we learn from these two stories?

- Sometimes we lose.
- Good play is not always rewarded with the pot.
- Bad play is sometimes rewarded.
- Don't fold on the River in 7-Card Stud when there is a large pot unless you are certain that you are beat. (That one mistake was worth 30 mistaken calls on the River.)
- When you have just lost a huge hand and feel awful, *eat!*

One of the hardest things to do in poker is to get up and leave and miss a hand or many hands when you are behind—especially when you are far behind but still have some money left. It is hardest among competitive poker players. They want to stay and duke it out until they win or lose completely. Isn't that what we're taught in sports and in life? Quitters never win and winners never quit.

In poker, as we've seen with regard to playing with players that aren't as good as you, it's the opposite. If you never quit, you will lose. If you want to win in the long run, sometimes you must quit when you are losing.

I find that the best way to quit is to just get in the habit of standing up and walking away whenever I am really upset about the result of a hand. Therefore, let the energy of anger take you away from the table instead of keeping you there. If you start to just automatically stand up when you suffer a bad beat, walking away from the table will become second nature to you. That's what you want. Eventually, if you develop good self-control, you will be able to sublimate those feelings of anxiety quickly; you will need to stay away for shorter and shorter periods of time. At some point you might even be able to completely avoid those feelings of anxiety and go right on with the play of the next hand without any emotional reaction to a loss.

But for now, the best move you can make when you lose a big pot is to just walk away.

Summary. Think more about how you are playing than about whether you are winning. Self-control and patience are much more important to winning play than short-term luck.

Money Management

Money management is a term generally used to describe a system of betting that can give a player in a casino an advantage over the house in games like roulette or craps. The theory is that if you know how to leave when you're ahead in a casino, you can gain an advantage over the house.

It purports, falsely, to help players beat the house by varying their bets based on past results. Money management systems frequently talk about *loss limits* and *win limits*. These terms refer to decisions to stop playing a casino game based on how much you have lost or how much you have won, respectively. The theory being that if you can walk away from the table when you are up or down by a certain amount you can ensure a win. Similarly, if you *press* (increase) your bets when you are winning or limit your bets when you are losing you can take advantage of a hot streak and minimize the effects of a cold streak.

Of course, all of these systems are doomed to failure. The house edge in games of chance cannot be overcome no matter how cleverly or elaborately you increase your bet, decrease your bet, or stop betting entirely. Similarly, it matters not in the least how long or how short any individual session is. Leave when you want, continue to play when you want. The house edge is immutable. You can control only the speed with which you will eventually lose. In the long run, the house advantage will defeat you no matter what.

Even so, some authors of poker strategy books still talk about varying play based on whether you are running lucky or not. If the cards are hitting you, these authors opine, you should take advantage of that hot streak and press your bets by being more aggressive. But if your luck has changed, and the cards start to hit someone else—or maybe no one at all—it may be time for you to pack it up and call it a day.

The problem with this thinking isn't necessarily the conclusion but the logic involved in reaching the conclusion. That's why thoughtful poker authors are reluctant to talk about money management. It brings to mind fallacious systems that seek to get an advantage over the house when none can be gained.

So when poker players use the term money management it is usually met with scorn. We play a game of skill. We have no interest in betting schemes that determine when we stop playing or when we continue to play. Our decisions should, logically, be based only on game conditions. If the game continues to be good, and we continue to play at our best, we should stay. If the game is bad, and we can't make adjustments in our strategy to take advantage of it, we should leave. It's as simple as that according to many poker experts.

There is certainly something to these thoughts. You should not pay attention to streaks, how much you are up, or how much you are down in a particular session when deciding whether to stay or go. Obviously, you have to play within your means. And you only a have a finite bankroll. But I've already addressed the question of how much you should be prepared to lose as a whole to learn this new skill. In any particular session, the amount you are up or down should have no bearing on how much longer you should continue to play.

Better that you should be thinking, instead, on how you are playing relative to the other players. Are they too strong for you? Not the timid, loose, bad players you want to play against? Then leave. Are they the loosest, most awful players you've ever seen? Stay if you can hold on to your cards even if you are down.

That being said, you need to think about one other factor in deciding whether it might be time to leave. If you have been getting no decent starting hands, you probably have been folding nearly all of your hands early on as well. If you have been folding hand after hand after hand for a half hour or more, even some of the inattentive bad players are going to notice it. They are going to see you as a rock—someone who only plays premium hands.

When this becomes your image it can become harder for you to make any money with the good hands you will eventually get—with the straightforward style I have suggested in this book. That's because even some of the most dim-witted players will have figured out your general style of play; they will fold when you bet unless they have an extremely strong hand. When this happens, you could try to take advantage of your new image to steal some pots by betting hands that are less than optimal. But, for good reason, when you are first starting out, I've cautioned that you shouldn't vary your style from straightforward play.

So, instead, if you find yourself on the bad end of a long run of cold cards, the best strategy may be to walk away from the game for a while until the dim-witted are given a chance to forget who you are and how you play. And don't worry. For most of them, that isn't a very long time.

Staying Too Long

As I've mentioned earlier, I have a good friend named Jim. We play poker together. He's probably a better pure poker player than I am but he has a huge hole in his game. Simply put, he stays too long.

Here's what typically happens. He's playing solid poker. He's up a couple hundred dollars at $5/10. It starts to get late. But, hell, he only comes down to Foxwoods every couple of months or so. So we decide not to leave yet. For whatever reason, he starts to lose.

He is close to even and then plays a hand where he's ahead at the beginning. But his opponent catches a perfect River and beats him out of a large pot. So now he's down.

He's pissed, because he should be up. But he's down. He plays a little too aggressively for a couple of hands and doesn't win. He's down more.

Gradually, a wave of weariness rolls over him. It doesn't put him to sleep or even cause him to be unable to keep up with the action. But his eyes get this kind of glazed look.

He comes back to the table. He wins a couple of small pots and loses a couple. His stack however is still going down, though gradually.

He gets into this loose-passive zone of calling Third Street more frequently than he knows is correct, hoping that he'll hit a card that will give him the hand which will beat these inferior players. Sometimes the card comes; more often it doesn't. Either way, he is now playing more passively, less aggressively, and noticeably looser.

But because he's in this zone, he doesn't see it. He only thinks, occasionally, about how he has to get his stack back up to even. "Back to even" becomes his mantra.

Only even never comes. Because he is less aggressive, he doesn't win what he should on the hands he does hit. Because he is looser and more passive, he is tossing in more money, into more multi-way hands, which he loses.

Had he left when he first started to feel tired he'd be up. Had he left when he first noticed he was really tired, he'd be down a couple of hundred. As it is, at 2:00 A.M., he's down $600 and totally exhausted. He finally leaves, down $500, at 2:40 A.M. after winning a hand and being convinced it was really time to go.

Some players can play all night and still do great. Some players can sit for thirty-eight hours with no apparent decrease in their abilities. But you're not one of them. Even if you think you are, you're not.

Maybe you are. Maybe you're one of those freaks of nature who can keep 100 percent concentration all night long, after marathon sessions. But so what? Why run the risk of finding out that you're wrong? You can always come back another time.

Why not just plan a certain time to leave and stick to your plan. If you get up from the table and you find that you're really not tired, have full concentration skills remaining and really want to continue, you can always come back after a break. But take that break. Think about how you're doing. Then, and only then, think about continuing.

I know that some poker writers talk about how you shouldn't leave if the game is good. But how much are you really giving up by leaving too early, when you initially planned to leave? Give up a couple of hours of play, at the end of the night, beyond the time you expected to leave, in exchange for some more sleep. You'll be happy and healthier in the long run if you do.

One last thought on this. The problem with deciding when to leave based on game conditions is that, after you are tired, you start to lose the ability to correctly judge game conditions. When you're tired, and your judgment is skewed, you tend to inflate the value of the game you're in and your ability to beat it. It's like people who say they drive better after a few drinks. They surely don't drive better. But, because they're inebriated they think they do.

Simple rule of thumb: Leave the table after a few hours of play and evaluate how you're doing. If you're feeling tired, go home. If it's a few hours past when you had initially planned to leave, go home even if you think you're playing fine.

Buying In

How much does it take to play at any level? How much should you buy in for when you sit down? What level is right for you?

These are tough questions to answer simply. Much has to do with your comfort level. Some wealthy players won't play higher than the lowest game in the casino, because they just don't feel good about playing for more than a hundred bucks a session or so. Other players who have very little money always sit down in the highest stake game they can afford to buy in for. They are at a disadvantage by doing this, but they enjoy the thrill and gamble of the highest stakes they can play, even if it means going all in regularly.

Every casino has certain minimum requirements for play. For example, you can't sit down at a $100/200 game with only $100. They have table minimums. Generally, the minimum buy-in is about ten times the small bet for games up to $10/20 and twenty times the small bet for games of $15/30 or higher. Therefore, if the game is $10/20, the minimum buy-in is $100; $6/12, $60; $20/40, $400. In the spread limit games this varies, but in the casinos I've seen the minimum buy-in for the $1–$5 games and the $1–$3 games is $30. Check with your casino to find out what the minimums are.

This doesn't really tell you what you want to have in front of you, however, when you sit down. I suggest that you have at least enough money to take full advantage of any situation you may face. For me, that means wanting to have enough money in front of me at the start of the hand to cap every round of betting if necessary. Why be caught short?

In 7-Card Stud, that means at least sixteen big bets at the start of every hand. As a practical matter, I like to have at least double that in case I don't have time, after a monster hand that I lose, to buy in again for the next hand. Roughly speaking, that's thirty big bets. In $2/4 I should have at least $120; in $5/10, $300; in 6/12, $350; in $10/20, $600; and in $15/30, $1,000. For the spread limit games, ante or no ante, I want $100 to $150.

Keep in mind that this is a minimum, not a hard and fast rule. In fact, I feel more comfortable taking a larger mound of chips to the table . . . larger than I need. It helps me treat the betting as a more tactical matter and a less financial one. If I have $1,000 worth of chips in front of me in a $6/12 game, I'm not inclined to think about the chips as money, at least not as much as if I have only $120 or so.

Therefore, if you want to take three racks of reds to a $5/10 game, I won't argue with you. After all, it's how much you leave with that's really important.

At What Level Should You Start?

Where should you start your casino career? At what level of play should you start learning the game by actually playing the game?

Some take the attitude that they want to start at the absolute lowest level offered by the casino and then work their way up. So if there is a no ante $1–$3 game, that's where they'll begin. I don't suggest that approach.

If you have the bankroll for a slightly higher game, I'd recommend that you *not* play the low, no ante, spread limit games. I explain this in more detail in the next chapter in the section on the *rake*. But the bottom line is that the amount that the house takes out of the pot, relative to the amount you are likely to win, is often so high in these ultra-low spread limit games that even a good player cannot win enough to compensate for it.

My suggestion is that you start at no less than $3/6. Ideally, however, even if you are a beginner, I believe you are best by starting out in a $4/8 or a $5/10 game so you have a good chance of beating the rake if you can master basic strategy.

Keeping Records

I read a statistic a while back. It was in an AAA magazine. It was the results of its annual driver's survey. The question was, "How would you rate your driving?" There were three choices: "below average," "average," or "above average." The results were that 95 percent put down that they were above average.

Of course the survey can't be accurate. You can't have 95 percent of any group above the average for the group. But that's how we perceive ourselves on the road. We all think we're better than the jerk who just passed us or whom we just passed.

That's a lot like poker. Ask any casual player how she's doing. Most will say, "About breaking even, maybe a little ahead!"

Well, that's fine for the casual player. Think of them as the casual bowler or golfer. They don't have to keep score. It doesn't matter to them. They just like their hobby. And we should be happy to have them in our game.

You should be different. You're not satisfied *just* playing. You want to win. So you'll need to keep records to know whether you are, in fact, winning or losing.

Keep them on paper or on your computer. Don't keep them in your head. The bottom line in poker is like the bottom line of a business. How much are you making? Have you improved over the last year?

You need to face yourself with the cold hard numbers—as many numbers as you need to figure out exactly where the holes in your game are. You've got to identify them if you are to fix them.

This means getting a ledger, or a software program that allows you to keep one on your computer. Set it up so you can keep track of every session, with the following information:

1. Where you played
2. How long you played for
3. Time of day and date you played
4. What game and what stake you played
5. What your total win/loss was for the session
6. Notes from the session including notes on individual players you played with

Ideally, this will be recorded with running tallies or with a function in the program that allows you to generate immediate summaries of your aggregate play. You should be able to divide the data into useable statistics.

For example, you should know your hourly win rate for whatever game or stake you play. You need to be able to tell at a glance whether playing at night or playing during the day seems to be more remunerative. You should be able to see what your hourly rate is for $5/10, $1–$5, and $10/20—and how it compares with some of the other casino poker you play. Are you doing better at Texas Hold'Em or 7-Card Stud, Omaha/8, or 7-Card Stud Hi Lo.

This is wonderfully easy to recommend, but difficult to actually do. It takes some discipline. Here are some ideas to make the task easier. Buy a separate notebook that you can carry with you at all times. Bring it with you to the casino. Write in it every time you sit in a game.

Plan on thirty minutes before and after every session in which to make notes about the prior session, and to review your notes from your last session. Try to get in the habit of having space between arrival and play and departure and play.

Schedule at least one hour every month to review notes on poker and to think about how you're doing. Get a file folder (or open a computer file) where you can put your stray thoughts and musings on your play.

Bear in mind that these are the building blocks of your poker education. In that regard, every session is useful because it gives you information that can be used to become a better player. Though you may be losing money early on, if you review and analyze your play, this money becomes an investment.

Poker Thinking

Of *Luck and Logic*

Many poker players think of poker as a game of luck, not skill. When they do poorly they attribute it to the poker gods frowning on them. When they win they feel they've been blessed with good fortune and are grateful.

Poker to them is just like craps, roulette, or the Big Wheel. When you're hot you're hot; when you're not, you're not. We, as players, have little if any impact on the final outcome. The game of 7-Card Stud is not like that, of course. In this game, the ability to win is a product, at least in large measure, of our skill. If we become better, we will win more; if we cease to learn, we will be forever cursed with losing sessions. The way to increase our winnings and decrease our losses is to learn more about the game and to apply that knowledge with discipline and rigor.

Even so, many poker players who think they are thinking critically really aren't. They are almost schizophrenic about it. One minute they could be analyzing the play of a hand in terms of pot odds and expected value, and the next they're moaning about how they're ready to pack it in for a while to wait out their losing streak.

Consider the following comments that seem to fall off the lips of many otherwise serious players.

"Why'd you fold? If you had called I would have caught my card and won!"

"You can't beat players who don't think."

"Nice catch!"

"You can't beat that low limit game. It's just a crap shoot!"

"You should quit. It's clear you're just not getting cards."

"I can't believe you're moving seats. That seat was so hot!"

"He Rivered me with the case 9!" (and all the other bad beat stories).

My point is that people clutter up their minds with irrelevancies and distractions about poker. Even though they know, when they really think about it, that all of this talk is crap, they fall victim to thinking of poker as a game of luck. It's no wonder that their play reflects that thinking from time to time.

You know what it reminds me of? Ever talk to an avid professional wrestling fan? Unless they are truly dumb, they know, cerebrally, that the matches are staged and well-scripted exhibitions—really just high drama among skilled athletes more than an athletic contest. They know that a 300-pound behemoth can't really be jumping off the top rope and landing on the other guy's neck. They know that.

But when they are at the event, or watching on TV, or even talking about it afterward, all their intellectual knowledge is shoved aside. I remember my friend, a recent high school graduate who worked in a print shop in the place I worked. He and

I both loved to watch and talk about wrestling. I recall the following monologue.

> "Yeah, Ashley, I know it's fixed. What, do you think I'm an idiot? But did you see what Andre the Giant did to Hulk Hogan on television last week? I mean, you know Andre was just angry because he's not the champion. No way did Hogan deserve all those cheap shots. When they get together Friday night, there's going to be hell to pay. The Giant's going *down!*"

It was as if, though he knew better, he couldn't help himself from getting carried away with the spirit and energy of the play, as if it were real.

Poker is the same way. Many, many players know, intellectually, how to think about the game. They know what solid poker is. But when they play, they suspend that part of their brain that thinks; they act totally with their emotions and their gut.

How does this manifest itself? Good players, who should know better, stay too long, thinking they are "due" to catch a card. Good players, who otherwise understand the game, blame the bad play of others for their losses. Good players, who understand basic strategy, lose their cool and start to throw money in the pot when they clearly have the worst of it because they are out of control following a couple of bad beats.

Players think in terms of "getting even for a bad beat." They think in terms of "just getting lucky," of "running good," or "running bad." How does an otherwise sober poker player keep from being seduced by the apparent randomness of the results of his poker sessions? How does he stay focused on the correctness of his play, the development of his skills, and the need for discipline and self-control?

The best answer is to regularly take the opportunity to think about his game. Players need to reserve time on a regular basis, to reflect on how they're doing—to review their records and think about their play. My experience is that if this is done regularly it will become habitual.

Many ideas can provoke serious thought: *Card Player* magazine, books on poker, and now many online poker sites and discussion groups (RGP and TwoPlusTwo being only the first two that come to mind). I recommend making a steady diet of these thought supplements, until this kind of critical thinking about the game in general and how you are doing in specific becomes as natural as breathing.

Computer-generated poker simulations, such as programs from Wilson Software, can help. By generating hundreds of hands an hour for you to play, they help make your responses automatic and mechanical. Although this is not how you will eventually play 7-Card Stud, it does help to keep your play on an even keel—computer-like. Eventually, after you have gotten into the habit of straightforward play, you can deviate as your expanding poker judgment determines and your skills allow. But early on, it is most useful to just get in to the habit of playing by the book.

You should now have a knowledge of the basic strategy and general concepts necessary to start playing poker in a casino. In the next chapter, I will present you with concepts that will help you modify this basic strategy so you can take advantage of better players and games with fewer loose-passive players.

CHAPTER 3

Deception

In chapter 2, in the interest of keeping things simple and straightforward, I excluded a major poker concept from the strategy I presented. That concept is *deception*. Although you will be able to win a small amount of money from bad players with the straightforward style developed in chapter 2, as you move from games with rank beginners to games with better players, you need to employ deception in your game to maximize your wins. If you play only straightforwardly, you will give up some potential profit because the better players will know to avoid you every time you enter a pot. Similarly, you will be able to play more hands overall—learning how to make money from hands that aren't only high-quality hands.

To become a better poker player and beat better players you will need to understand both how to deceive your opponents and how to avoid being deceived yourself. Chapter 3 covers those poker moves that you can use to deceive your opponent. Chapter 4 shows you how to avoid being deceived and figure out what your opponent has.

Deceptive Poker Moves

We can divide our deceptive poker moves into two broad categories: First, there are those moves designed to fool opponents into thinking we're stronger than we really are. These are the bluffs, semi-bluffs, and semi-demi bluffs. Second, there are the moves designed to fool opponents into thinking we're weaker than we really are. These are check-raises and slowplays. This chapter covers all of these moves as well as the related subjects of ante-steals.

Bluffing

Bluffing is the act of making your hand appear stronger than it is, by betting or raising, in an effort to win the pot. For it to be successful you must have two ingredients: You must have an opponent who thinks about what your betting may mean, sufficient for it to affect what he does, and you must have an opponent who has sufficient discipline to fold his hand if he believes he is beaten.

You did not learn how to bluff in the strategy presented in chapter 2, because your opponents were unlikely to possess the necessary qualities for a bluff to work. At the lower stakes games, against the typical loose calling stations that you face, someone normally will "keep you honest" by calling you and forcing a showdown on the River. It's unusual for all of the players to concede the hand. So bluffing often doesn't work.

Better players fold more frequently based on your actions. I'm going to give you a list of factors to consider before bluffing and then I'll give you some examples of how you can apply them. Just a word of caution in advance: even at the intermediate level, when you will be facing better opponents, you should keep your pure bluffs to a minimum. As we'll see, there are other types of deception, variations on the bluff, which are much more useful at this level of play.

Factors to Consider When Bluffing

The quality of your opponent. Avoid bluffing bad opponents. Bad players who call too much and fold too seldom will often not fold to your bet. Don't try to win the pot against them with a weak hand by betting. Bluff strong opponents who will fold when you bet because they deduce from your bet that you probably have a strong hand.

You need to think about what type of player your opponent is. If they are very tight, even if they aren't very good, they can be bluffed more easily than if they are loose. Players who play too tightly are known as *weak-tight*. They are the perfect object of a bluff.

Your image at the table. Generally, do not attempt a bluff if you think that the other players see you as a loose-aggressive player. If they think you bet with anything, they are likely to call your bet. A bluff won't work that is designed to get them to fold. Similarly, if you are perceived to be a tight player, you can attempt a bluff more frequently because your opponents will be more likely to believe that your bet means that you are strong.

The prior betting action. Good players, whom you want to direct your bluffs against because poor players will call you anyway, will be more likely to respect your bet and fold if the betting action before the bluff would lead them to believe that you really have the hand that you are now representing. Your bet isn't going to be perceived in a vacuum. Consider how your action up until the point you attempt a bluff will be viewed. If it looks as if you've been weak the entire hand, the chances are that any attempt to bluff on the River "out of left field," so to speak, won't be believed and you will be called.

The overall quality of your hand. Pure bluffs, when your hand has absolutely no value and no chance to get better, make less sense than bluffs with hands that either have some value to them or have a chance to improve on later cards. I explain this more in the next section on semi-bluffs and semi-demi-bluffs.

Your opponent's likely hand. A bluff works better against an opponent with a lousy hand than against an opponent who has a fairly good hand. The better you can gauge what your opponent has, the better you can decide whether to attempt a bluff. Bluff against weakness, not strength.

How many opponents you have. It is easier to bluff fewer opponents than many opponents. Your bluff is more likely to succeed heads up than against a full table. Similarly, it is more likely to succeed if you act late in the betting action, after the majority of players have checked or folded. Bluffs from early position are less likely to succeed because of all of the players who may actually have a good hand and will therefore call you—even if they believe that you have the hand that you are representing.

The hand you have showing. Think about what your opponent will think you have, based on your exposed cards, when you bet. It is easier to bluff an opponent if the hand you are showing looks like it is likely to be a very strong hand. High cards on board, known as *scare cards,* are easier to bluff with because your opponents are likely to believe that you have a high pair. For example, you are more likely to have your bluff work if you show (6♠-2♠) K♥ than if you show (2♠-K♥) 6♠, or if you have (7♦-8♣) 8♠-J♠-Q♠-K♠ (2♦) instead of (7♦-8♠) J♠-8♣-K♠-Q♠ (2♦).

The money in the pot. You are less likely to succeed in a bluff if there is a lot of money in the pot relative to the size of your bet. If, for example, because of a lot of betting action on earlier streets there is $300 on the River in your $10/20 game, don't expect your $20 bet to cause your opponent to fold. Your opponents, especially your better opponents whom you generally will be more likely to bluff than your poor opponents, will notice the size of the pot and tend to call you when the pot is large. They'll understand pot odds and will be less likely to lay down their borderline hands to your bet when the pot is large.

Here's an example of when **not** to bluff. You started with three Hearts. Someone raised the bring-in and three people called. You called too, hoping to get two more Hearts and thereby a Flush.

On Fourth Street you got another Heart. Someone else bet, there were three callers, and you called as well. On Fifth Street and Sixth Street you failed to catch the fifth Heart you needed to make your Flush. You called bets on each round.

Finally, on the River, with four opponents, you got your last card. Everybody checked to you. You had to decide whether to check or to bet. You looked at your last card, only to find that it was a Spade, leaving you with nothing.

You are tempted to try to bluff your way to victory by betting. *Don't.* Here's why:

1. You're against many opponents. You're less likely to bluff many opponents than few opponents.
2. Your opponents showed strength by either betting or calling other bets.
3. The pot is relatively large with four of you calling bets all the way to the River.
4. You're likely to be against bad opponents. With all of those people who just called each of the four rounds of betting, you're probably against at least a couple of very weak players who don't have the sense to fold hands when they're behind.

Here are some situations when bluffing does make sense. You may observe some players who are so tight, even in the lower limit games, that they can be bluffed. They wait for the best hands, they back away from contested pots, and they don't like showing down a losing hand. These players pride themselves on their ability to fold good hands. When you're against these types you can practically win with any cards. Just raise, no matter what you have, and watch them fold. If you have a player like this in the game, and it's just you and he, exploit his weakness by betting into him whenever you detect weakness. Let's say, for example, he called the bring-in or the completed Third Street bet. If you are high on Fourth Street, if he hasn't paired his door card, or a suited or consecutive card, you should bet into him. He may have started with a small pair, a 3-Straight or a 3-Flush. If he didn't improve, he will fold right away. Don't give him a free shot at improving. Represent strength by betting.

Here's an example of what I mean.

Seat 4: 8	Seat 5, You: (6-Q) 6
Seat 3: K	Seat 6, Tight Player: 7
Seat 2: 9	Seat 7: J
Seat 1: 3	Seat 8: 8

You brought it in for $2, the 7 called, everyone else folded. Now comes Fourth Street.

You: 6, 9   Tight Player: 7-J (unsuited)

He checks. You don't have much of a hand—just a Pair of 6s with a Queen kicker. But you should take advantage of his weak-tight style and bet here, not because of the cards you have but because of whom you're playing against.

Now, if he weren't a tight player, you probably wouldn't bet in a lower-limit game. You'd correctly assume that he would continue to call you down with his likely Pair of 7s. So you'd be inclined to check behind him and fold to his bet on this or a later street unless you improved.

Similarly, if this tight player checks on Fifth Street, Sixth Street, or the River, you should bet, knowing that he is more likely to fold than call because of his style of play. Obviously, this only works if it is heads up with this weak player. If there are other players in the pot, you have to be concerned that one or more of them would call you. So you don't want to attempt to bluff more than this one player.

Other opportunities to bluff arise because of the situation you are in, more than because of the opponent you are playing. Specifically, if you know that your opponent is on a draw—trying for a Flush or a Straight for example—you can often win the pot on the River with a bet, even if you don't have any hand at all. Consider the following example.

Let's say that you are dealt a Pair of 3s in the hole and an exposed Ace. The bring-in 4♣ is to your left and everyone folds to you. It's just you and the bring-in. You know her to be a generally poor player who calls too much with substandard hands. You raise. The bring-in calls the bet. You get a King on Fourth Street and your opponent gets a 5♣. You are high on board and bet. Your opponent calls. On Fifth Street your opponent gets a 5♦ and you get a 10. Your opponent, with an exposed pair of 5♠, is high on board and checks. You bet. Your opponent calls. On Sixth Street you get a 9 and your opponent gets an unsuited 9. Neither of you improve. Your opponent checks and you bet again. Your opponent calls.

On the River you don't improve. Your opponent checks. What should you do? You should bet. You deduce that your opponent, who called your bet on Third and Fourth Street with two suited cards and then checked when she got an exposed Pair on Fifth Street was probably drawing to a Flush. Had she a Pair to start and then made Two Pair when she got her second 5 on Fifth Street, she probably would have bet. You're not certain of this. But you deduce it based on the cards she had showing and the action she took.

Had she made her Flush on the River by catching another heart, she surely would have bet into you. When she checked you could deduce that she didn't make her hand. You didn't make a good hand either, however, and if you checked you would lose with your Pair of 3s to her Pair of 5s. By betting as a bluff you had a good chance of getting her to fold if you correctly guessed she didn't make her Flush. If she had only the pair of 5s she probably would have thought that you certainly had a better hand than her lousy Pair of 5s.

Keep in mind that there is another reason to bluff other than to win the pot. You will win more money with your good hands. If you are thought of as someone who never bluffs, when you really do have a hand your better opponents will fold. If you're known as someone who occasionally bluffs, on the other hand, your opponents will have to fear that you might be bluffing when you bet—causing them to call you much of the time. These extra calls, when you have winning hands, will add extra money to your bottom line.

Players frequently ask whether they should sometimes bluff as *advertising*—meaning bluffing with the expectation that you'll be caught and can thereby show everyone that you bluff. I don't advise this in 7-Stud. I would save my bluffs for those occasions when you think you have a high probability of success—based on the factors I've provided. You will be caught enough of the time without doing so intentionally for your bluffs to be advertised. Bluffing with the intent of getting caught will just cost you money needlessly.

Semi-Bluffing

Semi-bluffing is a bluff with a backup plan. It can either win by fooling opponents that your hand is stronger than theirs—so they should fold. Or it can win by improving on the next card to the best hand. Accordingly, you can't semi-bluff on the River. There are no more cards to come. And you aren't semi-bluffing unless you have some expectation of winning the pot immediately by getting your opponent to fold. Therefore, if there is no expectation that your opponent will fold when you bet, it isn't a semi-bluff.

Here's an example of a semi-bluff. You have (A♥-10♠) K♥. A 2 brings in the bet and a Queen raises. It's your turn to act. You raise. This is a semi-bluff. You hope to convince the 2 and the Queen (whom you presume has a Pair of Queens) to fold—thinking you have a Pair of Kings. But if you don't succeed with that bluff you still have a chance of improving to the best hand on Fourth Street by catching another Ace or King. Then when you bet you will be in the lead and will probably win.

That's a semi-bluff. It can be done with a raise as well as a bet. Imagine it's Third Street again. You have (2-2) A. A King to your right raises the bring-in. You raise as a semi-bluff. On the one hand you hope he will fold thinking you have a Pair of Aces. But if he calls you, you still have a chance of improving to the best hand by catching a 2 or an Ace.

Here's an example from Fifth Street.

You have (6♥-6♠) 9♥-K♥-4♥. Your opponent has (?-?) A♠-7♥-7♠. Your opponent is high on board and bets. You raise. This is a semi-bluff. You might convince your opponent that you already have a Flush, getting him to fold. That's the bluff part. But you also might get a heart on the next card giving you a Flush that will probably win. It's a very good move but you must remember that you can only use it when there is at least some chance that it will succeed as a bluff *and* that your hand may improve on the next card.

Getting a Free Card

The above, from semi-bluffing, is an excellent example of another good poker move that you should add to your arsenal. It is called *getting a free card*. Here's how it works. You raise as a semi-bluff in order to induce your opponent to check on the next card. You then check after her so you can get the next card without putting in a bet. That's called "getting a free card" because you didn't have to call a bet to get it.

Consider the hand above again. You have (6♥-6♠) 9♥-K♥-4♥. Your opponent has (?-?) A♠-7♥-7♠. Your opponent, making a Pair of 7s, bets. You raise. If he calls you he is very unlikely to bet on the next card fearing a raise (thinking you have made a Flush). If he checks to you, you can decide to check as well and get a final card without putting in the price of a bet. That's called a *free card*.

Defense Against the Semi-Bluff

Keep in mind that when you are playing with better players, they will be semi-bluffing *you* from time to time. What is your best defense? I suggest one of three responses.

First of all, if you're in a game where other players are very aggressive and semi-bluffing regularly, consider finding another game. Remember, you should be on the Intermediate slope now, not the Double Black Diamond expert course. Don't play in a very tough game with tricky players if you can help it. And you can help it. If expert players are taking advantage of you, leave and look around for easier pickings.

But maybe the game itself is a pretty good game. There are a number of bad players to go along with the one or two experts. You don't want to leave, because there are enough weak-passive players for you to make a profit, even with another good player or two in the game. In that case, when you face a player who seems to be semi-bluffing you, fold. I go into this further in chapter 5 in the section entitled "Playing Against Good, Tricky Players." But the bottom line is that you can just fold and avoid playing heads up against someone whom you think is using this play against you.

That being said, you don't have to always avoid these confrontations by either leaving the game or conceding the pot to the semi-bluffer. A successful move that you can use against a semi-bluff is semi-bluffing back at the semi-bluff. Here's how it works. Let's say you are the bring-in with (K♥-A♥) 3. An opponent in late position, after other players have folded, raises with (?-?) Q. The remaining players fold and it's up to you.

You suspect that he really doesn't have a hand. You've observed that he's a good and aggressive player who has semi-bluffed in the past. In this hand he has raised from late position with the highest up card. You think he might just be trying to steal the pot with his raise—hoping that if you call he'll still be high on board and can bet Fourth Street and pick up the pot.

So you reraise! This reraise is a semi-bluff. You might convince him to fold, which would be fine with you. But even if he calls, you might improve by catching a King, an Ace, or a 3 on the next card. So again, it's a bluff with a backup plan.

Semi-Demi-Bluff

A semi-demi-bluff is a semi-bluff that is also a value bet. Consider three concepts separately: value bet, bluff, semi-bluff. A value bet is a straightforward bet made because you think your hand is likely to win in a showdown—because it is or will become the best hand. A bluff is a deceptive bet made by a weak hand trying to convince opponents to fold by looking like a strong hand. And a semi-bluff is a bluff with a backup plan—a bluff with a hand that may improve on the next card to the best hand.

A semi-demi-bluff combines these three types of bets. It is a bet that can win as a bluff, or win by improving to the best hand on the next card, or that may actually be the best hand when the bet is made. In that sense it is a semi-bluff that is also a partial value bet.

Here's a typical situation when this comes into play. You're not confident that you have the better hand. So you can't make a pure value bet. But your bet is not a complete bluff either because you may very well have the better hand. And you have the possibility of improving to the best hand on the next card. It's a semi-bluff with something extra: a *semi-demi-bluff.*

Consider this hand. You have an Ace up with a King and 9 in the hole. A 4 brings in the bet and everyone else folds. Now it's your move. Everyone else has folded. You raise the bring-in 4. You have three ways to win the pot. First, you might win as a bluff if your opponent incorrectly views your hand as a pair of Aces and she folds her smaller pair. Second, you might win as a semi-bluff if your hand improves on Fourth Street to the better hand by catching an Ace or a King. And, finally, you might actually have the better hand right then with your Ace-King high. In other words, your hand has sufficient value to warrant a bet when combined with the other factors.

Semi-demi-bluffs and semi-bluffs are especially useful on Third Street as a ploy to win all of the antes and the bring-in bet. This is known as an ante-steal. Let's take a look at the ante-steal in some detail.

Ante-Stealing

"Stealing the antes" amounts to inducing all players to fold on Third Street so you may win the pot that includes only the antes and the bring-ins. Ante-stealing is a type of bluff done on Third Street when only the antes and bring-ins are at stake. It is generally not a good idea to try to steal the antes in a typical low-stakes loose-passive 7-Stud game. So we haven't covered it until now. However, as the games get tougher, it becomes a crucial part of your game. If you don't steal some antes, but your opponents are stealing yours, you will eventually go broke. Here are some things to consider when deciding whether to try for a steal.

Your betting position relative to the person who must open the betting with the forced bet. You should be more inclined to steal the antes if the bring-in is to your left and everyone after her has folded. This way you have to convince only one player to fold when you raise. Be less inclined to try to steal from early position when there are many players left to act. It's harder to convince everyone that you have the better hand than only one person. And, with many people yet to act, you are more likely to run into someone with a very strong hand who will raise you.

The tightness of the players who have not yet acted. It's much easier to convince a tight player than a loose player to fold. Your ante-steals should generally be directed at tighter opponents.

The number of people who have already called the bring-in. You are more likely to get someone to fold if they have not already called the bring-in bet. Many players will automatically call a raise if they are already in for the bring-in.

The tightness of your image. If you are seen as a very straightforward and tight player, you are more likely to succeed with your steal attempts than if you're viewed as a maniac who raises with no hand at all. Consider stealing if you have been folding for many hands in a row or are otherwise viewed as a tight player.

The relative strength of your hand. Be more inclined to steal the antes when your hand has some value to it, as in a semi-demi-bluff. This way, even if your bluff doesn't succeed, you may have a hand that is already or ends up as stronger than your opponent's.

The possibility that you might improve to the best hand on the next card. You should be more likely to attempt an ante-steal if you might improve to the better hand on the next card. That way, even if your bluff doesn't succeed you may win by improving or appear to improve to a winning hand on the next card.

Your ability to get away from your hand if your ante-steal doesn't succeed. If you have good self-control and can fold if your bluff doesn't work, you can make more steal attempts. If you have trouble folding once you are in a hand, attempt these steals less often.

The size of the antes and bring-in as a percentage of your initial bet. If the pot is relatively large, compared with the size of your bet, you should be more inclined to steal the antes. It's worth more for you to do so. Conversely, if the size of the pot is relatively small compared with your initial bet, you should raise less frequently.

Ante-Steal Examples

Let's look at some situations when an ante-steal might make sense. Compare the two hands that follow:

Your door card is an Ace. The other up cards, starting with your left, are 3, 6, K, K, 7, Q, 4.

Your door card is an Ace. The other cards up are 6,K, K, 7, Q, 4, 3.

In the first example, because you are to the right of the bring-in, you are *last* to act and will get to see what every other player does before it is your turn to act. In the latter example, because the low card showing begins the betting to your right, you are *first* to act. You must act without knowing what anyone else will do.

In the former situation, where you are last to act, there may be some excellent opportunities to steal the antes. If, for example, everyone folds to you, you need only worry about whether one player, the bring-in, will fold to your raise. A raise may well win the pot for you right there and might make sense when you consider all of the other factors. But in the latter situation, where you are *first* to act, it probably makes little sense to raise. Any of the players yet to act might have enough of a hand to warrant, from their perspective at least, a call or even a reraise.

When you are last to act you have more information to make your decision than when you are first to act. Accordingly, ante-stealing usually works best from late position.

What information might you glean by watching other players? First, if you see that they all have folded, you know that you only have one player to worry about. But, let's say they don't all fold. Let's say that three of the players call the "cheap" bring-in bet. How might your action change?

In that situation, a raise would probably *not* make sense. You not only have to knock out the bring-in 3, but the other three players as well. They are far less likely to fold because they have already called two-fifths of your bet. Especially in these low- and mid-limit games, players are apt to think "I'm in this far, so I might as well call." And they do. By acting first after the bring-in, you are doing so without any information on what the other players have or are likely to do. Be disinclined to ante-steal from early position. But don't rule it out entirely.

Keep in mind that, in general, you want to concentrate your ante-steal attempts on as few players as possible. The more players who are left to act after you, the more people you have to convince to fold. They may have a pair or a couple of high cards. Even if they believe that you have what you are representing, they may not be good enough to fold to a Third Street raise. This is especially true for players who have already called the bring-in.

If three or four players have already called the bring-in, your ante-steal is less likely to succeed than if everyone up to you has folded and there's only one or two players left to act. In general, it's a bad idea to attempt to steal an ante if more than one player has called the bring-in. Though as you begin to figure out your opponents, you will see exceptions to this.

Ironically, if the game were relatively tight, and the players relatively good, you might be better able to steal the antes from early position—that is, when you have to act before many other players—than from late position—when everyone or nearly everyone else has already acted. Not to confuse things, but I think you will benefit by appreciating the ambiguity of poker in situations such as these.

Many good players understand the nature of an ante-steal. They will assume that if you are last to act with an Ace that you are probably attempting to steal the antes. So the bring-in might call your late position raise, assuming that your raise does not indicate a Pair of Aces. In fact, if he is a very good player, he might raise you, since he will assume that you have nothing but the exposed scare card.

On the other hand, if you raise up front, without the advantage of seeing the action of other players, the good player might assume that you really have a hand. Since your raise is early, he is more likely to give you credit for really having the Pair of Aces—since he knows that you know you are less likely to succeed with an ante-steal from early position. So too might the other players with marginal hands give you credit for a Pair of Aces. While they might have called the bring-in with a Pair of 6s, let's say, and then called your raise because they were already in for the bring-in, they would be less likely to call your up front raise, figuring that since you raised up front, without knowing what any of them had, that you were really loaded. They may also conclude that it isn't worth a full bet to call. If they had already invested the amount of the bring-in, however, they would call for just the small additional bet.

Again, this is a level of sophistication in your opponents that you should try to avoid. Even so, you will find good players in your midst from time to time, especially as you move to $10/20 and higher. And as you succeed and move up you will encounter more of them. Recognize that what works against simple players may need to be altered if you want to succeed against the better players you will encounter.

Ante-stealing can get you into trouble if you are not careful and thoughtful in subsequent rounds. Consider the following scenario. You have an Ace up with two low cards in the hole. You attempt to steal the ante against a bring-in 5. She calls. You get another scare card on Fourth Street and bet. She calls. Now it's Fifth Street. You figure, well, maybe if she doesn't improve her Pair of 5s by now she'll fold for the double-sized bet. So you bet out. She calls again. Now it's Sixth Street. You can't decide if she's a terrible player who's just playing her Pair of 5s (or some other unseen weak hand) way too long, a really good player who suspects that you're on an extended ante-steal, or a player who is just passively playing a hand that might be better than a Pair of Aces.

You're still high on board with your Ace. You figure that if she's called this far, she'll call now too. So you check. She checks behind you. Now it's the River. You don't improve. But you are still high on board. You can't win by checking, you figure, so you bet out. She pauses, checks her down cards, thinks, and then finally says, "Well, I've called this far I might as well call," and she calls you down. Her Pair of 5s wins.

Or maybe you decide to give up on the hand on the River and check it. She checks behind you and wins with her pair of 5s. Or you bet and she calls with Two Pair—the second pair caught on the River. Therefore, in a $5/10 game, instead of losing $5 by conceding on Third Street with your Ace high, your $5 ante-steal gambit to win $6 has turned into a $30 or $40 pure bluff that didn't work.

That's why my advice is that if you believe you are in a good situation for an ante-steal, attempt it. But if it doesn't work on Third Street, unless you really know your opponents well and have good control over them, don't continue it past Third Street. If they haven't folded, check into them on Fourth Street and concede if they bet. True, they may be betting as a bluff because they have picked up that you were bluffing. But better to concede early than to attempt an expensive bluff when your hand doesn't get better.

Like everything else in poker there are exceptions. If the card you catch on Fourth Street doesn't help you, but it looks like it might, and the card he caught doesn't seem to help him, then you might want to continue to bet. Let's say, for example, that you attempt to steal the antes with an Ace up and two low cards in the hole. He calls. On Fourth Street he catches one of the low cards you have and you catch a high card, especially one suited to your Ace. If he's a fairly tight player you might want to bet here. If he's reasonably astute he might put you on two high cards to start—a semi-bluff raise in his eyes. Though the second high card didn't pair your door card, he may think that it may well have paired one of your down cards. Or maybe he will think that you are semi-bluffing a 4-Flush. Either way, if he has nothing he might well fold here. So a bet in this situation might make sense.

Your image counts for a lot here too. If you've just won a bunch of conceded pots in a row or for some other reason might be seen by a good and observant player as someone who has been taking advantage of being on a rush by getting very aggressive, the ante-steal might not work. Perceptive opponents might be assuming that you're just trying to steal. Not wanting to allow you to walk all over them, they may be more inclined to call with borderline hands.

On the other hand, if you've been folding hand after hand, you might want to think about an ante-steal—if only to loosen up your image somewhat for when you do get a hand. Your primary objective, however, should be to win the pot with the ante-steal, taking advantage of your rockier appearance. Opponents who have come to think of you as someone who plays only premium cards are more likely to fold when you raise. Use this image to your advantage by attempting to steal the antes accordingly.

Finally, I'd like to emphasis something I brought up earlier in the chapter on semi-bluffing. A semi-bluff ante-steal is usually a much better idea than a pure bluff ante-steal. The better your chances for improving to the best hand on the next card if your bluff fails, the more willing you should be to attempt the steal.

For example, a steal attempt with (6♦-K♥) A♦ is better than an attempt with (6♦-9♣) A♠. 2-Flushes and 2-Straights (and of course 2-Straight-Flushes), which deserve a fold under normal circumstances, might provide the necessary edge to your expectations to warrant a steal attempt from the right position against the right type of player. So, in late position, with a 4 and 8 remaining, your (9♥-10♥) K♠ is a better prospect for a raise than (5♣-10♦) K♠.

Attempt an ante-steal when your opponents are likely to hold bad cards. There are ways of recognizing a devalued opponent who is more likely to fold to your raise. Let's say you're at a fairly tight table. You see the following.

Seat 4: 9	Seat 5: K
Seat 3: K	Seat 6: J
Seat 2: 9	Seat 7: 3
Seat 1: J	Seat 8, You: (Q-A) 10

An ante-steal attempt might make sense from this early position. Why? Though your 10 is not the high card showing, it is unlikely to be against a Pair of Kings or a Pair of Jacks. That's because both the Kings and the Jacks are duplicated, that is, there are two of them exposed. Therefore, it's less likely that either one has a Pair. Your early position raise might just be enough to scare off any other halfway decent hands who would surely put you on a Pair of 10s and might be afraid of being reraised by the Jacks and Kings yet to act. Plus, even if they call and you don't win the antes, you might improve on the next card to the best hand. And they, with their duplicated up cards, are less likely to improve.

Again, don't make a habit of this. You have to pick your spots. But I've found that when carefully executed, these kinds of ante-steals add some small profit to the game.

Check-Raising

A *check-raise* is a deliberately deceptive check made to feign weakness initially in order to get your opponents to bet, so you can raise them. Bluffing and semi-bluffing succeed by fooling opponents into thinking your weak hand is strong. Check-raising is the opposite. You succeed by making your strong hand look weak. You check to fool your opponents into thinking you have a bad hand so they will bet. Once they bet you show the strength of your hand and raise. You do this to get an extra bet or to cause your opponents to fold their hands when they see the true strength of yours. There are many situations when it makes sense—when you want an extra bet in the pot and when you want to knock other players out of the hand.

Let's say that you are dealt a split pair of Aces, one of them is in the hole; the other is face up. You raise the bring-in bet and get called by one person who happens to be an aggressive player. On the next card, Fourth Street, you might want to check your split pair of Aces, expecting this aggressive player to bet, so you can then raise his bet. You expect him to bet because you have noticed that he is very aggressive when his opponents show weakness. Not all players are like that. But some are. Some people will almost automatically bet when their opponents check. In this instance, he is likely to assume that your initial raise with your Ace on Third Street was an attempt to steal the antes with a bluff. When you then checked Fourth Street, he assumed that you really didn't have a hand and that he could win the pot by betting—expecting you to fold. You turn the tables on him by raising him—checking initially and then raising his bet. A check-raise.

The check-raise in this situation accomplishes two things. As we have just seen, you will get your opponent to put in an extra bet when you have the better hand. But that's only half of the value of this move. By check-raising your opponent you will make him more cautious in the future. This is good for you. He won't know if your check means you are weak or strong. So he won't know whether he should bet when you check or just check along with you. His confusion is good for you. Any time you force your opponent to wonder about what to do you have increased the chances that he will make a mistake. His mistakes are your profit.

Specifically, by causing your opponent confusion you will give yourself more opportunities to attempt ante-steals in the future. By making him fear a check-raise, he'll be less inclined to bet when you really are bluffing on Third Street and then checking on Fourth Street. He won't know if you're going to check-raise him, so he'll be less inclined to bet in to you when you check. This will give you a free card on Fifth Street. You can then take another stab at the pot if he doesn't seem to make a hand. He may very well fold to a bet, thinking he wisely avoided being check-raised on Fourth Street and can now safely fold.

A check-raise is also useful as a way of thinning the field when you hold a Premium Pair. It works because some players who would call your single bet might fold for an opponent's bet and your raise.

Let's say the game you're in is pretty loose. You raised on Third Street with your Pair of Aces and got four callers. Now it's Fourth Street. You didn't improve. You're high on board. You're concerned that if you bet that you'll get three or maybe four callers again. You don't want that because your Pair of Aces is much more likely to win if you are only against one opponent. So how do you thin the field if your bet won't accomplish it?

If you have an aggressive player on your right whom you think will bet, try a check-raise. Check your Pair of Aces on Fourth Street. When your opponent to your right bets, raise her. The other opponents, having checked initially and now having to call two bets, will be much more likely to fold.

Here's another example of how you might use the check-raise to increase your profit against good players. It's Fifth Street. You've led the betting up until now and been called by your two opponents. Here are your hands at this point.

Seat 1:   (?-?) Q♥-6♥   You: (A♦-7♠) A♠-5♣
Seat 2:   (?-?) 7♦-K♦

You could bet this hand. But you're concerned that the two other players would be likely to call with their possible Flush draws. You know that the Two Seat is very aggressive and is unlikely to let Fourth Street get checked around without a bet. So you check, planning to raise the Two Seat's bet. You plan to do this to get the One Seat to fold for the double bet (the Two Seat's bet and your raise).

Keep in mind that this play wouldn't work if both the One Seat and the Two Seat were bad passive players who were likely to just check after you. If that happens your check would be a very bad mistake. You would have allowed them each to get another card for free, something you don't want to do. So you must pick your spots for the check-raise carefully.

The check-raise is a useful play. But you should know that it is controversial in some circles. Some people ban it outright in their home games. Even in casinos, players may react negatively to it.

I was in Las Vegas for the first time playing in the now-defunct Harrah's poker room on the Strip. I was playing $1–$5 7-Card Stud; it was the only 7-Card Stud game they had going at the time. While I was watching the action, which consisted of five local rocks (very tight players) and a couple of tourists, I saw something that illustrates the controversy, in some circles, of check-raising. A local guy who played very tightly checked his paired door card on Third Street. A tourist, about fifty-five or so who clearly knew how to play from home games and tended to be aggressive, had a King and some small card and bet $5 into the local rock. The local raised him $5. The tough looking tourist went nuts. He shouted, "You sandbagged me you no good sonovabitch!" "Aren't you man enough to show your strength?!"

Now, don't get me wrong. I had always known that some people didn't allow check-raising in their home games. In fact, I've played in a few games where this practice was barred. And, before I knew better, I tried to reason with the people who had this rule. My arguments always fell on deaf ears.

Some people just view check-raising as an unfair, unethical

practice. They have no problem with bluffing. Deception that makes a weak hand look strong is fine. But somehow they can't stand it when players deceive them by making their strong hand look weaker than it is. Nothing you say can dissuade them from that opinion. I understand the argument, having heard it my entire playing career. But it really doesn't make sense. Check-raising is just the reverse of bluffing. Instead of pretending you are stronger than you are by betting, hoping to induce a fold that wouldn't be made if your opponent really knew your strength, you are pretending you are weaker than you are by checking to induce a bet that wouldn't be made if your opponent really knew your strength.

Slowplaying

Slowplaying is showing weakness when you are very strong by checking or just calling throughout an entire betting round. Don't confuse check-raising with *slowplaying*. Check-raising feigns weakness early in a round of betting with the intention of showing strength by raising at the end of the round of betting. When you are slowplaying a hand you don't show strength at all during the entire betting round. You only show strength on the next round. Your hand must be stronger when you slowplay than when you check-raise because you are giving your opponent a free or reduced price card by not betting your hand aggressively.

Here's an example of slowplaying. Suppose you are dealt Trips on Third Street. The bring-in is to your right. You just call the bring-in. Your opponent raises the bring-in. When it comes to you, just call. You want to suck him in on the next round of betting and are therefore not raising his bet on Third Street.

Beware! Many lower-limit players, especially those at the extremely low stakes games, slowplay much too often. They slowplay Premium Pairs. These should be bet strongly and without deception. Similarly, when you make Two Pair on Fourth Street don't slowplay.

Few hands are good enough to slowplay. You should generally have at least Trips—and probably high Trips on Third Street if you're going to slowplay. On Fourth Street you shouldn't generally slowplay anything but Quads. On Fifth Street, don't slowplay anything less than a high Flush or Full House. Don't slowplay any hands weaker than these. There are two reasons for this. First, you usually have enough poor opponents who will call a raise or an initial bet on Third Street in these low- and middle-limit games. They won't need to be sucked in. They'll suck themselves into the action, even when you make your bet. Second, you want that additional money in the pot.

For a slowplay to make sense you need to be so strong that you don't have to worry about your opponent improving to a better hand than yours on the next card. The worst mistake you could make would be to suck your opponent in by not making a bet only to find that her hand has now surpassed yours.

If you have a hand like Trips on Fourth Street or even a Flush on Fifth Street you usually want to win the hand right there more than you want to run the risk of giving your opponent a free card that could beat you. Save those slow plays for your truly huge hands.

Here's an example of a good slowplay. If you're fortunate enough to get Quads on Fourth Street, then absolutely do not initiate the betting or raise the action. Even if it seems obvious that you're slowplaying a huge hand, don't worry about it. Just check. You want to give players a chance to greatly improve their hands. The same can be said on Fifth Street, for the most part. If you have Quads, slowplay. And probably that's true for a high Full House on Fifth Street. But with just about any other holding, at this level of play, it usually makes sense not to slowplay.

Summary

You have now learned a number of plays that will help you deceive your opponents. You can make your hand appear stronger than it really is by bluffing, semi-bluffing or semi-demi-bluffing, or you can seduce players when you have a strong hand by slowplaying or check-raising. These moves will enhance your ability to win against good opponents. You will be able to make more money on your very good hands by eliciting more bets from your opponents. You'll be able to turn some weak hands into winners. And your deception will confuse your opponents, adding to the profitability of the hands you play straightforwardly.

Use these skills carefully, however. Just because you can play your hand deceptively doesn't mean you should. Straight-forward play is still, generally, the best way to bet your hand. Deception is best used sparingly—mix up your play somewhat but do not change it completely.

It's not uncommon for players who have been successful at the lower limits by playing straightforwardly to move up in limits and start playing more aggressively by using deceptive plays. They frequently see that they can make more money this way. They are often successful at first when they are using their deception carefully. But the experience is often intoxicating. Betting and raising is certainly a lot more fun than folding. These players conclude erroneously that the secret to making money at poker is to just play aggressively and wildly. They forsake the careful tight-aggressive style they initially developed. And they usually pay the price with a ruptured bankroll.

Bear in mind that your better opponents will be figuring you out as you play. When you first go from very tight to deceptive you will throw them off. But if you just become a maniac, the better players will adjust to your new style and patiently pick you apart. The key, again, is mixing up your play without aban-doning the tight-aggressive style you developed initially.

Your better opponents will be trying to deceive you as well. Though mixing up your game is an important part of becoming a complete poker player, it is only part of what's necessary. You need to learn how to figure out what your opponent has. We'll do this in the next chapter. And then, in chapter 5, we'll put the pieces together and see how you can expand your repertoire on each Street of 7-Card Stud.

Putting People on Hands

Putting people on hands means figuring out what hand your opponent is likely to hold. You would have a huge advantage in 7-Card Stud if you played poker with your hole cards concealed, but your opponent played with all of his cards exposed. We've learned in chapter 3 how to deceive opponents with our play so they can't deduce our hole cards. Chapter 4 shows you how to figure out your opponent's hole cards. You do this by using all of the clues at your disposal in 7-Card Stud.

No magic formula exists for figuring out what your opponent is likely to have. It is basically a matter of simple deduction. You must use all of the clues that are available for you at the poker table. Let's start with one of the basic skills you'll need to rely on as you try to figure out what your opponent is likely to hold.

Remembering Cards

One of the key clues that you'll be using to put your opponent on a hand will be the folded cards. I remember reading a general book on cards that had a section on poker. In it, the author stated that to play 7-Card Stud you would need to memorize all the cards that are dealt face up. He then illustrated his point with a hand in which the solid player, remembering that nine Hearts had been folded, knew with certainty that his opponent couldn't have a Flush.

This is just plain silly. I have played 7-Card Stud seriously for twelve years. I don't think I have ever been in a situation where I saw enough of a suit to rule out, with certainty, a possible Flush.

The truth is that while it may provide you with a razor-thin edge to be able to recall perfectly all of the cards that have been dealt face up, you don't have to remember every card that's dealt to be a good 7-Card Stud player. In fact, you don't really have to memorize many cards at all. A few things can give you an edge in this department. It really isn't that hard.

First of all, you only have to remember folded cards. After all, the other cards are staring right at you. Why memorize them? Generally, you need to remember only the rank of the card, not its suit. What I do is recite the rank of the cards as they are folded. So as I see the 8, Jack, 9, 2, and 3 get folded on Third Street I recite it to myself, "8Jack923." It helps me to rearrange them in numeric order and to then continue to repeat it to myself until Fourth Street is dealt. So I'll repeat, like a mantra, "2389Jack" over and over again. If additional cards are folded as the hand is played, I'll add them to my "list." When I'm competing for a pot with a player who pairs his door card Jack, I'll bear the list of folded cards in mind and maybe not give him credit for Trips. That's it—seven or eight numbers. Hey, a phone number these days is ten digits!

Of course, if you are drawing for a Flush you want to keep track of how many of your suit are out. So if you are dealt three to a Flush, keep track of how many of your suit are folded on Third Street. And if you suspect someone else is drawing for a Flush it helps to remember, roughly at least, whether or not a lot of her suit was out. But attentiveness, more than explicit memorization, is the best way to keep track of suits.

For example, when the cards are initially dealt, just mentally make a note if you see three or more of a particular suit. Don't focus on memorizing that fact. Just mention it to yourself. When you are wondering whether someone is likely to have a Spade Flush on Sixth Street, if you made a mental note that a lot of Spades were dealt, it will come back to you.

I've found that in this method, you will be able to stay focused on the play of the hand while also retaining enough card information to assist in figuring out what other players are likely to be holding.

Seven Clues in 7-Card Stud

Stud has many more clues for the observant player than any other form of poker. You can gain a significant advantage over your opponents if you know what they are and your opponent doesn't. There are generally seven types of clues that will help you deduce what hand your opponent is likely to be holding. Let's look at them quickly.

1. The cards you see
2. The cards that have been folded
3. Your opponent's betting action and position
4. The type of player they are
5. The type of player they think you are
6. The size of the pot
7. Other tells

Let's look at these clues in some detail and then use a specific hand to apply them.

1. The Cards You See

This is the simplest clue available to you. Look around the table. What cards are exposed? Look at your hole cards. What do you have? You make some inferences about what other players are likely to hold based on what you see.

Here are a couple of obvious ones. If you see many suited cards, it is unlikely that anyone is likely to get a Flush in that suit. So if you see four Hearts, and someone with a heart calls an initial bet, it's unlikely that he is trying for a Heart Flush with a 3-Flush to start. It's not impossible. But it's unlikely.

Similarly, if you notice that a couple of players show a card of the same rank (we call that being *counterfeited*), it's unlikely that either one of them is starting with a pair of that rank. If your opponent in the Three Seat raises with a K♣ and the person in the Five Seat also has a King, it's unlikely that the Three Seat has a pair of Kings. If you have an Ace and another Ace raises the bring-in, while it's not impossible for them to have a pair of Aces, you're less inclined to believe that they have what they are representing.

2.   The Cards That Have Been Folded

Folded cards are just like exposed cards. They are clues to what other players are likely to hold—and unlikely to hold. If three Kings and two 9s have been folded, the person raising with 10-Jack-Queen exposed is unlikely to have a Straight. If you see a 5 in front of the One Seat and a 5 has been folded by the Two Seat and the Three Seat catches a 5 on Fourth Street to give him a pair of 5s, then you know he doesn't have Trip 5s. Be observant and remember the rank of those folded cards and you'll have some extra clues.

3.   Their Betting Action and Position

Is your opponent raising from early position? He's more likely to be strong. Is he raising from late position when everyone else has checked? He's more likely to be bluffing. Did he call last round when he caught an Ace? It was unlikely to have given him a pair of Aces—or he would have bet. Betting action and position will tell you a lot about what your opponent is likely to hold.

An opponent who raised on Third Street with a high card is more likely to have a pair than 3-suited cards. Players with 3-suited cards tend to call hoping to get a fourth and a fifth suited card for a Flush. However, if a good player who raised on Third Street with a high card pairs his door card on Fourth Street and then bets he probably didn't make Trips because he'd be unlikely to bet it aggressively. He'd be more likely to check and try for a check raise or just slowplay it and come out betting and raising on Fifth Street when the limits double.

4. The Type of Player They Are

It's important to figure out what type of players your opponents are. Are they tight or loose, tricky or straightforward, passive or aggressive. When you do this you can get a read on the hands they are likely to have. Tight players play fewer hands. If they're betting they probably have what they are representing. If they're in early position and they begin the betting, tend to put them on a strong hand. Loose players may have many hands you might not play. Very aggressive players raise with any cards. So don't be as inclined to believe that they have the strong hands your tight opponents would need in identical situations.

If a tight player raises from early position with a Premium card, tend to give her credit for a Premium Pair. Similarly, if she pairs her door card, tend to give her credit for Trips if she raises a higher board. If a loose-passive player raises on Sixth Street with a 3-Flush showing, tend to give him credit for a Flush. Since he's not aggressive, why would he be raising unless he really made his hand?

On the other hand, if an aggressive player raises on Third Street with an Ace up, don't be so inclined to believe that she has a pair of Aces. Maybe she has only a small pair in the hole. Or maybe she's trying to steal the antes with a couple of high cards to go with her Ace.

5. The Type of Player They Think You Are

Here's a good time to be concerned about your image. If opponents think you are very tight, they will be more likely to bluff against you. You can use this fact to better gauge what they have. If your opponent raises from late position with a King up and you have been folding just about every hand for an hour, chances are that he doesn't really have the Pair of Kings but is trying to steal the antes. He is trying to take advantage of someone whom he thinks is a very tight player.

On the other hand, if you've been a passive calling station and no one seems to be able to knock you out of a hand, chances are that he wouldn't try this move unless he really had the pair of Kings. Think about how you are viewed and you'll have a good clue about what hands your opponents are likely to have against you.

6.   The Size of the Pot

How big is the pot? If it's large, expect your better opponents to try to win it with a bluff or semi-bluff if they think it will work. Small pots aren't worth the risk of a bet or a raise much of the time. So if it's small, expect them to have the hands they're representing.

7.   Other Tells

Good players sometimes exhibit traits that tend to give away the value of their hands. The best book on the subject is *Mike Caro's Book of Tells*. I recommend it highly for anyone who really wants to master this subject. In the meantime, let me share with you some of my money-making observations.

Generally, you will encounter two types of opponents: Those who think they can fool you by acting and those who are too simple even for this basic ruse. Decide first into which category your opponent falls. Most poker players are actors—poor actors to be sure, but actors nevertheless. But some players, maybe 20 percent or so at the lower-stakes tables, are really completely guileless. If their eyes bug out of their head or they have a big smile, they really have a good hand; if they frown or shake their heads, they really have a bad hand. Use your intuition for this.

Most of the time, your opponent will show weakness when he is strong and strength when he is weak. He'll challenge you by staring you in the eye when he has a mediocre or bad hand, but he'll look away or sigh when he has a strong one. These aren't 100 percent accurate but they give you some clues. Again, use your own intuition about what type of player you're facing.

And then apply the tells I provide below to figure out what your opponent is likely to have.

Giveaway Tells

I mentioned previously that in lower-limit games it is often a waste of time to look for "giveaway" tells. Even so, there are some obvious ones that will help add profit to your game. Here are a couple you can look for.

Staring at the Last Card

You're on Sixth Street with Two Pair. You bet and are called by someone with a 2-Flush showing. You suspect your opponent is drawing to a Flush.

It's the River. You don't fill up. You just have your Two Pair. You look over to your opponent. He is first to go. You are studying him as he looks at his last card. He doesn't know you're watching.

When he slowly turns up the corner of his card to see what it is you notice that he continues to stare at it. He then looks back at the rest of his hand and back at the seventh card. He does this once or twice and then stares you in the eye, grabs some chips and, while staring at you, says loudly "$10," while flinging his chips into the pot.

Chances are he's bluffing. Looking at his cards again, especially with great care, is a good sign that your opponent doesn't have a decent hand. He looked again to see if he could find anything worth playing. Bad players do this out of habit, but then, sometimes, they try to cover their weaknesses by acting strong—hence the staring and the flinging of chips. The man is bluffing. Call him and expect to take down the pot.

Talking

Talking is often an excellent tell. I've found that most players will talk more when they made their hand than when they missed. When players are bluffing, for the most part, they tend to shut up—sometimes freezing physically as well—as if to try not to disturb anything lest you notice they're bluffing. Of course, some players know this and other tells and try to fake you out by doing the opposite of what they know to be a general tell. Even so, for the most part, I am cautious against a talker and bold against someone who shuts up suddenly while betting.

Rechecking Down Cards

Average-to-poor players often recheck their down cards after they receive cards beyond Third Street. You, an aspiring winning player, won't do this. You'll look at your two cards and easily commit them to memory. But they won't. You can take advantage of this behavior.

On Fifth or Sixth Street, if an opponent catches a third suited up card she often checks her down card to see if she has a 4-Flush. When she sneaks that second peak you can be nearly certain that she doesn't have a Flush. If she did she wouldn't have to look. She would have remembered that she had four suited cards.

If it is your turn to bet, you can bet with confidence into opponents who do this. They don't have the Flush. (Unless they are smart enough to be familiar with this tell and are trying to fake you out. But few players at this level do this.) Similarly, if they recheck their hole card on Fourth Street or Fifth Street and they haven't gotten a Flush (or Straight) card, you can be pretty sure that they are checking to see whether they paired one of their down cards. Had they started with a pair in the hole, they would have remembered that without looking. The check was a giveaway that you can exploit.

Looking at Chips

I've found that when players hit a card that makes their hand, they instinctively look at their chips to get ready to bet. They don't do this for long. It's almost a reflex. But it has helped me figure out what my opponent had and saved me some significant money.

For example, if my opponent has a 4-Flush on Fifth Street and then catches another suited card on Sixth Street, he will often stare down momentarily at his stack of chips. He may then look away as if he's disinterested in the pot or otherwise fake a lack of interest in betting. But first he looked at his chips.

Putting Opponent On Hand, Sample Hand

You are not always going to use all of these clues. But you will usually use at least two to figure out what your opponent is holding. The key factor is to make sure that you are constantly reassessing what your opponent has as you get more clues. Here's a sample hand. It's $10/20 with a $1 ante and a $3 bring-in. Let's see how we would attempt to figure out what the Six Seat has. You're in the Seven Seat.

Seat 4: A♠	Seat 5: 2♣
Seat 3: A♥	Seat 6: A♦
Seat 2: 8♠	Seat 7, You: (Q♣-8♦) Q♦
Seat 1: 6♥	Seat 8: K♦

It's Third Street. The bring-in 2♣ is raised by the Six Seat with the A♦. You're sitting in the Seven Seat. We'll look at what you should do later. For now, we're concentrating on what the Six Seat has. Let's use our seven clues.

The Cards You See

The first thing you notice is that the raiser has an Ace. You may initially think, "He raised with an Ace. Does he have a pair of Aces?" You then look around at the table and see that two other players also have Aces. You start to doubt that he's raising with a Pair of Aces.

The Cards That Have Been Folded

No cards have been folded thus far. All the exposed cards are still face up. So there's no other knowledge about the cards that have been dealt that can help you.

Their Betting Action and Position

The Ace raised the bring-in from early position. Bets and raises from early position—with many players yet to act—generally indicate stronger hands than bets and raises from later positions. (Go back to chapter 2, to the section entitled "Seat Selection," if you forget why.) You start to think he might have a Premium Pair other than Aces.

The Type of Player They Are

The Six Seat is very tight. He plays very few hands. He's also a pretty good player. He notices other up cards and plays his hand accordingly. In other words, he's the type of player who would notice that two other players have an Ace. So we can deduce that he has a strong starting hand.

The Type of Player They Think You Are

You also know that every observant player would put you down as a good tight-aggressive player yourself. You fold most of your starting hands unless you have something of value. An observant player would notice that.

The Size of the Pot

It is Third Street with just the antes and the bring-ins. The pot is still small in this regularly structured $10–$20 game. It seems unlikely to you that your opponent would be trying to steal the antes from this position in this game.

Other Tells

This player has no tells that you've picked up on. You just know, based on his betting habits, that he tends to be very tight and aggressive.

So at this early stage, we might put this player raising with the Ace as having a Premium Pocket pair. We eliminate Queens since we have a pair of Queens. And we tend to rule out Kings since we see a King. We lean toward Jacks or 10s, since they're the two Premium Pairs that are not exposed anywhere yet. And, when deciding between them we lean a little toward Jacks because we conclude that this tight player is more likely to need a Pair of Jacks in early position to raise the bring-in.

(Note: *We make this preliminary assessment but we don't become wedded to it.* Remember, we will reassess constantly, based on all the additional information we take in. This is a preliminary assessment, subject to change. After all, he *could* have many other hands, including a pair of Aces. Even though we don't think it is likely at this stage, we can't rule it out completely.)

Let's say, for the sake of this example, that we call with our pocket Queens and everyone else folds. (In a real game situation it would probably be better to raise most of the time. But that's a subject for later.) The rest of the players fold leaving just the Ace and you.

Fourth Street

Seat 6:   A♥-10♠   You: (Q-8) Q-J

He's high. He bets. You call and reassess what he is likely to have (probably not the ideal play—but again, we'll deal with that later).

Let's use the seven steps again:

The Cards You See

He's showing an Ace and a 10. You have a Jack now to go with your two Queens and an 8. How does this information help you? You start to lean against his starting with Jacks since you now have one.

The Cards That Have Been Folded

A King was folded as well as two Aces. No 10s or Jacks were folded. You think some more about the possibility that he might have started with 10s in the hole and now might have Trip 10s.

Their Betting Action and Position

He bet initially from early position and is now betting when it's heads up. You're thinking that he might play a pair of 10s and then Trip 10s in this way.

The Type of Player They Are

You think about the fact that your opponent is very tight and aggressive. But you've never known him to be particularly tricky. You wonder whether he's capable of trying to bet some other hand, like a low or medium pocket pair to get you to fold. You conclude that he probably wouldn't.

The Type of Player They Think You Are

You have the image of a tight-aggressive player. You're not seen as tricky. You think that maybe your opponent is just trying to get you to fold.

The Size of the Pot

The pot was just heads up on Third Street. So it's relatively small. It seems unlikely that your opponent would be trying to steal the pot with a bluff here.

Other Tells

You haven't noticed any particular tells that help you.

Analysis: You put all of this information together. You think that your initial assessment may have been wrong. Maybe he doesn't have a pair of Jacks. If he did, would this tight-aggressive player have bet into you? He must be putting you on at least Queens based on your image and the way you've bet your hand. You think about whether he could have that last Ace for a pair of Aces.

Fifth Street

He gets a 3♥; you get the last Ace.

He: (?-?) A♦-10♠-3♥   You: (Q-8) Q-J-A

You bet with your pair of Queens. He raises. What do you do? First you must decide what he is likely to have.

Again, let's use our seven general clues:

The Cards You See

You have the last Ace. So you can completely rule out a Pair of Aces for your opponent. (This rarely happens, when you can rule a hand out with certainty. But when it does make sure you don't miss it.) He got a 3 that you doubt helped him.

The Cards That Have Been Folded

You don't recall any 3s being folded.

Their Betting Action and Position

He's raising your bet. You think that he might very well have the three 10s you thought he might have earlier.

The Type of Player They Are

He's tight and aggressive, unlikely to raise you twice in a row without any hand.

The Type of Player They Think You Are

He knows you're tight and would be unlikely to bet without a legitimate hand.

The Size of the Pot

It's just been heads up from Third Street, so the pot is relatively small compared with multi-way action.

Other Tells

He hasn't given you any tells that you can use.

Analysis: You put it together and think that a tight player like this, who has been playing his hand strong from the beginning, is unlikely to have been bluffing. Though you are tight, he isn't quite the maniac or tricky player he would need to be to raise you twice in a row to get you to fold a strong hand. You realize that the pot isn't very large since it was heads up the whole way. You conclude that in all likelihood he has the Trip 10s. You're not certain of this, but you are reasonably sure based on all of the clues you picked up. So you fold on Fifth Street. Had it been a multi-way pot up until then, with much more money for you to win if he was bluffing, you'd be more tempted to call. But it isn't large so you fold.

That gives you the method for putting an opponent on a hand. Notice that you didn't just stick with your initial assessment. If you did, you would have continued to think that he had a Pair of Jacks, no matter what new information came before you. But you wisely updated your view of his hand based on what you saw after Third Street and wisely concluded that a fold was in order.

Summary

Reading hands is not an exact science. At its best it can tend to help you figure out what your opponent has. Use these seven clues to help narrow down the possible holdings of your opponents. But don't get carried away.

Players get into trouble by making an initial deduction about what their opponent has and then not updating that deduction based on additional information. Make sure to continue to update your assessment of what your opponent has based on all of the clues that develop as the hand is played.

Deduction can get you into trouble in another way if you're not careful. Remember that we all would rather play out hands than fold them. Sometimes, against what should be our better judgment, we tend to put players on hands that we can beat to justify our calling or raising. If we're clever, we can always concoct some rationale for justifying a bad call or wild raise. Make sure you don't throw away your generally sound poker judgment just because you think you have a good read on your opponent.

In chapter 5 we'll revisit each street and see how we can add a few more plays into our play book so we can play more hands profitably. We'll still be playing a tight-aggressive style, but we'll be expanding our list of playable hands, taking into consideration our ability to play deceptively and our ability to pick up deceptive plays from our opponents.

CHAPTER 5

Expanding Your Repertoire

Playing More Hands

You will be able to play more hands as you develop your ability to read other players. You will not have to assume that they have what they are trying to represent. I provide some moves you can make on different streets. These can provide some additional profit to your game. I would not suggest that you use these moves against the worst players you are likely to play against. They will work best against players who are good enough to be predictable.

Most of these plays are for play on Third Street and Fourth Street. I've divided them accordingly. I've also added a few that apply to many streets.

Third Street Plays

The ante-steal is the primary weapon that you'll be able to employ against better players. We covered that in chapter 3. Your playable hands increase greatly with the ante-steal. This makes you less predictable and thereby allows you to make more money on your strong hands—as opponents will be more likely to call you, not knowing that you are strong.

As your skills increase, you will also be able to play other hands of marginal value more frequently, depending on your opponents, your position, your image at the table, and your ability to fold these hands on later streets if they don't improve. For example, though you shouldn't make a habit out of playing such borderline hands as low pairs without high kickers, three low-suited cards, or three high cards, under the right circumstances you can call with these hands.

In general, you can play these hands if you have weak-passive opponents who are also in the hand and will call your bets if you make powerful hands on later streets. This is especially true if you can see Fourth Street for only the bring-in and/or the hand is multi-way going in to Fourth Street. And, of course, the cards that improve your hand must be very live.

Here's an example of when you might play a hand of marginal value on Third Street when it has been completed to the full bet. You hold (4♥-5♥) 5♠. You see the following lineup in this $10/20 game:

Seat 4: (?-?) J♥	Seat 5: (?-?) J♣
Seat 3, You: (?-?) (4♥-5♥) 5♠	Seat 6: (?-?) 10♣
Seat 2: 9♣	Seat 7: (?-?) 4♠
Seat 1: (?-?) 10♠	Seat 8: (?-?) 2♦

Eight Seat brings it in for $3. One Seat calls. Two Seat folds. It is your decision. If you know the other players are loose and passive—calling stations for example—go ahead and call the $3. If someone does complete the bet and there are three or four callers of the completed bet, call along as well. If someone else reraises, or if everyone else folds to a completion of the bet, fold as well—losing your initial $3 call.

You're experienced enough now to be able to fold that hand if you don't catch a third 5 on Fourth Street or to use a deceptive move like a bluff or a semi-bluff to gain an advantage if possible. So go ahead and put yourself in the hand even though you probably don't have the best of it yet. When you think that you can outplay bad opponents, sometimes it makes sense to call with these marginal hands so you are in a position to take advantage of their suboptimal play later in the betting.

Let's follow along with this hand and see some examples of how you might take advantage of your opponents, once you've developed some hand-reading skills. Assume that the hand was called by a few more players for just the bring-in, so on Fourth Street, this is what you see:

Seat 4: (?-?) J♥-6♣   Seat 5: (?-?) Folded
Seat 3, You: (4♥-5♥) 5♠-A♥   Seat 6: (?-?) 10♣-9♥
Seat 2: Folded   Seat 7: (?-?) Folded
Seat 1: (?-?) 10♠-8♦   Seat 8: (?-?) 2♦-K♣

You're high. You know that the One Seat is a very aggressive player and that the Four Seat and Six Seat are weak-tight—they play selectively but fold under pressure. The Eight Seat you know to be a calling station—he tends to call more than he should and raise less than he should.

You could try for a check-raise here. You check. The Four, Six, and Eight Seats check as well. But the One Seat, being an aggressive player and not seeing any strength from anyone else, bets. You go ahead and raise. Your raise is likely to knock out the Four, Six, and Eight Seats who all fold to the double pressure of a bet and a raise. The One Seat calls your raise and you both see Fifth Street.

You've greatly improved your chances of winning by thinning the field to two players. You are unlikely to be far behind the One Seat, if at all. You doubt he has a Pair of 10s, since you noticed that another player held a 10. Maybe he has a Pair of 8s now, but you doubt that he started with 10-9-8 since two of the 9s are gone. You think that he probably has no better than a small pair, since he would have raised had he a Premium Pair on Third Street. There's a strong likelihood that he just has a couple of high cards and was trying to steal the antes on Fourth Street by betting after seeing everyone check. You conclude that he's just calling you to see if he gets another high card. If he doesn't, you can go ahead and bet Fifth Street and expect to pick up the pot.

As you gain experience you can also afford to be more liberal with your calls when other players raise. Some players will be raising as bluffs or semi-bluffs on Third Street. While your initial strategy was to assume the worst and generally fold when high door cards raised you, you can modify this somewhat as you gain experience.

For example, when you started out it was generally a good idea to fold when you had a Premium Pair if someone with a higher up card than that pair raised the bring-in in front of you. So you would usually have folded your pair of Queens, for example, if a King in front of you raised (and you didn't have an Ace kicker). You would generally give him credit for two Kings and concede right away.

With a better ability to read your opponents, you can call or even raise with that same Pair of Queens if you think that your opponent may be trying to steal the antes with that exposed King. You'll have to take into consideration the many factors that we've already outlined in chapter 4. But when you do so, if you believe that you may well have the better hand, then the best strategy is not to fold.

Let's say, for example, that you are in the following $5/10 hand:

Seat 4: K♦	Seat 5: (Q♥-7♠) Q♠
Seat 3: 9♣	Seat 6: 2♠
Seat 2: K♠	Seat 7: J♥
Seat 1: 9♥	Seat 8: 8♣

The 2♠ brings in the bet for $2. The J♥ folds, the 8♣ folds, the 9♥ folds, the K♠ folds, the 9♣ folds, and the K♦ raises. It's $5 to you. What do you do?

In our early strategy, presented in chapter 2, I recommended that if you didn't at least have a higher kicker, you should generally fold—not wanting to go up against someone who was likely to have a pair of Kings. However, now that you have some experience under your belt and are better able to figure out what your opponent is likely to have, you can vary that response to suit your circumstances.

In this case, you'd notice that there was another King out, you'd consider the late position of your opponent when he raised and you'd consider the type of player he was and the image you had at the table. In many situations you'd conclude that he was on an ante-steal. You could then either reraise him or call and then raise his bet on Fourth Street if he didn't seem to improve. If he raised you back you'd tend to give him credit for Kings and fold, although as in all poker decisions you'd have to consider what type of player he was before making your decision. Again, your ability to expand your repertoire of hands increases as your skill at reading your opponent's cards goes up—provided you have the discipline to get out of a hand when you deem yourself to have the worst of it.

Fourth Street Hands

In general, after some experience and some development of your ability to read other players, you'll be able to play more hands on Fourth Street than a relatively new and inexperienced 7-Card Stud player. You will not have to automatically fold your Flush or Straight draws just because you failed to improve on your fourth card.

For example, if you started with a high 3-Flush like (A♦-J♦) 6♦ and called a raise on Third Street, along with two other players, you might be able to call a bet on Fourth Street even if you caught a blank. This is true because if your cards are still very live and the pot is large and you are against opponents who play relatively straightforwardly, it is worth it to draw a fifth card. Here's a specific example of that:

Third Street

Seat 4: 8♥	Seat 5: 3♣
Seat 3: Q♥	Seat 6: 10♣
Seat 2: 2♠	Seat 7, You: (A♦-J♦) 6♦
Seat 1: 8♠	Seat 8: 7♠

Seat Two, with the 2♠ brought in the bet for $3 in this $10/20 game, was raised to $10 by the Q♥ in the Three Seat, called by the 8♥ in the Four Seat, you in the Seven Seat, and the bring-in 2♠. The other hands folded.

On Fourth Street you saw this:

Seat 4: 8♥-7♣

Seat 3: Q♥-2♣   You: (A♦-J♦) 6♦-K♠

Seat 2: 2♠-6♠

Assume that the other players are relatively straightforward players. You would check with your King. If the Two Seat checked and the Three Seat bet with the Q♥ again and the Four Seat called, you could call as well. While it is a 9.4:1 long shot that you'll make your Flush, when you add in all the other factors it is often worth a call in this situation. Based on the cards that have already been played, you'd have to figure that the Three Seat was just betting a pair of Queens again, the Four Seat was either on a straight draw or maybe had a medium pair (a start of 7-8-9 or 8-8-x might have been possible, for example).

Your diamonds are completely live—none have been exposed yet. Your Ace and Kings are live and might improve to the best hand on the next card. That means that sixteen cards will help you on Fifth Street. You've seen eighteen. That leaves eighteen that don't help you. So you have a nearly even chance of either improving to a Flush draw or what is likely to be the best hand on Fifth Street. The eventual size of the pot you'll win, if you win, is likely to be very large considering that there are four people who have seen Fourth Street. And, your opponents are unlikely to outplay you—given that they are straightforward and predictable. All in all, then, you'd conclude that it was worth another call to see if you either improved to a Premium Pair or a 4-Flush on Fifth Street.

The above notwithstanding, you need to be careful not to automatically start calling bets on Fourth Street when your Flush or Straight draw hasn't improved. The example I gave you was deliberately crafted to highlight a situation that favored drawing a fifth card. That type of situation is unusual. Your hand is rarely that live, the pot rarely that large, and the opponents rarely as predictable and straightforward all at the same time. Just because your increased skill and experience gives you the *option* of calling doesn't mean you should routinely do so.

The Check-Raise Semi-Bluff

Let's say you played Fourth Street with wired 6s and an Ace kicker. You raised the bring-in in late position and got called by a good player. On Fourth Street you caught bad—neither pairing your Ace nor hitting another 6. Your opponent seemed to be unhelped by her Fourth Street card.

If you are up against a particularly good aggressive opponent who will likely bet if you check, then try for a check-raise. You have a good shot at getting her to fold right there, fearing that you have a Pair of Aces, Aces up, or Trips. If she calls, follow up this check-raise with a bet on Fifth Street if your good opponent doesn't seem to improve. Expect her to fold.

This is not a move you can use habitually, as your better opponents will eventually figure you out. But used sparingly you'll accomplish a lot. You'll often win the pot with it. You'll also slow down your more aggressive opponents in the future when you try for an ante-steal and don't connect on Fourth Street and then check. They'll be reluctant to bet into you, fearing that you have just been setting up a check-raise. By keeping them from bluffing or semi-bluffing you on Fourth Street when you check, you'll often be able to see Fifth Street for free—giving you another chance to improve your hand and win the pot.

Playing Pairs on Fourth Street

What's the best way of taking advantage of a paired door card on Fourth Street? I've found that the right play is not always the obvious one. Let's look at two common scenarios that exist when you pair your door card and consider how you might vary your play based on the circumstances you're in.

You bet your Premium Pair on Third Street and now have Trips on Fourth Street. If you raised or completed the bring-in on Third Street with your split pair and you had the good fortune to pair your door card, you now have Premium Trips. You have an excellent chance of winning the pot. You want to maximize the amount you will win.

Conventional poker thinking dictates slow play here. The theory is that you don't want to be too aggressive lest you scare off all of the other players. Some experienced players and writers caution that you should check or bet the lower-tier amount. For example, if the game is $5/10 when there is a pair showing on Fourth Street you may bet either $5 or $10. Some suggest only betting the $5 or checking on this street to avoid having everyone fold to your Trips. They conclude that you want to win a large pot on the River, not just a small pot on Fourth Street.

I sometimes follow that advice. If I am against a player whom I know will bet if I check, I'll check. If I'm in a game where I'm sure that players might be lured into calling my lower tier $5 bet but be scared off by the $10 bet, I'll bet the $5. But most of the time, against typical or better-than-average opponents, however, when I make Premium Trips on Fourth Street I make a full bet. Let me explain why.

It's certainly true that everyone else may fold if the complete amount is bet. But, on balance, that risk is worth the potential reward that generally seems to accrue from the more aggressive bet.

In the typical low- and mid-limit games that I play in, players who pair their door card will often make the higher tier bet when they don't have Trips. Their opponents often suspect that the larger bet doesn't indicate Trips, so they tend to call. In fact, if someone bets the lower tier amount when they pair their door card most players become suspicious wondering why they bet the lower amount. They suspect that their opponent is trying to seduce them with the lower bet and are thereby more likely to fold. I want to take advantage of these expectations.

The typical early aggression, bluffing and semi-bluffing in

these low- and mid-limits, is also accompanied by a fair amount of disbelief and calling. Not betting this hand, or betting the lower tier amount, would raise more questions and doubts than the full bet. By betting at the lower tier amount, and raising these questions, I might actually slow down or stop their betting action as the hand progresses. I don't want to do that.

Typically, when I bet with the Premium Pair, I am often called by at least one and sometimes two, three, or four other players who think that I'm misrepresenting my hand (or who don't have the sophistication to suspect that I probably have Trips). This is advantageous for two reasons: The pot I am the favorite to win is made larger by my larger tier bet and their call on Fourth Street. And, because the pot is now larger, they may be seduced by its size into making more bad calls as the hand progresses.

The size of the pot, after my Fourth Street double bet and their calls, will be larger than normal. Many of my opponents may use this as an excuse to justify "going to the River" with many drawing hands like 4-Flushes, 4-Straights, and Two Pair. If, for example, they called my larger tier bet on Fourth Street because they had a 4-Flush, and they failed to get their Flush card on Fifth Street, they will erroneously conclude that it makes sense for them to call every bet I will make until the River. Since they didn't give me credit for Trips (or, if they did, they didn't properly value it against their 4-Flush) they mistakenly put themselves into a disadvantageous position for every street thereafter. Furthermore, they run the serious risk of making their hand, gleefully raising my bet on the River when they make a Flush, only to be reraised by me when I make a Full House or Quads.

In fact, I have played in many games with these typical loose low- and mid-limit players who will call me even when I have made another exposed pair (and thereby my Full House). If they reasoned at all, they probably thought that since this happened on Sixth Street, they were obliged to call on the River, having "gone this far." Even somewhat sophisticated players may have concluded that by betting the full amount on Fourth

Street, I didn't have Trips (if I made Trips, they conventionally reasoned, I would have slowplayed my hand because I wouldn't want to scare them off). So they didn't give me credit for anything better than Two Pair when I made my open Two Pair on Sixth Street.

Ironically, then, slowplaying Premium Trips on Fourth Street, when you pair your Premium door card, often causes players who would call a full bet to fold, suspecting a trap. And if you check, and they check behind you, they will often fold as soon as you bet on Fifth Street, suspecting that you have the Trips. The full bet on Fourth Street often doesn't raise these suspicions because it is the expected play. And that's why, in the games I usually play in, it is often the better play.

You called with your 3-Flush or 3-Straight on Third Street and now have a non-Premium Pair. Your hand has improved here, but only slightly. Conventional play would usually dictate a check and then a fold if someone bets into you. But what I do in this situation is usually dependent on how many callers there are on Third Street.

Against many opponents, I will usually do the conventional thing and check my low pair with the expectation that I will fold to a bet. Sometimes, however, if I have a very tight image in a game and haven't played a hand for a while, I will try a different play. Here is that play.

I check my pair, but if a player bets (and is a fairly solid player) and subsequent players fold, and I am the last player or the next to last player to act, I may then raise. This would be, technically, a check-raise semi-bluff. I checked initially showing weakness but then when my opponent bet I raised him as if I really did have the Trips. I'd be happy if he folded, but I would still have a hand that could improve to the best hand on the next card.

My reasoning is that a good player may well bet if he has a pair, having seen apparent weakness by my check. But when I then raised him with my paired door card he will probably release his hand, concluding that I really did have Trips after all. I don't make this move often, and I only do it if I believe that my image at the table is very tight and if I'm against a player whom I have observed to be at least reasonably good. But when the conditions are as I've described them, it often succeeds in winning me the pot right there.

Against one or two other players, however, if I think they are at least slightly observant and less than completely loose, I might try betting the lower tier amount (but only after a slight pause). My goal is to pick up the pot right there.

That's right, I said the *lower tier* amount, *not the higher tier* amount. Remember that on Fourth Street, with a pair showing you have the choice of either betting the lower amount of the structure or the higher amount. Conventional thinking might dictate that you bluff with the largest amount possible. But I bet the lower amount in this situation for two reasons: First of all, if no one else has improved, any bet will probably win me the pot with my pair. So I am picking up the pot while only risking half a bet.

The second reason is that against players who think they are sharp, my slight pause before the lower tier bet will often be enough to convince them that I really have Trips and that I am trying to lure them in with only the smaller bet. My small bet is meant to be seen as an enticement for them to call. If they are halfway decent, mildly observant, and have not greatly improved their hands, they will often concede the pot to me right then. But even if they do not do so, they will rarely, if ever, raise me. This enables me, for the lower tier bet, to see my Fifth Street card cheaply. If I don't improve, I can check and fold here if they bet into me. But, more often than not, I find that these typically weak and passive players do not bet into me. If they haven't improved, they usually don't bet. This gives me another card for free—sometimes two more cards. All this for one half-sized bet that had some expectation of winning the entire pot.

Of course, this play does not always work, especially against very good players. The better, more observant, more aggressive players will sometimes see through it and will often raise my half-sized bet by the full bet. If this happens I usually give up on my gambit right there if I have only the exposed pair. But even so, it was a gambit waged cheaply, with only half a bet.

As you can see, for the thoughtful and experienced player there is nothing automatic about pairing your card on Fourth Street. Depending on the type of game you are in, you may want to consider making this play that deviates from what conventional wisdom dictates.

Fifth Street Plays

The Semi-Demi-Bluff on Fifth and Sixth Street
Simply put, this is a bet with three ways to succeed: by winning as a bluff, by winning by improving on the next card, and as a value bet where you actually are in the lead. It has an application for these two later streets as well. Consider this example from Sixth Street. It is heads up and you have the following hand:

(King♦, 9♦) 4♦, 7♦, 9♥, 4♥

You are up against a fairly good, reasonably tight player with:

(?-?) J♠, 8♠, 3♦, 8♥.

He has bet the whole way up until this point. And he bets again. Sometimes you should raise here. You probably do not have the better hand here, since his early betting indicated that he probably had a Pair of Jacks to start. You probably won't succeed in getting him to fold, and you aren't at all certain that you will improve to the better hand on the next card. But the addition of all of these three possibilities is probably sufficient to make this the correct play.

Look at it more closely. You've paired your 4s giving you Two Pair—9s and 4s. You put him on a higher Two Pair because of his betting. The pot is fairly large at this point since he's been betting and you've been calling the whole way. There's only a small possibility that he will fold to your bluffing attempt to represent that you've just received Trips. There's no way to pinpoint what the chances are that he'll fold, but just for the sake of estimating it roughly let's say it's a 20 percent possibility. If this were just a pure bluff, it probably wouldn't make sense.

There's also only about a 20 percent possibility that you will make your Flush, and only about an 8 percent probability that you'll make your Full House. So the chances that you'll improve on the next card (the addition of 20 percent and 8 percent) don't alone warrant a bet here.

Finally, consider that your opponent probably bet initially with a Pair of Jacks. But there is the possibility that he had a pocket pair or even that he was raising with a 3-Flush or a 3-Straight. Not much of a possibility. And again, it's impossible to pinpoint the chances. But for the sake of putting a number on something that is intangible, it's a small but not microscopic number, let's call it 20 percent. Standing alone, this doesn't make sense as a value bet since you are probably not in the lead. But when you add it to the possibility of a bet succeeding as a bluff and the possibility of your hand improving on the next card, it may tip the scales in favor of a raise.

Again, this isn't a play you want to make routinely. But by making it occasionally you will keep your better, more observant opponents from being able to read you well. And that will add to your profit.

Two Wrongs Can Make a Right

Imagine this scenario. On the deal you have an Ace with wired 6s. You raise on Third Street to steal the antes. Everyone folds except a 10 (who may have a pair of 10s) and who calls you.

On Fourth Street, with your table image as a tight aggressive player, you assume that your next bet might take the pot. You know your opponent is aggressive and that if you check, he will bet and you will have a tough call to make. So you bet. He's a loose player, so he calls you.

On Fifth Street you don't improve; neither does he. You still have only that Pair of 6s with the Ace kicker. You bet again. He looks at the pot with the antes and the four small bets from Third and Fourth Street, pauses a moment and then, though he hasn't improved at all, he calls.

Ironically, he is making two mistakes but doing the right thing. Your bets on Third, Fourth, and Fifth Street have convinced him that you have a Pair of Aces. That conclusion is wrong. Since he's a bad player, however, he also mistakenly believes that with the bets already in the pot he is correct in calling your Fifth Street bet, even though you have Aces. He's wrong again. But because of these two wrongs he makes the correct play and calls you.

If you can help it, don't give a loose opponent an opportunity to make two wrong decisions that back him into the right action. What could you have done differently that might have gotten him to take the wrong action?

If you had established yourself as someone who check-raises, you could have bet Third Street in an attempt to steal the antes but then checked on Fourth Street. You could check on Fourth Street because your earlier check raises would have made your opponents worry that you might check-raise them if they bet. Not wanting to be check-raised, or not having the temerity to bet into you, your opponent would also be likely to check. If you then bet on Fifth Street your inexpert opponent might very well have concluded that you were attempting a check-raise on Fourth Street (which he skillfully avoided) and that you were now betting with your Aces. It wouldn't be worth a call from him because the pot would be small compared with what it would have been if you had bet Fourth Street.

This may seem like a very unlikely scenario. But I have seen it many times. I've seen many loose opponents who will call all the way to the River if an opponent bets each round. But if there's no bet on Fourth Street, they fold to a bet on Fifth Street.

Use this analogy: you need to take out one of the stairs on the stairway. As long as your opponent is walking up one step at a time, you are less likely to succeed in your attempt to win the pot. It's too easy to walk up to the next step. But take out one of those steps and he might well decide to call it quits rather than take the double stride to the next level.

There's another use for the check-raise; it can help you thin the field. Do this when your hand is strong but not superstrong.

Here's an example of what I mean. Imagine you are dealt a split Pair of 7s with a King kicker. You bet on Third Street and get called by three players: a Queen, a 9, and a 2.

On Fourth Street you catch a King giving you Two Pair, the 2 catches a suited card, the 9 catches a 10, the Queen catches a blank. The Queen is to your right. Consider a check-raise. You check. The 2, with perhaps a 4-Flush, checks hoping to get a free card, the 9, maybe with a Pair of 9s or a 4-Straight, checks. The Queen, with a Pair of Queens, sees that you checked. Because you checked, even though you showed a King, he assumes that you don't have a Pair of Kings. So he bets. You raise—a check-raise. You do this to knock out the two players who checked. They are very likely to fold for the double-sized bet (the Queen's bet and your raise).

Had you bet with your Two Pair each of those two players may very well have called. If they were drawing to a Flush and a Straight they may have figured it was worth one bet to see Fifth Street. But for two bets they're unlikely to call. Your check-raise helped thin the field and increased your chance of winning.

I'll give you one other example of a useful check-raise that you can make on the River—the last round of betting. Imagine that you had a Premium Pair on Third Street and started the betting. Your hand improved to Two Pair on Fourth Street and you continued to bet. On Fifth Street you bet again and were called by one other player who showed two to a Flush. On Sixth Street you still had Two Pair but your opponent caught a third suited up card. You decided to bet. He raised you. You called.

On the River, you make a Full House. You are high on board. Go for a check-raise here. His betting indicates that he caught a Flush on Sixth Street. He will bet that Flush after you check. You can raise him expecting to collect two bets instead of just the one you would collect had you initiated the betting on the River.

Ninty-nine percent of the time your raise will be called either because your opponent suspects that you might be bluffing or because most players at these moderate limits don't fold when they have a Flush even if they're certain they're beaten.

You might wonder if there's a chance that this move will backfire on you. What if he checks after you check, you might ask. Won't you be missing a bet? Let's look at that possibility.

If, in fact, he was bluffing on Sixth Street (or semi-bluffing) without the Flush, he might check on the River if he doesn't make his Flush. But this won't mean that you'll lose a bet by checking. The reason is that he wouldn't have called your bet anyway if you had initiated the betting on the River. He would have folded to your bet if he didn't make a hand. So you lose nothing by checking.

If, in fact, he didn't have a hand on the River, your check might cause him to bet as a bluff on the River. That's because he might reason that if you checked, the only way he could win the pot would be to bet—hoping you would fold. Had you bet out on the River he would have folded and you would have lost that bet.

Drafting and Poker

Have you ever watched a bicycle or auto race? If you have, you're probably familiar with a racing strategy called *drafting*. It works something like this. You get behind your opponent. Because he's in front, he's expending a lot of energy to cut through the air. You, on the other hand, are conserving energy by staying back—following in the slipstream behind him. While he is leading and you are following, he may be convinced that you are weak and unable to pass. But he is using more energy while you are saving energy. You use the energy you saved to pass him near the end of the race. He is tired from having led for so long and can't keep up as you go on to win.

A similar situation can arise in poker. You follow along behind your opponent, not using all of your strength. You lull her into thinking that she is ahead because she is acting stronger without any challenge from you. You only reveal your strength at the end when it is too late for her to do anything about it.

Consider the following example. You are dealt a split Pair of Aces. A two, to your left, brings in the bet. Everyone folds to your opponent who has a Queen up. He raises. Two more opponents fold to the raise. The bet is to you.

Well, conventional strategy says you should reraise. You're in the lead. Get more money in the pot while you are ahead. This is an opportunity, however, to draft behind the Queens. Don't raise. *Call!*

If you were to reraise, the Queen would probably conclude that you had Aces and might very well fold. By just calling you allow your opponent to incorrectly assume that they are the stronger hand, encouraging them to lead bet for the rest of the rounds.

The bring-in is likely to fold. So it will be heads up. Now it's Fourth Street. You check. The Queen is likely to think you had a 3-Flush or a small wired pair on Third Street. Let the Queen bet into you. You call.

Now it's Fifth Street. The Queen is now fairly convinced that you have a low pair. You should try for the check-raise here. The Queen, whether he's improved or not, is likely to bet. And you should raise. What you have done is used the Queen's speed to get him into trouble.

If you've made Aces Up on Fifth Street, you can continue to draft behind his lead betting by checking and calling. Then, on Sixth Street you can bet out or go for the check-raise. He's unlikely to fold by this time, seeing how large the pot is. Even if he suspects that you have the superior hand, he may figure that he has the right pot odds to call you down.

Similarly, on the River, if he has even a Pair of Queens, and surely if he has Queens Up, he'll call your bet. So there's a strong likelihood that by having your Aces draft behind these Queens, you'll be able to extract many extra bets with very little additional risk. Not a play you should make a habit of, but surely something that can help mix up your play once you have some experience under your belt.

Playing in Different Types of Games

Nonstandard Poker Games

Most 7-Card Stud games in a casino are played eight handed. Most of the players tend to be of average ability, with an average mix of tight and loose players in every game. The strategies that I've outlined apply to those average games. For the most part, even when those conditions change, you'll be able to adapt to the changing conditions with the strategy and tactics that I've outlined. Even so, there are some changes in your general strategy that you should use for special circumstances. I address those special types of games next.

Playing Short-Handed

Playing short-handed is a very different game from playing full. I consider short-handed to be five players or fewer. You need to consider the effect of the smaller game on your strategy. I'd suggest a few things to think about. First of all, you will be tempted to bluff more. You figure that there are fewer players to beat, so bluffing will be easier.

This is a common mistake. You shouldn't bluff more in a short-handed 7-Card Stud game. You should bluff *less*.

You bluff less because you are fighting for a smaller initial pot than at a full-handed game. It is diminished because there are fewer antes in the pot. In a full eight-person $10/20 game the initial pot you are trying to steal is $11 ($1 in antes from each player and a $3 forced bet). But in a five-person game the initial pot is only $8. In the full game you are betting $10 for $11, in the short game $10 for $8. Your potential win for making this play just dropped by about 25 percent, so you need to be that much *more* sure of success.

Even so, you should be playing more hands. And you'll be playing some hands more aggressively in a short-handed game than in a regular-sized game. But this isn't because you're bluffing more.

Rather, you are just value betting more. Many (though not all) hands go up in value when you are short-handed because there will be fewer players who will be drawing against you. The best hand you are likely to be up against will be worse than in a full game.

For example, in a three-handed game, if you have a Pair of 4s on the deal, you are likely to have the best hand against random opponents. But if you are in an eight-handed game, you are more likely not to be in the lead unless you have at least a Pair of 10s. So, roughly speaking, on Third Street your Pair of 4s in a three-handed game is worth about as much as a Pair of 10s in a full game. Its value has gone up.

Think of it this way. If you are playing eight-handed and everyone has folded to you and the bring-in you can raise with hands much weaker than you would need to raise with if you were first to act, when six players were left to act after you. Short-handed games are like full games when you are in late position and the players before you have all folded. But the pots are smaller.

Pairs, especially middle pairs, go up in value in a short-handed game. While they often will be folded in a full game, you should often raise with them for value in a short-handed game. On Third Street in a four-handed game, for example, you should play a pair of 7s, 8s, or 9s as you would play Jacks in a full game.

Some hands, however, go down in value because of the unlikelihood of having pots large enough to justify chasing. While you will often consider calling with a 3-Flush or 3-Straight from early position in a loose full-handed game, if the game is four-handed, you should probably fold—unless you have something strong to go with it like an Ace and another high card. In that way, it's like playing a 3-Flush from early position in a very tight full game. If you knew that it would be heads up, you'd fold all but your best 3-Flushes in a tight full game. Same in a short game.

It's important that you not be seduced into playing too aggressively in a short-handed game. It's easy to be. Because there are fewer players, you will be winning a larger percentage of your hands—and hence may find yourself winning quite a few hands in a row. That can fuel a mistaken view that you are unbeatable. This causes some players to go on tilt, to start betting and raising with little regard for card value, and little sense of the true relative value of their hands. There is the sense that with just enough aggression any hand can be turned into a winner. And that is wrong and potentially disastrous.

In fact, I'd recommend that beginning casino 7-Card Stud players stay away, as much as possible, from short-handed play. Part of the strategy for winning poker that you have learned depends on many loose calls from opponents. With fewer players in the pot to start with, you can't rely nearly as much on that aspect of the strategy. There will be fewer players; others will play more aggressively to compensate, meaning, generally more raising and reraising. You don't want to be in that type of game until you have become more experienced playing 7-Card Stud.

That being said, if you have played 7-Card Stud for a while, and are ready for some atypical games, short-handed play can be very lucrative. You will see many more hands an hour than in a full game. If you are better than your opponents, you can play many more hands an hour and thereby win more money per hour.

There is, however, another potential disadvantage to short-handed low-limit games. The effect of the rake may be much greater than in full games. This is because there is a much greater chance that the hands will end up heads up with the pots, thereby, considerably smaller than in a game that is contested three-way or more. The amount of money raked from the pot is going to be a larger percentage of your winnings. (This is covered fully in the next chapter.) Your advantage over the other players in your game will have to be all the greater for you to see any profit.

Playing in Tight Games

While you will surely seek out the loosest, most passive games you can find, you will occasionally find yourself in a tight game. This is inevitable. Loose players eventually lose their money. They, in turn, are often replaced by tight players who have been eyeing the good game waiting to get in. The more tight players, the more likely it is that the loose players won't stay as long. When they leave, they are replaced by more tight players until, sometimes, what was once a wonderful flower patch of loosey-goosey players has turned, sadly, into a barren rock garden. But don't despair. Once you have been playing for a while and learn the rudiments of solid play, you can turn this situation to your advantage.

Tight players fold. That's why we call them tight. Often they are passive, raising little and avoiding confrontations. These tight, conservative players who fold to even a small amount of pressure, are often very predictable. You can use their predictability and their tightness to your advantage.

You should play slightly more hands early on than you would normally play, and play them more aggressively. But if you are met with stiff resistance, you should not hesitate to quit.

Here's an example of what I mean. Let's say it's Third Street. You are in fifth position with a split Pair of 8s. No 8s are out. Your kicker is a Queen. Following you are three players, with a King, a 6, and a 5, and the bring-in 2. The King is a rock. The rest are average players. The players fold to you. Go ahead and raise here.

In a normal, looser game you wouldn't raise. You might call. And if the King were a particularly tricky and aggressive player (or any of the other players were especially tough for that matter), you might even fold. But since you know the King is a rock, who never calls or raises without the goods, take your ante-steal shot against him here. Statistically, 83 percent of the time he won't have a pair of Kings. He and the lower valued up cards, held by typical straightforward players, are likely to fold.

However, if the King calls or raises you, you know you're in trouble. If he comes out betting on Fourth Street, you should fold unless you've improved. You know that he wouldn't bet into you without a pair of Kings (or maybe a Premium Pair wired). And you're a big dog in that situation. So get out!

Similarly, on later streets, be more inclined to be aggressive and less inclined to call than you would normally be. Tend to believe your opponent's bets mean exactly what they seem to mean.

Some of this is fairly obvious. If your tight opponent has a 3-Flush showing on Fifth Street and you have a Premium Pair, tend to give up the hand if he bets (assuming, of course, that there aren't a lot of his suit that have already been folded). If he was high, checked, and then called your bet on Fourth Street and then comes out betting with the third suited card on Fifth Street, chances are very strong that this rock has hit his Flush. So fold.

If he pairs his door card and bets, and you haven't seen another of that rank, give him credit for Trips. Even if you have Two Pair, be inclined to fold right away. True, he could have Two Pair as well, with a wired pair and an open pair to go with them. But you have two reasons to believe he has Trips. First of all, it is twice as likely that a pair is split than that it is wired. So the chances are much greater that a paired door card is, in fact Trips, and not Two Pair. Add to that his conservative style of play, which would be much more likely to check Two Pair than to lead bet it. The overwhelming likelihood is Trips. So you either have a small chance of being a slight favorite, with a higher Two Pair, or a large chance of being a big dog, with Two Pair against Trips. Why buck this rock when he probably has you beaten? Wait for another hand when you will be in the lead.

On Fifth Street, Sixth Street, and on the River, be more inclined to bet your hands, even if you haven't made them, when you are facing a rock. If, for example, you started with a wired pair, and have improved to a 3-Flush on board by Fifth Street, don't get cute. Bet into him. This play may, in fact, make sense against most opponents. But against a tight player it is imperative. Take the opportunity to win the hand as soon as you can, based on the scare cards. If he plays back at you, be inclined to fold.

On Sixth Street, if you are on a Straight or Flush draw, but have a scary board, bet it. Normally, you might assume that you would be called down from this point until the showdown. Typical players have a hard time folding on Sixth Street or the River (and, by the way, they generally blunder into a correct calling frequency this way). So your bets here, against typical opponents rarely have a chance of success. But against a rock who hasn't made his hand, or who imagines that his opponents have the best hand possible, bets on the later rounds become crucial. Especially if the pot began multi-way, and is thereby large, your bet needs only a small chance of success to make it worthwhile. When the concession frequency of your opponent is high, you must make these bets to maximize your profits.

Similarly so on the River. Some opponents are so tight that I will bet my hand as a matter of course on the River. At times I will even make a bluff raise because my opponent's timidity and self-control are sufficient for him to fold otherwise winning hands. These rocks can be bullied into folding. So you should not be afraid to shout!

Playing Against Good, Tricky Players

If you play in a casino regularly, before too long, you are going to encounter the very good, solid, aggressive Tricky Player. He has all the moves. He check-raises bluffs, he slowplays, and he reraises with second best hands to get heads up. He mixes up his play so much that you really never know what he's doing or why he's doing it. And he wins regularly. Maybe he normally plays a higher stakes game, but from time to time you are up against him. How do you handle him?

In general, fold more frequently than you normally would early in the hand but check and call more often than you normally would later in the betting. For example, let's say it's Third Street. He is to your right and raises with an 8. Two folds to you and five players left. One of the remaining players has a King. You have a split pair of 9s and a low kicker. Fold this hand.

It's a borderline hand anyway from early position. He's made it a complete bet. There are five players to follow you, one with a higher up card. Sure, you may be the best hand. But you're not giving up much of anything by folding. But by calling, you run the risk of being heads up with a guy you can't figure out who seems able to make your head spin.

Why bother? Wait until he's not in the hand or you have something really solid.

Similarly, imagine you have a low 3-Flush with an exposed 6. One of your suit is out. This good tricky player is to your left. The bring-in bets $2, five folds to you, leaving just this player and the bring-in. Fold this hand.

True, 3-Flushes can be played profitably for just the bring-in with three players. But the player on your left who has yet to act is aggressive and tricky. He may well raise you after you call. The bring-in is likely to fold to a raise (which this tricky player knows). So you're likely to end up heads up against this player when you only have a low 3-Flush. Not a good idea. (Compare it with playing against a very passive player who is very unlikely to raise the bring-in. Then, you'd figure to be able to see Fourth Street for only the bring-in and could correctly call here.)

On Fourth Street, same thing. Be less inclined to enter a hand without a lot of strength. Let's say that you are last to act on Third Street and call the bring-in with a 3-Flush. Three other players in the hand including this deceptive player are in the hand. On Fourth Street you don't get a Fourth Street suited card but improve by pairing your door card 5. The other three players have caught cards that don't seem to help them. The deceptive player is to your left. You are high. What do you do?

You think about betting. Should you bet the higher or lower tier? Neither. You should check and fold to a bet.

You didn't catch the card you wanted, which was a suited card. Your pair is low and you don't have a high kicker. You would only be betting as a semi-bluff. But it's a bad semi-bluff because you're unlikely to get all three other players to fold. And, you run the risk of having this aggressive, deceptive player reraise, get it heads up, and then eat you for lunch. Much better to check and hope that it's checked around, but if it isn't, fold to a bet. Save your money for a time when you're clearly in the lead.

Let me interject here that it is very hard for poker players to avoid confrontations like this. This is especially true if we are winning players. It hurts the ego to admit that there is someone at the table who is better and whom we actually try to avoid. It offends our sense of machismo. Even so, it will help your bottom line to avoid contests with good, tricky players. And that's the sign of being a good player—taking advantage of profitable situations while avoiding unprofitable ones. As we've said, playing against better players is an unprofitable situation.

On Sixth Street and the River, be more likely to check and call and less likely to initiate the betting or raising. Be less likely to fold. That's not to say that you don't bet your very strong hands or fold to obvious strength. But be careful.

Let's say for example that you were dealt a Premium Pair that you bet on Third Street. Your tricky opponent raises with a lower upcard than you; everyone else folds and you call making it heads up. On Fourth Street he catches a blank as do you. You bet. He calls. On Fifth Street you both catch blanks, but his is a second suited up card. You bet. He calls.

On Sixth Street he pairs one of his cards and bets. You catch a blank. You are tempted to fold. You have an over pair, but he seems to have Two Pair.

Don't fold. If this is a tricky aggressive player, you should call him down. True, he may have raised you on Third Street with a pair—maybe even a higher pair than yours. But he's unpredictable. He might very well have had three suited cards. Don't take the chance of him stealing a very large pot at this point. Call him.

Similarly, on the River, don't bet even if you have Two Pair. Just check. But make sure to call if he bets. He may very well have you beat, but the size of the pot combined with his unpredictable pattern of betting make a call essential.

Finally, let's talk about trying to figure out aggressive, tricky players. My advice is that you don't try to figure them out. Sure, they may have some giveaway tells that a world-class player might spot in a minute. But it's more important that you have been able to characterize them as tricky. Leave it at that. Avoid confrontations when possible. Play back at them as blandly as you can . . . unless of course you have a real monster in which case you should be as aggressive as the cards warrant.

The best analogy I can think of is Ping-Pong, known as table tennis by serious players. In the last thirty years the game has become increasingly dependent on the ability of the player to apply great spin to the ball. Faster and "spinnier" rubber and sponges have been developed for the serious table tennis player so he can impart greater and greater amounts of spin. What's the best defense against an experienced player who has some of this super fast, super spinning rubber on his paddle?

Well, for all but the very, very best table tennis player, the best defense is to have, on one side of your paddle at least, a type of rubber called *anti-spin*. It acts as a buffer to the spin. Now the player with this type of rubber can't put much spin on the ball himself. He gives up that ability. But because he can cancel out the spin of the attacking player, he can at least neutralize his opponent's advantage.

With a fast, tricky, aggressive poker player, you should either get out of the way completely by folding or respond with the poker equivalent of anti-spin. The more passively you play back at him, the less effect his tricky aggressive play will have on you.

Playing in Poker Tournaments

You should be able to apply what you've learned to another format for poker—poker tournaments. Many casinos have them. They can be great fun as well as an excellent way of playing poker against excellent players without running through your bankroll. And where else but in poker can a rank amateur actually play against the world's best players and have some shot at winning.

I played in the $1,000 buy-in 7-Card Stud tournament at Foxwoods' World Poker Final. I got half of my buy-in paid for by backers who wanted to have a piece of my action. So it cost me just $500 to play with the "big boys."

Along with me, 150 people entered the tournament, including one of the world's best—Huck Seed. He won the Championship No-Limit tournament at Binions at the World Series of Poker and a few dozen other major tournaments. And I was in the same damn tournament as he. Wow!

There were forty-minute stages. At the end of each the stakes went up. After two hours there had been considerable consolidation of the tables. I was moved, with a little less than the median amount of chips in front of me. When I looked around at my new table, whom did I see to my left but World Champion Huck Seed! Only in poker! For those of you not familiar with the big names in the poker world, it would be like going to the municipal golf course and being put in a foursome with Tiger Woods or Phil Mickelson.

Huck Seed, seated on my left. I tried not to show my awe.

I rocked around for a few hands, watching my stack slowly slip perilously close to the pathetic level. I won a small pot and got a renewed burst of confidence.

The next hand I was dealt a Pair of 7s, wired, with an exposed Ace kicker. A low card brought in the pot. A few players folded and it was to me. I, as naturally as I could, completed the bet, hoping everyone would allow me to steal the antes. Unfortunately, Huck called my bet with a nine. Everyone else folded.

Fourth Street: blank for Huck, Queen for me. "Well, big shot, what do you do now?" (I silently asked myself). Again, as calmly as I could, I bet (hoping Huck would fold). He looked at me blankly for half a second and called.

Fifth Street and I got a 10. Huck got a blank. Well, I figured that he must assume I have *something*! I wouldn't bet against the world's champion with nothing, would I? So I bet again. He called without hesitation.

On Sixth Street I didn't improve. I went all in with my last chips. He called.

The River didn't help me. And I was humiliated when I turned over a bare Pair of 7s. He won with a Pair of 9s.

Huck Seed knocked me out of the tournament. He went on to win it and a $50,000 first prize. So, naturally, I took credit for being the second best player in the tournament!

Tournament play is different from regular ring game play. (*Ring game* is the name they've come up with to distinguish regular poker from tournament poker.) I'm not going to provide an entire study of optimal tournament play, but here are the fundamentals so you can start to play tournaments without being intimidated.

With very few exceptions, tournaments are generally structured like this. Participants pay an entry fee that buys them a predetermined number of chips, which have a nominal value much greater, usually, than the amount paid for them. For example, a tournament entry might cost $35, but each participant would start the tournament with $500 worth of tournament chips. They can't be cashed in but are just "play money," which is used throughout the tournament.

You play poker with these chips, which often may be supplemented with additional chips, called *rebuys*, that may be purchased during the first hour or so of play. If there are no rebuys in the tournament, or once the rebuy period is over—usually after an hour or so—when you lose all of these chips you are out of the tournament. Play continues until one player has all of the chips. He is declared the winner and gets first place. The last player to be knocked out wins second place, the next to last third place, on down to the last place that is paid in the tournament. Typically, about 10 percent of the entrants or so win some prize, though this varies quite a bit among tournaments and the number of entries. First place usually pays 30 to 50 percent or so of the total prize pool (made up of all of the entries minus some fee for the casino), with each successive finisher receiving less money. Check with the card room to find out the exact payout structure of your tournament before you enter.

Usually, a tournament comprises more than one table of players. When players lose all of their chips, and empty seats arise, poker tables are eventually consolidated.

Say the tournament starts with eighty players—ten tables of eight players each. As soon as eight players in the tournament are knocked out, they will eliminate one table from action and reassign players to new tables accordingly.

Tournaments come in many different shapes and sizes. Many casinos and poker rooms have relatively small buy-in tournaments. These may attract anywhere from 30 to 200 players or so, for buy-ins of $10 to $100. Often these tournaments are weekly or even daily events. Some places have a different tournament every day of the week: Limit Texas Hold'Em on Monday, Omaha 8 on Tuesday, No Limit on Wednesday, 7-Card Stud on Thursday, and so forth. Some even have more than one tournament a day.

Tournament buy-ins typically include both an entry fee and an amount that goes into the prize pool. So you might see a tournament listed as $25 + $5, meaning that $25 goes into the prize pool, which is divided among the winner and other high finishers. The $5 goes to the house to pay for the dealer and other overhead.

For the $25 fee a player may get $500 in tournament chips to play with. These chips have no real value. They can't be cashed out or exchanged for any real chips. They are solely to be used in the tournament as symbols of value. The house could decide to make them worth $5 million dollars. It would have no impact on the size of the prize or the nature of the game.

Typically, tournaments have an escalating bet structure. Every thirty minutes or so the stakes go up. So the game might begin as $15/30 7-Card Stud, then after thirty minutes go to $30/60, after another thirty minutes $50/100, and so forth. The structure of the game would increase accordingly, with the antes and bring-ins rising along with the stakes. You should also know that the time limit for these rounds vary from tournament to tournament. In general, the smaller the buy-in, the shorter the rounds. This tends to increase the action of these small tournaments. In the eyes of some, that makes the fastest tournaments little more than crapshoots, with the stakes rising so quickly that players have little ability to show the patience necessary to demonstrate skill. These critics are mistaken, in my view. While quickly escalating stakes mean that luck may play a larger factor, there is still a great skill in making adjustments in play necessary to play correctly and win.

As I mentioned earlier, some tournaments, most in fact, have what are known as rebuys. This means that if you wish, typically for the first hour of play or so, you may add to your stack by buying more chips. There are limits, usually, on how many rebuys you may make, how many chips you may rebuy for, and how large your stack of chips may be to allow a rebuy. Typically, for example, you must have no more than the initial buy-in if you wish to rebuy.

Sometimes, the house allows *add-ons* in tournaments. This type of rebuy may be made only at the end of the rebuy period. Usually they may be made irrespective of how large your stack is. Typically, you may add on an amount equal to your original buy-in for half or some other fraction of the full cost of the initial entry. So, for example, if you were in a $25 + $5 7-Card Stud tourney with $10 rebuys and a $10 add-on, you'd get $500 worth of tournament chips for $25 when you started; you could rebuy $200 worth of chips for $10 during the first hour at any time you fell below $500 worth of tournament chips; and then you could add on another $500 worth of chips for $10 at the end of the first hour.

It is very important to know, before you sit down in a tournament, exactly what the structure is. Rebuy tournaments play very differently from tournaments without a rebuy. Players are often much more aggressive and loose during the rebuy period figuring that if they run out of chips they can reload. Things don't usually settle down with this tournament until after the rebuy period is over.

It is also important to know how the payout works. Some tournaments are winner-take-all; others pay the winner a huge percentage (as much as 60 percent) of the entire prize pool. Still others are much more flat, with the winner getting closer to 35 percent; second place, 30 percent; third place, 25 percent; and so forth. Your strategy would vary accordingly.

Some general strategies to consider include, first of all, the lowest stakes tournaments—$30 or less—often contain the very worst poker players in the casino. These players frequently play the very low spread limit games like $1–$3 or $1–$5 and are willing to gamble a little money for the chance of winning big in a tournament.

Frequently, they play very, very loosely and aggressively (if not maniacally), especially early on in the tournament if there are rebuys (which there usually are). They will raise and reraise seemingly without reason. In fact, their only reason for raising may be to have fun.

You must adjust to this. If there are rebuys, you can loosen up some as well—provided you don't become seduced by the crazy play around you and copy it. Play more 3-Straights and 3-Flushes on Third Street than you normally would. If the pot is multi-way and large you can even call from late position with a gapped 3-Straight like 7-8-10. Fold of course if you don't hit a 9 on Fourth Street. And only make this play if all of the 9s and nearly all the 6s and Jacks are live.

Similarly, you can play three high cards if the game is especially loose. Call with A-Q-J or K-Q-10 and other similar hands. Do this when they're live, in unraised pots. And fold on Fourth Street if you don't pair up. But since you're likely to be the best hand if you do pair, if you can get to Fourth Street relatively cheaply, do so.

I'd also suggest that if the Fourth Street pot is large and multi-way, you can take a fifth card for one bet on your 3-Flushes. If, for example, you have a 3-Flush and five or so others called a completed Third Street bet, but you failed to make a 4-Flush on Fourth Street, it would still be worth it to call a single bet, from late position, if there were likely to be four or more callers to

Fifth Street. Of course, make sure your suit is extremely live. This is a frequent occurrence in these low-limit tournaments.

For the remainder of the streets play straightforwardly, avoiding fancy plays or thinking too deeply about what your opponents are likely to have. Most of them are too aggressive and too loose for your clever plays to affect.

The higher stake tournaments generally contain better players. Some of them concentrate on tournaments. Their play is understandably stronger.

One thing that you might consider: Early on, these higher stakes tournaments are often very, very tight. Players are reluctant to drain their chip stacks early on, at least until and unless they have very strong hands. You can use your position and scare cards to your advantage, early in a tournament, to steal the antes by bluffing and semi-bluffing more.

This is especially true in no rebuy tournaments or immediately following the rebuy period. I've often noticed that players, who had been very loose and aggressive before the rebuy period ended, suddenly become rocks when the break is over. For the first couple of hands at least after the break is over, you can sometimes capitalize on players by raising with scary door cards even if you have nothing else to back it up. Of course, if anyone plays back at you, fold.

Tournaments have different stages to them, so adjust your strategy accordingly.

I'd suggest that, in general, you think about tournaments in three stages.

The first stage is during the rebuy period if there is one—or during the first hour or so if there isn't one. This is when loose and aggressive play predominates among the poor players. You can exploit them with solid play—nothing fancy or particularly aggressive. Your aim here is just to accumulate chips, not to knock other players out.

A standard rule of thumb is that you should double your stack by the end of the first hour or so. Admittedly, this is much easier said than done. And it doesn't really address any strategy considerations. But, insofar as it gives you some general goal of where you want to be to stay competitive with the field, bear it in mind.

The next phase, the middle phase, follows the end of the rebuy period. By the second hour, the stakes have risen sufficiently to knock out many of the poorer players and the maniacs. Play tends to slow down as people watch their stacks more carefully. It's important that you do the same. But you must also be more alert to the possibility of stealing antes and pots with selectively aggressive play. This phase changes as you near the point when players who remain will be in the money.

Let's say, for example, you entered a $30 tournament with 100 players. There were rebuys the first hour. After four hours there are 30 players left, with the final 16 players finishing in the money.

At this point, your play should be dictated by the size of your stack. If you have a large stack, you should become very aggressive against the smaller stacks. You are trying to take advantage of their fear of elimination before they make the money. They will be much less likely to risk elimination with medium-strength hands. So you need to play aggressively against them.

Similarly, if you are a large stack, you want to avoid confrontations with other large stacks. Don't risk getting eliminated in a war with someone who could knock you out unless you have a vastly superior hand.

On the other hand, if you are a small stack, you need to be very, very selective about entering pots. Don't play those 3-Flushes or 3-Straights. Only enter a hand if you have a hand that figures to be in the lead. You will become much more selective.

The final stage is when everyone is at the final tables where money is paid. You must continue to keep a careful eye on your stack relative to other players' stacks. At these final stages, every deal may mean elimination for someone. Pay close attention to that. Sometimes, even if your hand figures to be the best hand, it makes more sense to stay out of a pot and let other players battle it out.

Here's an example of that. It is late in the tournament. There are six players left. Nearly all of the prize money is in first, second, and third place.

Let's say you are dealt a split Pair of Aces. You have a small stack and will be all in by Fourth Street if you enter the hand. Two large stacks are to your left. The bring-in, to your immediate left, begins the betting. The King to her left with a large stack raises. The Queen to his left with an equal stack calls as does a 10 with a small stack like yours. An Ace folds. Another card, which matches your kicker also folds. It's to you.

Consider folding. The pot is four-way. True, you might win a monster if your hand holds up. But you will be all in if you call. You have little chance of improvement. And you can't thin the field or increase your chances of winning by raising.

Your best play is probably to hope that one of the big stacks knocks out three other players, putting you in third place. So you should think strategically for the situation you are in and fold your hand, even though it is almost surely the best hand out there at the moment.

One final consideration. Many players pay little attention to their play once their stack has become very small. This is a serious mistake. You should carefully consider how you spend your few remaining chips. Stories abound of players who were down to their last couple of chips and staged a comeback, winning the tournament.

I remember playing with the late, great poker author David Spanier in the World Poker Finals at Foxwoods. He was the tightest player I had ever seen. He was down to a tiny stack—but he made it last for well over an hour until he was hit with the deck, won six pots in a row, and went to finish just short of the money. It inspired me to take my chips seriously, no matter how few they were.

The next tournament I played in was in the Orleans in Las Vegas. About sixteen seats away from the final table, I was down to my last three chips. I resisted the urge to toss them carelessly into the pot on a low percentage hand.

The very next hand, I was dealt Aces. I went all in, won, and then went on to win three hands in a row. I made the final table, played well, and took home second place. I secretly thanked David Spanier for inspiring me not to give up just because my stack was small.

CHAPTER 6

General Poker Concepts

Psychology: Getting Your Mind Right to Win

One of my favorite movies with poker in it is *Cool Hand Luke*. There's that great little poker scene at the beginning when the hero played by Paul Newman gets his eponymous prison nickname. The prisoners are playing 5-Card Stud. Luke feigns a disinterested attitude toward the other players and their hands. He's dealt in anyway. He raises very casually while not looking at the other players or the cards as he raises. "Kick a buck," he says. The other player with a pair of Kings in is intimidated into folding. Luke has nothing. He was raising on a pure bluff. "Sometimes nothing is a pretty cool hand," he says.

However, another scene from that movie comes to mind when I think about psychology and poker. The head of the work camp, a sadist, is explaining the importance of learning how to be a prisoner. He talks about how the prisoner must follow the rules of the camp. "You must get your mind right!" he lectures in his shrill voice. This theme comes up repeatedly in the movie. The prisoners, Luke especially, must get their mind right if they are to stay out of trouble in that prison environment. If they don't they are severely punished.

This is especially true at the poker table. If you don't get your mind right you will be severely punished. Self-control is the first step in this endeavor. The emotions that flow around the table like a strong breeze must not distract you. It's hard to do this at first. I've already mentioned the problem of ego—of caring about whether you appear to be a good player to the other players at the table or in the room. Although it feels good to be recognized as a superior player, it is irrelevant to good play. Get your mind right.

Situations come up that tend to throw players out of their right minds. They tend to get upset and lose self-control when they are losing. Some lose control when they are winning. Others lose control when they have suffered a few bad losses in a row or taken a particularly bad beat. The common expression for this is *going on tilt* or *steaming*.

I know the feeling. Early in my casino career I was playing at Foxwoods. I had been playing tightly for a few hours, waiting for some decent cards, when I was finally dealt a great hand. I got Trips on the deal and bet them the whole way. I filled my Full House on the River. A guy who seemed to have a Flush raised me on the River when I bet. He was a loudmouth who always criticized everyone's play as weak or bad. I raised him. He reraised me. I raised him back. He reraised me. I called. He turned over quads—well hidden without even a pair showing.

I couldn't believe it. It was the second hand in a row that I had lost on the River, having led the whole way. I wanted to tear up my cards and scream. As it was, I pounded the table uncharacteristically and said "damn" before getting up and walking away.

I sat back down, vowing to make up the money I lost before I left. I started playing much more aggressively than I usually did. I raised with low pairs, I reraised with a Flush draw. And, the funny thing was, I started to win. Players, who had known me as a tight player, figured I must have what I was representing. So they folded. And twice I hit miracle cards on the River to win. I almost accomplished my pie-in-the-sky goal of getting back to where I was before the two bad beats.

My success fueled my frenzy. I started to raise blind, reraise raisers, and reraise reraisers. I lost three or four hands in a row and was down to my last $100. I decided that there was no point in playing conservatively. So I raised and reraised until I was all in. I lost and went home—down $900.

This doesn't have to ever happen to you. There are some things that I've found helpful in keeping me from going on tilt even when I have suffered some very bad losses.

Once I was playing at one of the nicest poker rooms in the United States, Canterbury Club in Minneapolis. My brother plays there regularly in the $3/6 7-Card Stud games. He generally does well, enjoys the regulars, and likes the atmosphere. He didn't have to ask me twice to join him.

At the time, they had a $15/30 7-Card Stud game (I've since heard that they don't get players at that level in 7-Card Stud anymore). I sat down to a short-handed table—a table with fewer than the standard eight poker players. There were only six of us.

I had a good run of cards for the first couple of hours. But they were just good enough to take me to the River, not good enough to win. Many of my Premium Pairs were outdrawn—meaning that players who were trying for hands like Flushes and Straights drew the necessary cards to fill those hands and make their Flushes and Straights. I lost with a Flush to a Full House a couple of times, and with a Full House to a higher Full House on a couple of other occasions. It happens to any regular 7-Card Stud player. By the fourth hour of play I was down $800.

I was disappointed. I recognized, however, that I was playing against very loose-passive players. This was good for my tight-aggressive style of play. When I bet they generally called. Over time, I was bound to get the money because I was playing hands that were statistically more likely to hold up and win at the end than the other players were. In the short run they were getting lucky. But that didn't change the fact that statistics and probability were on my side.

Though there were only five to six players, the pots were typically three-handed on the River. Some players always called Third and Fourth Street—programmed to see their hand develop at least until they had five cards. Frankly, I had rarely seen such a good game. Still, I had gotten beaten many times on the River, was feeling frustrated and angry at my misfortune, and ready to call it quits.

At that moment I remembered a posting I had made to the online poker discussion group Rec.Gambling.Poker—known familiarly by its initials RGP. I advised a new player about what to do when he faced a similar situation. I advised him to step away from the table for a while, collect his thoughts, analyze his play and the play of the other players, maybe get something to eat, and then—if he was convinced that the game was a good one and that he had calmed down enough to play his best game—he should reenter it.

This is exactly what I did. Just as I had advised, I took a seat in their nearby snack bar. I ordered some chili and took out my notebook. I wrote down what had happened. As I wrote, I forced myself to think through some of the hands I had lost. I gradually became convinced that I was playing well, making good decisions, and that I was playing against inferior opposition. After an hour, I decided to go back to the game.

One of the players had left. The game was now five-handed. I played another four hours. I didn't win right away. But after a couple of hours it was clear to me that my assessment was correct. The other players were all very, very loose and very passive. They called my raises and rarely raised me.

I played selectively but I called a few more hands early on than I normally would because I was nearly certain I wouldn't be raised on Third Street. I played my mediocre hands a little further because of the lack of betting pressure from the other players.

After four hours I had won back the $800 I had initially lost plus another $750! By the time I had reached this point, the game had dwindled to three-handed. So we decided to end it there. I had made a $1,550 dollar recovery in four hours.

Now I'm not saying that this will always happen. Of course it won't. But it surely won't happen if you allow yourself to get rattled or intimidated.

Psychology: Ego

It's sometimes tempting for the aspiring player to show off his knowledge. Let's face it. Winning at poker is tied in to our ego. We want to win so others will say, "He's a great player." But this ego need can really work against us at the table. I'll give you an extreme example of what I mean.

I was playing at the $10/20 table at Mohegan Sun. It was back when I worked in Connecticut for a union that represented broadcasters. The trip from my home to my assignment was about a two-hour ride, so I'd sometimes stay overnight. It gave me an opportunity to stop at Mohegan Sun and play. I was doing this a couple of times a month. My game was never sharper than it was then.

Anyway, I sat down at this $10/20 table. There were some familiar faces and some I had never seen. The room was very smoky. I was wearing my gas mask.

One of the players I recognized as a *table bully*. By that I mean that he always wanted to be the initiator of the betting action. He'd never call; he'd always raise. He peppered his conversation with insults and daggers at the other players, always putting down their play, rehashing the hand to show how smart he was and how he should have won, and how his opponents had played the hand wrong. He often got into arguments with the other players.

He and I had an interesting and telling battle one night. He was the bring-in with a 4. I completed the bet showing a 7 and with a wired Pair of Kings. He raised me. Everyone else folded. I called.

The hand progressed to Fourth Street. He got an Ace up and bet. I called. He got a blank on Fifth Street and bet. I got another King to go with my Pair of Kings in the hole and raised him. He reraised me. I decided he probably had, at best, Aces Up, figuring that if he had made Trip Aces he wouldn't have been so aggressive. So I reraised him. He reraised me back. I figured that, with this rereraise, he might have Trip Aces after all so I just called. On Sixth Street he and I both got blanks. He bet and I called. On the River I didn't improve, still having the Trip Kings. He bet and I called.

He turned over Aces Up and I turned over Trip Kings. He slammed his fist on the table and flung his cards at the dealer. "Damn!" he said. I said nothing. Then he looked at me with a half smile and said, "Well, you might have had the better hand but you'll never back *me* down!"

And he meant it. He was pleased with the way he had bet the hand even though his overvaluing of his Aces Up cost him at least two extra bets. It was more important to him to think of himself as a tough aggressive player than to make the right play.

Ego. You must do away with it at the table. It interferes with optimal play.

Here's another example from a game I played in. It comes up all the time. And it is a mistake I used to make more often than I'd like to admit. I don't make it anymore, but I'm sure many players do.

I was playing $5/10 7-Card Stud at Foxwoods. It was a relatively loose game with a few bad players. On Third Street I had an Ace showing and tried to steal the antes with a raise from late position. The bring-in 3 wasn't having any of it and called my raise.

On Fourth Street I got another high card, but still no pair. I was high. Rather than conceding that my steal attempt didn't work and checking, I tried betting again, thinking that my opponent might fold without any obvious improvement on his part. So I bet. He called.

I didn't improve on Fifth Street, nor did he have any obvious improvement. I thought that maybe for the double bet he'd fold to my high cards—crediting me with a high pair by now. So I bet $10. He called.

Sixth Street. I nervously thought that I was at risk of looking absurd by continuing to bet with nothing. If I were called on the River and had to show my awful cards, the other players would know I was just a bluffing fool who couldn't play serious poker.

So I checked—hoping that he'd bet so I could fold and avoid being humiliated on the River. But he checked.

On the River I actually paired one of my low cards. I think I made a pair of 2s. I thought about betting but figured he'd just call and then I'd be humiliated by having to show down my lousy pair. Everyone would think that *I* was the worst player on the planet for betting so often without a legitimate hand. So I checked. He checked behind me. He showed down a pair of 3s and won the pot.

I made about five mistakes. I tried to ante-steal from a bad player who would probably call me even if he had nothing. I compounded the mistake by betting Fourth Street against a bad player. I did it again on Fifth Street. And then, I checked the River when my only hope of winning the large pot was by betting.

But the biggest mistake was my motivation for betting. I was betting based on the image I wanted to avoid. I was made timid on the River by my fear of looking foolish.

This has no place at the poker table. You cannot play as if you care what other people think of your play. Worrying about your image sabotages optimal strategy. In fact, sometimes it's better to look like a bad player. And yet many, many players ask me how they can avoid looking stupid at the table. Why worry about this? Go ahead and look like an idiot! If people think you are clueless, they may play bad hands against you thinking you must have a worse hand. Or they may try some tricky moves to confuse you when their best play would be something more straightforward.

The Rake

The house takes money from every pot in a low- and medium-stakes poker game. Known as the *rake*, it generally comprises 10 percent of the pot up to a maximum of $4. So if you're playing $1–$5 Stud and you win a pot of $30, the house will rake $3 before they give the pot to you.

This is how they make their money in poker. Unlike all of the other games in the casino, poker players play against each other. You do not play against the house. They have no financial interest in the outcome of any hand. But they have to make their money somehow. How else would they pay for the overhead of tables, chairs, chips, dealers, cashiers, floor people while turning a profit?

You can generally expect to pay a rake on all games $15/30 and lower. Some casinos rake the $20/40 game as well. If the games are higher, the house generally charges *time*—an hourly fee paid directly by each player to the house every thirty minutes. No money comes directly out of the pot. In the $20/40 game, for example, each player simply pays $7 to the dealer every half hour. Think of it as a rental charge. The higher the stakes of the game, the higher the rental charge for playing in the game.

Most players pay no attention to the rake figuring that it's only paid when they win. This is a mistake. In fact, the rake can have such a great impact on the game that, at times, it can make the game completely unbeatable even for the very skilled player.

Here's a simple quiz that illustrates the pernicious power of the rake. Imagine there are eight of you—buddies from home who decide to come to a casino to play. You all sit down at the $1–$5 7-Card Stud table. You each have $100. You start to play at 4:00 P.M. on Saturday and play until midnight. The rake is 10 percent of the pot up to a maximum of $4.

The dealers are efficient. They average a little more than twenty-five hands an hour. For the sake of this example, imagine that there are exactly twenty-five hands that reach $40 or more every hour. If the best player is 50 percent better than the worst player, and they all play the same number of hands, how much money will the best player and the worst player have when they go home? Assume that they are all very cheap, didn't eat anything, didn't tip any waitress for their free drinks, and never tipped the dealer.

The answer is simple and easy. You only need third-grade

math to figure it out. The best player and the worst player will have the same amount of money at the end of eight hours. They will have $0.00! In fact, all the players in the game will have lost all of their money.

Here's the math. The casino takes $4 out of every pot, twenty-five pots an hour. That equals $100 in rake an hour. If they play eight hours, that is $800! They only brought $800 among them. All of it goes to the house!

Then why, you might ask, does anyone even play in a casino? If the house is going to rake the games to death, how can anyone ever win money? Good question.

The answer is, in my mind, that even these highly raked low-stakes games may be beaten because of the many bad players, with very deep pockets (at least collectively) who continue to take the seats of other bad players who bust out. The example I gave was for a strictly limited world of only eight players. In the real world of casino play, the worst players who bust out are continuously renewed with more bad players with more money. An expert player can win money in those situations.

Keep in mind, however, that it's much more difficult to beat this kind of a raked game than to beat a home game with no rake. And, significantly, some rakes are much tougher to beat than others. In some casinos, the lowest stakes games are raked at a higher rate than the higher stakes games. This is true in my home casino, Foxwoods. They rake the $1–$5 game more aggressively than the $10/20 or $20/40 game, for example. Although they take 10 percent with a $4 maximum rake in $1–$5, they rake the $10/20 game closer to 2 to 3 percent. All raked games have $1 taken when the pot is at $10 and the second dollar taken when the pot is at $20, but at $1–$5 the third and fourth dollar come out at $30 and $40, respectively. At $10/20 the third dollar doesn't come out until the pot reaches $80 and the fourth dollar doesn't get raked until the pot is at $160. At $20/40 it's an even better deal, with the third and fourth dollar not being raked until the pot is at $120 and $240, respectively. In case your math isn't too hot, that's less than a 2 percent rake at the top end of the $20/40 game.

You also need to think about the eventual size of the pot in the game you're in. A $1–$5 game may be raked at 10 percent, because there's a maximum of $4 that is taken out, but you're much better off if the game tends to have huge pots. If the pots tend to be small, you're always paying the maximum 10 percent to the house. But if the pots are large, your percentage paid in rake goes down. A $40 pot is raked $4, which equals 10 percent. But an $80 pot, also raked at the maximum $4, is raked at only 5 percent. A $160 $1–$5 pot (a rarity indeed) is raked at 2.5 percent.

So if the game you're looking at tends to be tight, with nearly all of the players folding on Third Street, you're going to have to beat a huge rake to win. That 10 percent, by the way, isn't 10 percent of your winnings in a hand. It's 10 percent of the entire pot. If it's just you and another guy, half of the money in the pot is yours, meaning that a 10 percent rake is really a rake of 20 percent of your winnings.

It's important that you know *how* the rake is taken. Not all 10 percent, $4 maximum rakes are the same. Consider these two examples of $1–$5 games. Both charge 10 percent and both have a $4 maximum.

In the first casino, the first $2 is taken right out of the antes. Each player antes $.50 for a total of $4. The house takes half right away. They take the next $1 when the pot reaches $30 and the final dollar when the pot reaches $40.

The second casino also charges a 10 percent $4 maximum rake. But they don't take the first rake until the pot reaches $10. They then take the second $1 when the pot is at $20. The Third and Fourth Street dollars are taken at $30 and $40, respectively.

Does this really matter? Absolutely. Your strategy must take it into consideration if you are to maximize your winnings. In the first game, which rakes $2 right out of the antes, it doesn't pay to play too aggressively on Third Street. If you win the antes, the house is going to rake 50 percent or so of your winnings! Think about it: 50 percent. That's the worst house *vig* (vigorish—the percentage of a bet retained by the house) of any game. You'd be better off playing the Big Wheel or Keno!

Now the second casino is no joy ride for the player either.

They still have a rake that will take nearly 20 percent of the player's winnings by the showdown if the hand is heads up. But at least the pot isn't touched until there's at least $10 in it. Therefore, your strategy can still include some aggressive play on Third Street. In fact, winning the antes, if it's possible with the loose players in the game, is about the only way to win without any rake whatsoever—making it a very good play (again, if it can be done against the typical loose player). Especially at the lower limits, the rake plays a major role in your strategy.

Can the typical 10 percent $4 maximum rake be beaten consistently in the $1–$5 game though? Experts disagree. My opinion is that it can. I'm not speaking from my own experience. I moved up to $5/10, $4/8, and $6/12 very quickly. But I have gotten to know a few players who claim to beat it. In fact, I became good friends with a player who is a $1–$5 professional poker player. He manages to eke out $15,000 a year (on which he doesn't pay taxes). He supports himself (though not his wife anymore—she's now his ex-wife) but lives very, very frugally, doesn't own a house (indeed, will never qualify for a mortgage if he doesn't pay taxes), and eats most of his meals in the players' lounge at the casino.

I know only a few others who are consistent winners at these very low-limit games. My advice is generally to avoid them if you can. If you have the bankroll, you're better off concentrating on beating the slightly higher stakes games of $4/8 and above where the rake is a considerably smaller percentage of the pot.

Summary. The rake may make very low-stakes games impossible for even excellent players to beat. If you can afford it, even if you're a novice, you might be better off starting at $4/8 or $5/10.

Odds and Ends

Many home game players are intimidated by the math of poker. They imagine playing against geniuses who can do elaborate computations in their heads. They figure that since they aren't similarly adroit, that poker for serious money in a casino just isn't for them. So they stay in their home games.

You don't have to be a math whiz to be an excellent 7-Card Stud player. In fact, if you are too focused on calculating your precise odds for drawing hands, you may hurt your game by missing the bigger and simpler picture.

The math of 7-Card Stud is actually very simple. Let's start at the beginning. First, understand that every decision in poker comes down to this. Is it a good or a bad bet? That's all you have to decide. Will your call, bet, raise, or fold be a good move or a bad move. Or, to put it in the language of a gambler, you need to know when you have the best of it and when you have the worst of it.

What makes a bet good or bad? You first must have a basic understanding of pot odds. Don't get scared. Yes, there is a little bit of math involved. But **no**, you don't have to have a calculator or knowledge of anything but fourth-grade math to master this.

Let's forget poker for a minute. Make sure you understand the difference between a good bet and a bad bet. Let's say you're back in fourth grade. A friend of yours is flipping a coin. You decide to gamble with him. You tell him that you'll give him $1 if the coin is heads and he'll give you $1 if it's tails.

That's a fair bet. It is neither good for you nor bad for you. Why? Because the odds are even and the payout is even. You will have heads 50 percent of the time, on average, and tails 50 percent of the time. You get the same amount when you win as you give to him when you lose. You are getting even money ($1 for $1) when the chances of winning and losing are even—1:1.

So it's a fair bet. Neither one of you has an edge; neither one of you has the better of it. In fact, the gambler in you might say, "What's the point?"

Now let's change the bet. You find some dumb third grader and you get him to accept the following bet. Every time the coin is heads, you will pay him $1. Every time it is tails he will pay you $2. Is this a good bet for this poor schlub?

No. He is going to have to pay out $2 when he loses but he will only get $1 back when he wins. The odds of him winning are still 1:1 but he is paying out 2 when he loses and only getting 1 when he wins. In other words, he is paying out 2:1 on a 1:1 probability. That's a bad bet.

You need to look at calling a bet in poker in the same way. Is it a good bet or a bad bet? Remember that poker is about the long run. In the long run you must get more from your call than you put in the pot. That seems obvious. You should get more from the game than you put into it. Of course.

But many players don't think about this at all. They call, bet, or raise based solely on the hand they have, without any consideration given to the size of the pot. This is a mistake. Let's look at the simplest example.

You are playing $5/10 Stud. It is Sixth Street. You have six cards. There is one more card to come. You hold a 4-Flush. There are just two of you left in the hand. Based on your opponent's exposed cards and bets thus far you are certain that she holds a Straight. You are going to need to fill your Flush to win the hand.

Okay. With me so far? Good.

Your opponent is high on board and bets $10. Do you call her $10 bet? If you answered "Yes" or "No," you don't understand the concept of pot odds yet and must read on.

The correct answer is that you *must* have more information to answer correctly. Before you know whether the $10 call is correct, you need to know the size of the pot. You need to know how much money you will win if you win the hand compared with how much money you must put in the pot to call the bet. This ratio of the size of the pot to your bet is called *pot odds*.

Okay. Still with me? Let's say that the pot is bet and raised early in the betting, with many people staying in until Fifth Street, when all but you and your opponent folded. So the pot is big. Let's say, to make this easy, that it's $100 on Sixth Street when your opponent bets $10.

That means that if you call his $10 bet, you are getting 10:1 odds from the pot. The size of the pot, $100, is ten times larger than your $10 call. $100 to $10 or, to simplify it 10:1. Easy, right? But it still doesn't tell you whether to call or fold. How do you know?

Some basic memorizing helps here. You need to know that the odds are about 4:1 against you making a Flush with just one card to come (actually 4.25 to 1 against you). I provide a table later that gives you some of these basic odds.

On average, therefore, every five times you go for that Flush on Sixth Street, you will make it one time and not make it four times. Again, on average, for every five times you call this $10 bet, you will win the pot one time and win $100. The other four times you will lose $10—or $40 total for all four times. That's $100 you win versus $40 you'll lose. $100 to $40.

Let me ask you the question again. If you are on Sixth Street and your opponent has a made Straight and you are drawing to a Flush, *and the pot is $100,* should you call your opponent's $10 bet? The answer is, yes.

In the simplest terms, if the pot odds offer you a better pay-out than your odds of drawing your hand, then it pays for you to call the bet. In this example you are getting 10:1 pot odds and the 4:1 probability of drawing your hand. That's called an over-lay. It is a good bet. You are getting the best of it.

Let's look at another example. Let's say that the hand was practically heads up the whole way with very little betting. In-stead of a pot of $100 on Sixth Street, the pot is $20.

The rest of the facts are the same. You have a 4-Flush and your opponent has a made Straight. Your opponent bets $10. Should you call the bet?

Well, let's do this simple math. The odds of drawing the Flush are the same as they were before: 4:1. The pot is $20 and your call will be $10. That's 2:1 pot odds. You're only getting 2:1 money for a 4:1 possibility. That is an underlay—meaning it is a bad bet—so don't make the call. That's all there is to it. It's that simple.

So all you need to know on Sixth Street are the odds of draw-ing your hand and the amount of money in the pot. The rest is up to you. Not all examples are that easy of course. You're not always certain that if you draw your hand you're going to win. Sometimes you have to take into consideration his additional chances of improving as well.

If, for example, you are going for your Straight and he has Trips and is drawing to a Full House then you both might improve. You might make your hand and still lose. Or, you might not know, exactly, what your opponent has. You might be pretty sure that he only has Trips but not completely sure that he doesn't have a Full House.

You must also consider the cards that you've seen. If you are drawing for a Flush and have seen a number of your Flush cards, you must lower the chances that you will hit your Flush. For example, if you have seen all of your suit folded before Sixth Street, there is zero chance you can draw your Flush. There are no suited cards left, so it's impossible.

It will help you to do more than memorize the general odds for drawing hands that I've listed later in the chapter. These odds apply to situations when you don't remember any cards that have already been folded. But if you can remember folded cards and observe cards that are still exposed, you can better estimate your chances of making your hand.

Now I'm going to complicate matters slightly by telling you two other factors that you might want to consider when faced with a bet: First of all, your decision isn't quite as precise as I am making it out to be. Remember that you want to compare how much you will win from your call compared with how much it will cost you to make your call. Thus far, we have had you consider the size of the pot when your call is made. So if the pot is $100 and the bet to you is $10, figure out whether to call based on the $100:$10 ratio.

But, in reality, there is another round of betting on Seventh Street—after you make your draw. The complete picture must take into consideration the amount you will eventually win if you win the pot. And that involves thinking about the last round of betting on Seventh Street.

The pot may be $100 on Sixth Street in the example above. But there is still one round of betting to come. So the amount you may eventually win is greater.

Look at it this way. If your opponent has a Straight and you are drawing to a Flush, and if you hit your Flush on the River and your opponent bets her Straight, you will win at least another bet—this $10 bet of hers on the River. And, you might win two bets if she bets, you raise, and she calls! Similarly, you'll win it even if she doesn't initiate the bet. If she checks, and then you bet with your Flush and she calls, you'll still win $10 more.

Compare that with how much you'll lose if you don't hit your Flush. If you draw for it and don't hit it, will it cost you another bet? No! Because on the River, if she bets and you haven't hit your Flush, *fold!* These are called *implied odds:* the amount you *expect* to win if you eventually win your hand compared with the amount you *expect* to lose if you don't hit your hand.

Let's look at a closer call. You have a 4-Flush on Sixth Street. Someone whom you credit completely with having a Straight bets $10 into a $40 pot. Do you make the call?

If you just used your understanding of pot odds, you'd be faced with winning the $40 pot versus the $10 call. The true odds of making your Flush are 4.25:1. So you'd be tempted to decline: $40 to $10 is worse than 4.25:1, so you'll have the worst of it, making this a bad bet.

But wait! You realized that if you did call and made your hand you'd actually be able to pick up at least another bet on the River, giving you $50 for your $10 call. You'd realize that you'd fold if you didn't make your hand—so you wouldn't have to put in any more money on the River if you didn't make your hand. So the implied odds would really be 5:1 for a 4.25:1 chance, making this a good bet and worth the call. In fact, it's even better than that if you believe your opponent might initiate the betting with his Straight and call your raise when you made your Flush. In that scenario you'd be getting $60 (the $40 in the pot, the $10 he would be with his straight and your $10 raise, which he'd call because he wouldn't fold his Straight when you raised him on the River) when you won the pot, versus losing $10 when you lost. The odds 6:1 versus 4.25:1 are certainly worth a call.

Now, it would be useful to know a few sets of odds automatically, without having to figure them or look them up. Use the following charts as your guide to call, raise, or fold in different situations. Memorize them!

Odds against improving with one card to come

4-Straight becoming a Straight (open-ended)	5:1
4-Straight (inside only)	11:1
4-Flush becoming a Flush	4.25:1
Two pair becoming Full House	11:1

Some other probabilities for you to use

Trips on Third Street becoming Full House or better	1.5:1
Two Pair on Fourth Street becoming a Full House	3.5:1
4-Flush on Fourth Street becoming a Flush	1.25:1
4-Straight on Fourth Street becoming a Straight (open-ended)	1.5:1

Peter O. Steiner, in his excellent poker book *Thursday Night Poker*, puts poker statistics in a format that you might find useful. He addresses the number of cards that will actually give you the hand you want on Fifth Street when there are two cards to come. So if you need a 3, for example, to fill an inside straight on Fifth Street, there are only four cards that can help you. He gives you the odds of that possibility. Similarly, if you have an open-ended straight but have seen three of the cards that will make your Straight, then five cards will help you. He gives the odds of that happening with two cards to come. His complete list follows.

Number of Cards That Will Make Your Hand	Probability	Odds
4 or fewer	.22 or less	3.5 to 1 or more against you
5	.28	2.6 to 1
6	.33	2.1 to 1
7	.37	1.7 to 1
8	.42	1.4 to 1
9	.47	1.2 to 1
10	.51	even money
11	.55	1.2 to 1 in your favor
12	.59	1.4 to 1 in your favor
13	.63	1.7 to 1
14 or more	.66 or more	2 to 1 in your favor*

*From Thursday Night Poker, by Peter O. Steiner.

The following shows you how your odds of making a hand change as your hand progresses.

Odds against making a straight

3-Straight (open-ended)	4.2 to 1
3-Straight (4 cards)	8 to 1
3-Straight (5 cards)	21 to 1
4-Straight (open-ended)	1.5 to 1
4-Straight (five cards)	2.1 to 1
4-Straight (six cards)	5 to 1
3-Straight (K-Q-J)	6.3 to 1
3-Straight (A-K-Q)	12.8 to 1

Odds against making a flush

3-Flush	4.5 to 1
3-Flush (4 cards)	8.4 to 1
3-Flush (5 cards)	23 to 1
4-Flush	1.13 to 1
4-Flush (5 cards)	1.86 to 1
4-Flush (6 cards)	4.1 to 1

Odds against making a full house

One pair (3 cards)	12.3 to 1
One pair (4 cards)	18 to 1
One pair (5 cards)	39 to 1
Two pair (4 cards)	3.3 to 1
Two pair (5 cards)	5 to 1
Two pair (6 cards)	10.5 to 1
Trips (3 cards)	2 to 1
Trips (4 cards)	2 to 1
Trips (5 cards)	2.4 to 1
Trips (6 cards)	4 to 1

It's also helpful to know how good a starting hand is. This means knowing the odds that it will turn into the quality hand on the River that you desire. So here are some stats that point you in the right direction.

Column one depicts the first three cards, and the odds *against* you making the hand in column two are listed in column three.

Trips	Full House	2 to 1
3-Flush	Flush	4.5 to 1
3-Straight	Straight	4.2 to 1
Pair	Two Pair	1.3 to 1
Pair	Trips	9 to1

Random Thoughts and Observations

Some random thoughts that might help you as you observe your game follow. Players who are about to leave the game rarely bluff. Thus, if you see someone who has either announced or has acted like she's leaving, and she bets or raises, believe her bet and fold unless you have a powerhouse.

Players who have just won a large pot and are still stacking their chips will rarely enter the pot unless they really have something worth playing. Players don't want to be distracted by playing a hand while they are "busy." If a player is in the middle of counting and stacking his chips, and raises, believe him.

Players who have just sat down tend to play conservatively at first. Bluff and semi-bluff against these players more frequently. Players who have just lost a huge pot, but still have a significant amount of chips in front of them, will rarely bluff. They often react to their large loss by tightening up. ("I won't make that mistake again," they think.) So you can more easily bluff. But don't do this against someone who has lost a large pot and has only a small stack in front of them. They are more likely to call any bet, thinking that they have nothing left to lose. They've given up and are either going to leave if they lose their whole stack or buy in again. Don't try to bluff them.

When you have a 3-Flush, with a Premium card or two in the hole and a low card up, you can sometimes raise the bring-in from early position to mix up your play. You do this with the expectation that you will bet again on Fourth Street no matter what you catch if your opponent doesn't catch anything scary and checks to you. For this to work, your opponent must be likely to be high on board on Fourth Street. This sets up a number of situations that are favorable for you.

First of all, he might fold to your bet, assuming that you had a wired Premium Pair. Second, if he calls you, he's likely to check to you on Fifth. If so, if you receive a fourth suited card you can check behind him for a free card, which might give you the Flush. Or if you catch something scary like a pair you can bet with the expectation of taking the pot right there on Fifth Street.

Taking It to the Next Level

Let's see where we are. You started with a basic strategy, capable of beating really good games while you learned the ropes of casino poker. You studied, you kept notes, and you recorded your wins and losses assiduously. You learned as you played and you started to feel more confident playing slightly more aggressively and against better opposition. You tried a few moves out and found out how to make them work for you. You became better at reading other players, dividing them into basic categories, and taking advantage of their general tells.

You have become a steady, self-controlled, disciplined player who understands how to find good games and how to find the right seat. You avoid going on tilt by leaving the table when you are distracted by a bad beat or a bad run of cards. You are able to concentrate on figuring out the right poker action to suit each situation. You aren't discouraged by your losses, but have learned from them and improved your play as a result of the mistakes you have made and seen others make.

After 1,000 hours of casino play or so you should be winning between one small bet and one large bet an hour. So you're thinking that you're ready to move up out of the lower and middle echelon of poker games into the higher regions of $15/30, $20/40, and above. What do you need to know before you take a stab at these games?

First of all, this book does not pretend to give you all the skills to beat those games. A thorough reading of David Sklansky, Mason Malmuth, and Ray Zee's *7-Card Stud for Advanced Players* would be in order. But I can give you some insight into what you need to do with your game to move up.

A Plan for Moving Up

Players often ask, "When am I ready to move to a higher limit game?" Of course, there's no definite answer. But, since I'm about trying to quantify the unquantifiable, let me give you my opinion on the matter. You need to be beating $4/8, $5/10, or $6/12 7-Card Stud before you should give serious consideration to taking a stab at $10/20 or anything higher. That's not to say that you can't do so sooner. Hey, it's your money! If you have the bread, there's no rule that says you can't sit down and start playing $100/200 whenever you damn well feel like it. I play with a guy in a home game who is not good at all. But he is very, very rich. His first experience was at $30/60. He loved it. Of course, I suspect that his opponents loved it even more than he did. But everyone's entitled to his own sort of fun.

So let's say you've been winning at $5/10. You aren't getting rich, but you have logged a good 500 hours of winning play and are now ahead about $10 per hour (one big bet) for your efforts. That would be a good point to start thinking about playing higher.

Players often ask how much they need to sit down at $10/20. This is a more complicated question than it first appears to be. Technically, all you need is the minimum buy-in. That's $100 in most casinos.

There's an advantage to this strategy, by the way. It's not one that I choose, but there are some things to recommend a minimum buy-in. First, if it's your first time at the game, you may not want to risk any more than the minimum amount of money. You might not even want to think about winning. You're just getting your feet wet, just getting into the mind-set of playing for a higher stake. Sit in a few hands, expecting that you are outclassed, overmatched, and ready to retreat at the first sign of pressure or difficulty.

Now I'd argue that you could do this without handicapping yourself with just the minimum buy-in. After all, even if you have $10,000 on the table, you could decide to leave as soon as you are down $100. No one forces you to stay.

Even so, many players tell me that they don't really have the self-discipline to leave in these situations. If they have money on the table, they play with it. They force themselves to leave if they run out of chips.

Essentially, what they're doing is putting up $100 just for the experience of sitting in a $10/20 game. But what kind of an experience is it likely to be when they're so short stacked? What can they really hope to learn from it? In my opinion, not much.

You'd be better off just standing and watching a $10/20 game for a couple of hours. You don't risk any money; you see how a particular game is played; and you can even get a feel for some of the players. Why blow $100?

If you're going to take a stab at $10/20 or any higher game, do what I did. Start with enough money to at least give yourself some room to absorb some bad beats and bad cards. For me, that meant at least $500. If I lost my first $500, I'd take a long break and think about what I was doing. If I was too rattled or tired or distracted to do a thorough evaluation of my play, I'd leave right then. If my evaluation concluded that I really was out of my element at the higher level (or if I wasn't sure where I stood), I'd leave as well, and drop back down to my comfort level. If I honestly assessed the situation carefully, however, and concluded that I was at least on par with the other players but had been suffering a string of bad luck, I might play on with the second $500.

Ideally, if I took this stab at a higher-limit game, I'd find out quickly that I was well suited to the game, was able to win at it, and could play it any time I found the right combination of poor players to suit my game. I could then continue to take stabs at it until my bankroll was sufficient to warrant a serious move to this higher level on a regular basis.

How much bankroll do you need to make this *complete* shift to a higher game? This depends on whether you have a renewable supply of money if you lose your initial stake. If you do—if you can continue to replenish your stake—you don't need any bankroll larger than your initial stake. Just renew it when the need arises.

But if your funds are finite, my simple answer is that you need to be able to play 500 hours to see if you can at least break even at a new level of play. That would mean, in my estimation, the ability to lose one to two small bets an hour for the entire period before I concluded that I wasn't really ready. That would mean a $5,000 stake to really play $10/20. And if you seem to have mastered that it means having at least $10,000 to really play $15/30. You'd want relatively more money to try out $15/30 because the games tend to be more aggressive, given the normal ante structure that encourages faster play. I have no empirical evidence for that. It's just my seat-of-the-pants estimate of what it takes to really try out a new level of poker. The key to all of this is the ability to critically analyze how you are doing. That's why I'd suggest that you study your game for at least a year or so, at the lower limits, before you attempt the higher ones. Even if you seemingly set the world on fire with winning play at $5/10 or $10/20, you should weigh the experience before you tackle the higher-limit games. How else will you know whether your winning ways at $5/10 or $10/20 were the result of great play on your part, incredibly bad play on the part of your opponents, or just a wonderful infusion of dumb luck. You need to have played long enough to be confident in your tools of self-criticism and analysis. They are your greatest weapons. That doesn't come with a bankroll. It comes only from experience.

Some poker theorists answer the question in a very different way. They estimate that players should have a bankroll of $15,000 or so to take on $10/20. But this assumes that this is all the money they had in the world with which to play poker. When they lost it they would be broke. In these calculations, the player needed to guard his bankroll more carefully as the stakes increased because of the difficulty of rebuilding a sizable bankroll. In other words, the bankroll itself became more valuable and less replaceable as it grew.

Accordingly, you can't just use an arithmetic progression to determine the necessary bankroll size: $100 for $1/2, $500 for $5/10, $1,000 for $10/20, $2,000 for $20/40, for example. You need to have more of an exponential progression: for example, $50 for $1/2, $1,500 for $5/10, $15,000 for $10/20, $150,000 for $20/40.

An interesting aside. When I first made the jump from $5/10 to $10/20 I did not beat the $10/20 game. I was clearly a loser. The tactics that worked for me in $5/10—essentially trapping bad players by playing more tightly and more carefully when I had weak or average hands and then much more aggressively when I did have a hand—did not suit the tighter, more aggressive $10/20 game. My records for the first year of my transition to $10/20 show a clear difference in my performance at $5/10 and $10/20. I was a "two big bet an hour" winner at $5/10 and about a "three small bet an hour" loser at $10/20.

Even so, the early experience I had at $10/20 helped my $5/10 game. I thought less about the money in $5/10 and was better able to think of the chips as markers in an intellectual exercise. I was significantly less intimidated by any action directed at me—allowing me to more readily loosen up when proper strategy demanded it.

My $10/20 game also got better as I played it. I remained thoughtful and made adjustments in my play. I could see, after reviewing my records every few months, progress in my game, moving from a large to a small loser over time.

After about fifteen months of moving between $5/10 and $15/30, I crept into the black for both $10/20 and $15/30. Eventually I became a winner of a little more than one big bet an hour at $10/20 and $15/30. I can now confidently practice good game selection among these four levels: $5/10, $10/20, $15/30, and $20/40. But it took a while, with many losing sessions, before I was fully able to master the higher stakes games.

Keep in mind that there's nothing wrong with dropping down in stakes to take advantage of a good game—especially if you're in a bad higher stakes game. If the $10/20 game is really juicy and you're playing with a bunch of excellent $20/40 players, you might do much better at the lower stakes game.

Remember, never let ego get in the way of winning. So what if other regular players see you in the more plebian setting of a $5/10 game. You're not running for office. You don't get a bonus for beating the toughest players. Even after you've made the jump to a higher stakes game, if it seems more profitable to take advantage of a good lower stakes game, you should do it!

Poker Quiz

Choose the best answer(s) to each of the following questions. The correct answers are listed at the end of the test.

1. Which of these is *not* a good reason to play 7-Card Stud?

    a. Can exploit players with bad card memory
    b. Availability of good-loose games
    c. Tend to be higher stakes than Texas Hold'Em
    d. More betting rounds in 7-Card Stud

2. How many hours should a good 7-Card student expect to play 7-Card Stud before he can expect to consistently win?

    a. 10–50
    b. More than 500
    c. 100–500
    d. It doesn't matter

3. Which of the following is the best example of the difference between home games and casino poker?

    a. Stakes
    b. Value of the hands

    c. Skill of the players

    d. Speed of play

    e. All of the above

4. What should you do before sitting down to play poker in a casino for the first time?

    a. Grab a bite to eat.

    b. Read a poker magazine.

    c. Buy a pair of sunglasses.

    d. Closely study every player at the poker table.

    e. Learn the rules for the casino.

5. Which of these is *not* necessarily a good habit to get into after a poker session?

    a. Record your win or loss for the session.

    b. Evaluate how you did.

    c. Write down the time and date of your session.

    d. Write down notes on players in your game.

    e. Point out to your opponents the bad plays they made during your playing session.

6. When starting out in a casino, which of the following *shouldn't* you generally do in a typical low- or middle-limit 7-Card Stud game?

    a. Make a lot of strategic bluffs and semi-bluffs.

    b. Converse with the other players.

    c. Alter your style based on the other players at the table.

    d. Stick to your plan of action even if you are losing.

    e. Leave the game if the players are tough.

7. A string raise is

    a. A raise that puts you all in

    b. Another word for a reraise

    c. A raise made in two motions

    d. A semi-bluff raise

    e. None of the above

8. Which of the following are generally allowed in casinos?

    a. Pulling in the chips when you win a pot

    b. Putting chips in the pot

    c. String raises

    d. Check-raising

    e. Going light

9. In a casino, the tip to the dealer must be

    a. No less than 10 percent of the pot

    b. No less than 5 percent of the pot

    c. No less than the smallest denomination chip on the table

    d. $.50 or more

    e. None of the above

10. True or False

    All casino 7-Card Stud games have an ante. _____

11. In a typical $10/20 7-Card Stud game, the most money you will have to put into the pot on Fourth Street is?

    a. $40

    b. $60

    c. $80

    d. Unlimited

12. In a $1–$5 spread limit game, the most a single bet on Fourth Street can be is

    a. $2

    b. $3

    c. $4

    d. $5

    e. $6

13. If someone bets $3 on Fifth Street in a $1–$5 Spread Limit 7-Card Stud game, which of the following raises is permitted? *(You may pick more than one.)*

    a. $5
    b. $2
    c. $8
    d. $1

14. Which of the following hands might you raise less than the full amount on Third Street in Spread Limit, which would nearly always warrant a raise in fixed limit?

    a. (A-3) A
    b. (9-9) 9
    c. (J-10) J
    d. (7-8) 9 suited

15. Which of the following might be accurately said of betting rounds in spread limit games after Third Street?

    a. Bluffing, semi-bluffing, and check-raising are done more frequently than in comparable fixed limit games.
    b. Large pairs go up in value and should be played more aggressively.
    c. Check and fold on the River more frequently than in comparable fixed limit games.
    d. Your hourly win rate should be less than in a fixed limit game.
    e. It is very similar to fixed limit.

16. If your spread limit game opponents tend to be looser and more passive than those in your fixed limit game, how should you adjust for this?

    a. No need to adjust. Poker is poker
    b. Play more aggressively with Premium Pairs.
    c. Generally play Jacks and Queens less aggressively on Fourth Street.

d. Raise less than the full amount on Third Street.

e. Be more inclined to call a reraise on Fifth Street than in a fixed limit game.

17. If you are playing in a casino, and you see a player with a baseball cap, sunglasses, and a silk jacket with a poker room logo on it, what should you do?

    a. Copy his play because he's a professional.
    b. Be intimidated.
    c. Tend to be less aggressive when playing against him.
    d. Tend to be more aggressive because he plays more tightly.
    e. Study his play as you would any other player.
    f. Make sure to play as aggressively as possible so he won't think you're a weak player.

18. If you were to summarize basic 7-Card Stud strategy, what would it be?

    a. Vary your play so you're unpredictable.
    b. Play as many hands as possible without going overboard.
    c. Take control of the table.
    d. Take advantage of your opponents overly aggressive play.
    e. Wait for good hands to play.

19. In general, if you find that you are playing against players who are better than you, what should you do?

    a. Quit the game.
    b. Tighten up play.
    c. Loosen up play.
    d. Raise more frequently.
    e. Raise less frequently.
    f. Use their strength against them.

20. Which of the following starting hands would you generally *not* play? *(Pick all that apply.)*

    a. (A-K suited) 8
    b. (9-8) 7 (unsuited)
    c. (A-6) 6
    d. (4-6) 5 (suited)
    e. (2-7) A

21. Which of them would you generally *raise* with? *(Pick all that apply.)*

22. In general, which of the following statements is most accurate?

    a. Though position is certainly important in every type of poker, it is less important in 7-Card Stud than in Texas Hold'Em.
    b. Position is more important on the later streets in 7-Card Stud than on the earlier streets.
    c. Since you don't know your position in advance of every street in 7-Card Stud, it really can't be taken into consideration.
    d. Even though your betting position may change on every round in 7-Card Stud, it's just as important in 7-Card Stud as it is in Texas Hold'Em.
    e. Because of the extra betting rounds in 7-Card Stud, position is actually *more* important than in Texas Hold'Em.

23. In a typical $3/6 7-Card Stud game, what action should you take in the following scenario?

    You have a split pair of 6s with a Queen kicker. The Deuce to your right opens the betting for $1. The Jack, 5, 4, 7, Ace, Ten, and Jack are yet to act.

    a. Fold   b. Call   c. Raise

24. Which of these statements is incorrect?

   a. Even under the best of circumstances, playing Straights is an iffy business.
   b. In deciding whether to play a Straight, the most important factor is whether the Straight is two suited.
   c. It's important to consider how high the cards in the Straight are before you decide whether to play it or not.
   d. You need to consider how live the cards are that might make the Straight.

25. You should generally fold your 3-Flush for what reason(s)?

   a. More than two Flush cards are exposed on Third Street.
   b. For any raise.
   c. If there are four players or fewer who are likely to play against you.
   d. Only one of your Flush cards is a Premium card.
   e. All of the above.

26. Which of the following statements is generally correct?

   a. Aggressive play on Fourth Street is usually the way to go.
   b. If you played on Third Street, you usually want to play on Fourth Street.
   c. The most important consideration on Fourth Street is the amount of money you have already invested in the hand. If you've called a raise on Third Street, stay for a bet on Fourth Street. But if you only called the bring-in, fold unless your hand is very strong.
   d. When you're starting out with 3-Flushes and 3-Straights, you should improve or fold.

27. On Fifth Street, which of the following statements is generally *true?*

    a. If your Premium Pair hasn't improved, tend to fold to any bet.
    b. If you figure to be the best hand, bet.
    c. If you've made your Flush or your Straight, go for a check-raise.
    d. If you have a Premium Pair and are up against a 3-Flush, you should generally bet.

28. On Fifth Street, if you have Queens up and your opponent pairs her door card King and bets, you should usually

    a. Raise
    b. Fold
    c. Call

29. If you are on a Flush or Straight draw on Fifth Street, and it's heads up, which of the following is generally correct?

    a. Plan to call all the way to the River.
    b. Fold if two or more of your cards have hit other players.
    c. Raise if one of your cards is an Ace.
    d. Fold to any bet.

30. In general, on Sixth Street, you should do which of the following?

    a. Tend to fold.
    b. Bet with a pair of Aces or better.
    c. Call if you are on a draw unless you see a board that is scary.
    d. Generally raise, unless you know you are behind.

31. Of the following, which is the biggest mistake you can make on the River?

    a. Not raising enough with the best hand
    b. Not bluffing enough

    c. Bluffing too much
    d. Folding too often
    e. Calling too often

32. In general, how important is game selection to a poker player's success?

    a. Perhaps the most important factor
    b. Not as important as studying your opponent
    c. Not nearly as important as most people think
    d. As important as a deck change

33. What is the key ingredient to a good game?

    a. A good dealer
    b. Lots of raising
    c. Good heads up competition
    d. Bad players who call a lot
    e. A serious mood so you can concentrate on your play

34. Of the following, which are signs that the game is good?

    a. The table is near the poker room entrance.
    b. The dealer is fast and talkative.
    c. The players are laughing and maybe a little drunk.
    d. There is a lot of cigarette smoke hanging over the table.
    e. There are many women and young players in the game.

35. True or False

If you are a good, solid player, you will win more, in the long run, in a game with at least a couple of solid players than you will win in a game with all bad players. _____

36. If you see a game that is usually four handed on the River, it is probably

    a. A good game
    b. A bad game
    c. Either a good or bad game; you need more information

37. True or false

    If a game is very tight, it probably isn't beatable by a good solid player. _____

38. What questions should you ask if you see a loose and aggressive game?

    a. How large is my bankroll?
    b. Are there any better games available?
    c. Do I have the stomach for big swings?
    d. All of the above.

39. What tends to happen to good games?

    a. They tend to get better as players go on tilt.
    b. They tend to break up as players lose their money.
    c. They tend to stay the same, as similar players cycle through them.
    d. They tend to tighten up as bad players get replaced by good players.

40. What is *not* a sign of a bad game?

    a. Few showdowns
    b. Short stacks
    c. Big stacks
    d. Aggressive play
    e. A lot of heads up action

41. Generally speaking, which is the best seat in a typical good game?

    a. To the immediate left of the tightest player at the table
    b. To the immediate right of the tightest player at the table
    c. Directly across the table from the most aggressive player
    d. With the most aggressive player to your left
    e. With the loosest player to your right

42. Pick the correct statement below.

    a. It's generally not a good idea to ask for a seat or table change more than once an hour; it makes other players angry and can hurt your play.
    b. The worst seat at a 7-Card Stud table is the one to the right of the dealer because when you fold, you can never see what card you would have gotten.
    c. In general, if you're a good player, where you sit doesn't really matter.
    d. It sometimes makes sense to disguise your reason for changing your seat.

43. Which of the following statements is incorrect for low- and middle-limit 7-Card Stud?

    a. The most important skill you can develop when starting out at casino poker is learning each player's idiosyncrasies or tells.
    b. Studying the individual mannerisms of your opponents is generally overrated.
    c. It is more helpful to put your opponents into general categories like "loose" or "tight" than to look for a telltale mannerism, twitch, or behavior.
    d. It's important to keep track of what your opponents do at the poker table.

44. If you have won three monster pots in a row, which of the following statements is most likely to be true?

    a. You may be able to use this winning streak to your advantage.
    b. You are more likely than normal to continue to get great cards.
    c. You are less likely than normal to continue to get great cards.
    d. Your three monster pots should have no bearing on how you play your next hand.

45. You should most seriously consider leaving your table, leaving the poker room, and going home when

    a. You lose at least 50 percent of your total bankroll.
    b. You have lost more than 100 big bets.
    c. You are tired.
    d. You have lost three times the minimum buy-in for the table.

46. True or False

    If you have had a long streak of bad luck and haven't gotten any decent starting hands for a long while, it can become harder for you to make money in the future at your table.

    _____

47. True or False

    A developing poker player can benefit by setting loss limits, win limits, and time limits when he is first starting out at casino play.   _____

48. What's generally the minimum buy-in for a $10/20 7-Card Stud game?

    a. $25
    b. $30
    c. $50
    d. $100
    e. $300

49. Generally speaking, how much money should you have with you if you wish to sit down in a $5–$10 game?

    a. At least $300
    b. At least $500
    c. At least $1,500
    e. At least $10,000

50. True or False

    Generally speaking, it makes sense to start your casino poker career at the $1–$3 table.

51. Once you've learned to play well enough to consistently win at the lower stakes tables, what are two major skills you'll need to develop to consistently beat the tougher higher stakes games?

    a. Money management
    b. Detecting cheating
    c. Reading other players
    d. Becoming deceptive
    e. Knowing how to dress like a high-roller

52. In a typical short-handed 7-Card Stud game your bluffing frequency, compared to a full game should generally

    a. Increase
    b. Decrease
    c. Remain about the same

53. Which of the following are factors you should consider when bluffing? Choose all that apply.

    a. The quality of your opponent
    b. Your image at the table
    c. The overall quality of your hand
    d. Your opponent's likely hand
    e. How many opponents you have
    f. The money in the pot

54. A bluff with a backup plan would be called what?

    a. Semi-demi-bluff
    b. Value bet
    c. Slowplay
    d. Check-raise
    e. Semi-bluff

55. Which of the following is *not* one of the seven clues to your opponent's hand. Pick all that apply.

    a. The cards that have been played
    b. Your opponent's betting action
    c. The size of the pot
    d. The type of player your opponent thinks you are
    e. The betting action and position of your opponent
    f. The sex of your opponent

56. Generally speaking, if your opponent rechecks his two down cards on Sixth Street, with two suited cards showing, what hand can you rule him OFF?

    a. Pair
    b. Two pair
    c. Trips
    d. Straight
    e. 4-Flush

57. In general, how would you adjust your regular strategy when playing in a tight game?

    a. Play more hands early, play them more aggressively, but if met with stiff resistance be more inclined to fold.
    b. Play more passively early, don't respect your opponents raises as much, and call more on the River.
    c. Be tighter and more aggressive.
    d. Be tighter and more passive.
    e. Do not make any significant adjustments in your strategy.

58. In general, how should you adjust your play when facing good tricky players?

    a. Be careful not to back down just because they play aggressively on Third Street.
    b. Play more aggressively early and more passively on Sixth Street and the River.

   c. Be more selective early and fold less on the River.

   d. Never play against them—leave the table if they are in your game.

   e. In general, do not adjust your play at all.

59. True or False

    When playing in a poker tournament, you need to adjust your strategy according to what stage of the tournament you are in. _____

60. Provide the best ending for the following:

    If all players in a casino poker room are evenly matched but they are all losing money, the reason is probably

    a. Someone is cheating.
    b. The stakes are too high.
    c. They have no self control.
    d. The rake.
    e. There are too many bad players in the game.
    f. Other players in the game.

Answers

1. c	21. None	41. e
2. c	22. d	42. d
3. d	23. a	43. a
4. e	24. b	44. a
5. e	25. a	45. c
6. a	26. d	46. True
7. c	27. b, d	47. True
8. d	28. b	48. d
9. e	29. a	49. a
10. False	30. c	50. False
11. d	31. d	51. c and d
12. d	32. a	52. b
13. a	33. d	53. a, b, c, d, e, f
14. a	34. c	54. e
15. e	35. False	55. f
16. c	36. a	56. d
17. e	37. False	57. a
18. e	38. d	58. c
19. a	39. d	59. True
20. a, e	40. c	60. d

Bibliography

The following books have helped me become a winning player. I recommend them all.

Brunson, Doyle. *SuperSystem*. Las Vegas: author, 1979.
This poker classic is excellent even after all of these years. Even in the sections on games that are rarely spread, like 7-Stud Hi-Lo no qualifier and 5-Draw, Brunson shows a serious poker player how to think about situations profitably. The other sections, especially on no-limit play, are as good as any of the more contemporary strategy books.

Card Player Magazine
This magazine comes out twice a month. It is the best source for news about America's card rooms, including a listing of tournaments, wonderful photo essays about the larger rooms, and excellent strategy articles. It is available online as well.

Caro, Mike. *Body Language of Poker: Mike Caro's Book of Tells*. Los Angeles: Caro Publishing, 1994.
An invaluable guide (available on video as well) on the general patterns of behavior and mannerisms of poker players, indicating the strength of their hand. Though the book has dated

photos from the 1970s and '80s, the analysis is 100 percent applicable today. I can tell you, without question, this book has taught me how to make a lot of money in correct calls, folds, and raises.

———. *Fundamental Secrets of Winning Poker.* New York: Simon and Schuster, 2002.
A great and very readable overview of general concepts necessary for winning play. Perhaps the best starter book for someone who has never played in a casino before and wants to understand, generally, what it takes to win.

Ciaffone, Bob, and Jerome Reubens. *Pot Limit and No Limit Poker.* Bob Ciaffone.
The Ciaffone sections are a must if you want to read about how to play No Limit or Pot Limit. They have turned me from a break-even player at Pot Limit Omaha into an overall winner. And they have helped me think more critically in limit poker as well.

Jones, Lee. *Winning Low Limit Hold Em.* Pittsburgh: ConJelCo, 2000.
This is the other excellent low-limit hold'em book. The conservative style advocated by Jones may not be a lot of fun for the action seekers, but in the no-fold'em hold'em games that are most common on the West Coast and in some Vegas casinos, this book is most useful.

Kreiger, Lou. *Poker for Dummies.* New York: John Wiley & Sons, 2000.
A thorough and eclectic mixture of information, humor, and strategy about poker. Though the poker strategy is somewhat superficial (you're surely better with Kreiger's other book on hold'em, for example) this book provides a very accessible and thorough overview of the poker world—from online casinos to home games.

———. *Hold'em Excellence.* Pittsburgh: ConJelCo, 2000.
One of the two best texts for beginning low-limit casino hold'em players. Even though I am not much of a hold'em player, I can hold my own with this simple and direct strategy.

Malmuth, Mason. *Fundamentals of Poker.* Las Vegas: Two Plus Two, 2000.
A great tool for beginners. No one will be burdened with too much to read. The two- or three-page summaries of strategy for each casino game are excellent, but obviously don't give you enough winning at the table. Even so, it will get you off on the right foot.

———, and Ray Zee. *Poker Essays,* Volume III. Las Vegas: Two Plus Two, 2001.
Three volumes of somewhat long winded and very interesting essays on poker concepts.

Silberstang, Edwin. *Winning Poker for Advanced Players.* New York: Cardoza Publishing, 1992.
A surprisingly good book from an author more associated with gambling than serious poker strategy. The author has a compelling style, making general concepts easily understood. Little in depth analysis but a good grasp of the basics that every winning player needs to know.

Sklansky, David. *7-Card Stud for Advanced Players.* Las Vegas: Two Plus Two, 1999.
The best book for advanced Stud play. It has helped me master the $15/30 games. The concepts contained in this book are also useful for all levels of play. Most readable after you have at least a few hundred hours of serious poker playing experience. Text not entirely clear to a relatively new Stud player.

———. *Sklansky on Poker.* Las Vegas: Two Plus Two, 1994.
Another useful book for getting you to think critically and

logically at the poker table. His analysis of Razz (a low version of 7-Stud) helps make complex poker thinking somewhat easier to understand.

————. *Texas Hold 'Em Poker for Advanced Players.* Las Vegas: Two Plus Two, 1999.
The best book for advanced hold'em play. I don't recommend it for learning basic strategy. But once you have mastered the Jones or Kreiger text and want to move up, this is the book to read.

————. *The Theory of Poker.* Las Vegas: Two Plus Two, 1999.
An excellent explanation of how to think about poker. Not without errors. But as good a general approach to poker as has been written.

Wallace, Frank. *Poker: A Guaranteed Income for Life by Using the Advanced Concepts of Poker.* Reno, NV: I/O Publishing.
An interesting and sometimes odd mix of basic poker strategy and general skills necessary to perpetuate profitable home games. Wallace obsessively looks at all of the skills needed to exploit those lesser skilled home game players whom you are likely to know socially. But he also provides many ideas for the serious poker player to ponder. If you are looking for a compendium of every possible home game edge you can create, this is the book for you.

Williams, Ted. *Science of Hitting* New York: Fireside, 1986

Software

Wilson Turbo Series
Wilson Turbo is simple to use, very fast, and has made complex poker software highly accessible. The series covers all the major games, as well as tournament simulations.

Masque World Series of Poker

A fun bit of simulation that creates a virtual World Series of Poker. The software isn't nearly as challenging as the toughest players on the Wilson software. But the mimic of the WSOP makes this worth having.

Newsgroups

TwoPlusTwo

A more cerebral and serious poker discussion group, moderated by Twoplustwo staffers. I find the interface more difficult to deal with than RGPs.

Rec.Gambling.Poker

This is the most popular online poker discussion group, with all of the advantages and disadvantages attending thereto. As expected, there are a good number of flames, spams, and otherwise worthless posts. But there are also many worthwhile things to read about the game we love.

Glossary

All-in Having used all of one's chips to call a bet or a raise.

Ante-steal Winning the antes on a bluff.

Ante An amount of money that each player must put into the pot before they are dealt a hand.

Balk A baseball term that describes a pitcher's motion to home base in an attempt to get a runner on first base to attempt to steal. It is not allowed. The runner is awarded the base when a balk is declared.

Bellybuster An inside straight draw. "Hitting a bellybuster" means hitting an inside straight.

Bet A wager. The act of making a wager.

Blank A card of no apparent help.

Bluff A bet designed to get other players to fold by misrepresenting a strong hand when a player really has a weak hand. The act of making such a bet.

Board The up cards.

Bring-in To initiate the betting by being the lowest card showing. The initial bet itself. The person who is required to bring in the bet.

Brush A casino employee who often directs players to tables.

Button The player who is designated as the dealer for betting purposes in Hold'Em and other games with community cards such as 5-Draw, LoBall, and Omaha. The large disk, usually made of plastic, used to make such a designation.

Call To place into the pot an amount equal to the bet of the immediately prior bettor. The amount placed into the pot when making a call.

Calling station A person who calls a lot and raises little.

Cards speak A poker rule that declares that the best hand wins, regardless of what the player declares. Often invoked in hi-lo games.

Check A declaration by a player that he chooses not to initiate the betting in any betting round. The act of making a check.

Check-raise A check with the intention of raising when someone else initiates the betting in any round of betting. The act of making this check and then the subsequent raise.

Check-raise bluff A check-raise designed to induce an opponent to fold by misrepresenting a strong hand when the player really has a weaker hand.

Check-raise semi-bluff A check-raise designed to induce an opponent to fold by misrepresenting a strong hand when the player really has a weaker hand but still may improve to a stronger hand on the next card dealt. The act of making such a check-raise.

Comps Complimentary goods or services, such as free meals, given to players after a certain amount of play.

Connectors Cards in sequence. Often with "suited" as in "suited connectors."

Counterfeit A second card of the same rank dealt to another player in Stud.

Dead Some or all cards that will improve the hand unavailable because they have already been exposed.

Dealer's Choice A type of poker game where each player may declare which poker game is being played, either for his deal or for some predetermined number of hands.

Dog Underdog. Not likely to win.

Door Card First up card.

Down Card A card dealt to a player that remains unexposed until the showdown.

Drop A rake taken from the pot at the beginning of the betting, instead of at the end.

Fast Usually used to describe game conditions with a lot of raising and reraising. Very aggressive play.

Fifth Street The third round of betting in 7-Card Stud, when each player has five cards—two face down and three face up.

Fish A bad poker player, especially one who is too loose and passive.

5-Draw Also 5-Card Draw. A common variation of poker where each player receives five down cards and then may exchange some or all of his cards. It is rarely played in casinos, though a variation of it, where the low hand wins, is still occasionally spread.

Fixed Limit Stakes that are limited to a specific amount on each betting round. For example, $10/20 would allow for only $10 bets or raises on Third Street and only $20 bets or raises on Fifth Street and all latter Streets of betting.

Floorperson A casino employee who helps settle disputes and otherwise attempts to keep games going and running smoothly.

Fold To decline to participate further in the hand, typically done when faced with a bet that a player declines to call. The act of making a fold.

Force The person who must make the forced bet.

Forced Bet The required bet of the lowest card showing on the first round of betting.

Frequent player points Points typically awarded by casinos or poker rooms as credit for players to use for the purchase of goods or services at the casino.

Fourth Street The second round of betting in 7-Card Stud, when each player has four cards—two face down and two face up.

Go light In a game that is not played table stakes, the act of taking out of the pot and putting to the side an amount of money equal to the amount of money owed to the pot by a player who does not have enough money in front of him to call a bet or a raise. This is typically not allowed in casino games.

Hold'Em Texas Hold'Em. A popular casino poker game in which each player gets two down cards, with five mutual cards dealt face up. The player makes his best combination of the mutual cards and the hole cards.

Implied odds The odds that the pot will eventually offer you if you make all of the expected bets and your opponents make all of their expected bets.

Kicker The third card when a player has a pair in three cards. Typically this is a high card. For example, a player dealt the 4♥, the 4♦, and the Ace♠ would have "A Pair of 4s with an Ace kicker."

Live Not having been exposed in front of other players and thereby available to improve your hand.

LoBall A variation of 5-Draw with the low hand winning the pot. Often played with a Joker as a wild card.

Lollapaloosa A freak hand of five unmatched cards, not including face cards, which beats every other hand.

Loose A style of play typified by a lot of calling.

Maniac A very loose player who also raises a lot, seemingly without reason.

Maximum rake The most the house may rake from a pot. Typically, this is expressed after the percentage of the pot that the house takes. For example, a 10 percent $4 maximum rake means that the house takes 10 percent of the pot up to a maximum of $4 a hand.

Newbie An inexperienced poker player.

NL No Limit.

No Limit Stakes that are not limited. A No Limit game, played table stakes, would allow for each player to bet, at any time, all of the money he has in front of him.

Offsuit Not of the same suit.

Omaha A popular casino game where each player receives four down cards with five mutual cards. The player may use two and only two of his down cards combined with three and only three of the mutual cards to make his best hand. Often played Hi-Lo 8 or better.

Omaha/8 Omaha, played Hi-Lo 8 or better. A popular casino game.

Online On the Internet.

Overbet To bet more than the value of the hand would normally call for.

Pass To check. In some places, this also means to fold.

Passive A style of poker or type of poker player characterized by little or no raising.

Pocket Pair A wired pair. A pair in the hole, especially on the deal of the initial three cards.

Pot The amount of money in the center of a poker table that is awarded to the winning hand (or winning hands in a split pot).

Pot limit Stakes that are limited to the size of the pot.

Pot odds The odds that the pot is offering you for calling a bet.

Protected pot A pot with more than two remaining players, especially on the last round of betting.

Push A home game variation of poker wherein each player may "push" an up card to another player.

Quads Four of a Kind.

Raise An action by a player that increases the size of the bet. The act of taking this action.

Rake The amount taken out of the pot by the house. Also the act of taking this amount out of the pot.

Replace A home game variation of poker wherein each player may exchange a card, usually for some predetermined amount of money.

Reraise A raise of a raise. The act of making a raise of a raise.

RGP A poker newsgroup: Recreational. Gambling. Poker

River Another name for Seventh Street, the fifth and final round of betting in 7-Card Stud, when each player has seven cards—three face down and four face up.

Rock A very tight player.

Rockaramma A situation in a game when there is a lot of folding. A game full of rocks.

Round Each betting interval, after which another card is dealt or the final showdown of the hand takes place.

Runner runner Hitting two perfect cards in a row to make a hand. Getting a "runner runner" Flush would mean getting two suited cards in a row to make the Flush.

Scare card An up card that looks like it might help an opponent, especially a high card.

Seventh Street The fifth and final round of betting in 7-Card Stud, when each player has seven cards—three face down and four face up.

Semi-bluff A bluff that has some expectation of improving into the best hand on the next card dealt.

Semi-demi-bluff A bet that may be representing the strongest hand, may win the pot as a bluff, and may improve into the best hand on the next card dealt.

Set Trips. Three of a Kind.

7-Card Stud A standard casino game played with seven cards, four of which are dealt face up. The hands consist of the best poker hand among five of the seven cards.

7-Stud8 7-Card Stud, Hi Lo, with an 8 low or better necessary to qualify for the low half of the pot, played cards speak (not declared). This is the typical 7-Card Stud Hi-Lo game found in casinos.

Side pot That pot established after a player is all in between the remaining players who are still entitled to betting action.

Sixth Street The fourth round of betting in 7-Card Stud, when each player has six cards—two face down and four face up.

Skeet A freak hand consisting of a 2, a 5, a 9, and two cards in between a 2 and a 9 without making a pair. Typically it beats Three of a Kind but loses to a Straight.

Skeet Flush A freak hand that is a skeet and a flush. It typically beats every hand except for a Straight Flush.

Slowplay To deliberately hold off on making a bet or a raise in order to represent a weaker hand than a player actually holds.

Softplay To deliberately play a hand less aggressively than it would typically be played against another player. Done, usually, to avoid confronting a friend, colleague, partner, or family member.

Splashing the pot Putting money directly into the pot, especially in such a way as to make a determination of the amount placed in the pot difficult.

Split Pair A pair dealt with one down card and one up card on Third Street.

Spread Limit Stakes that can vary between a preestablished range. For example, $1–$5 Spread Limit would allow betting of between $1 and $5 at any time in any of the rounds of betting.

Stakes The betting structure of a game that limits how much may be bet or raised.

Steam To tilt. To play very aggressively and erratically when out of control.

Street A round of betting in 7-Card Stud, typically preceded by a number indicating the total number of cards each player has. For example, Fourth Street would be the second round of betting when each player has four cards—two face down and two face up.

String-raise A raise made in two motions, wherein someone moves chips in to the pot to call the bet and then returns to his stack and makes a second motion to raise the pot. This is not allowed in a casino.

Stud A type of poker where some of the cards dealt to each player are dealt face up. The typical casino stud game is 7-Card Stud. Other variations include 5-Card Stud and Razz, which is 7-Card Stud low.

Suited connectors Cards in sequence and of the same suit. The 7♥ and 8♥ would be suited connectors.

Sweat To watch the play of another player.

Table stakes Stakes that are limited to the amount of chips a player has in front of her when a hand begins.

Tells Actions, usually unintentional, made by players that may reveal to other players the true strength or weakness of a hand.

Third Street The first round of betting in 7-Card Stud, when each player has three cards—two face down and one face up.

Tight A style of play typified by a lot of folding.

Tilt A condition whereby a player's betting action is out of control, often typified by a lot of loose calls and inexplicable raises.

Time An amount paid to the house by every active player in a game typically collected every half hour.

Toke A tip, especially to the dealer. To give a tip.

Twist A home game variation of poker whereby each player may exchange a card, usually for some predetermined amount of money.

Underbet To bet less than the value of the hand would normally call for.

Up card A card intentionally dealt face up to a player.

Value bet A bet made based on the superior value of your hand relative to the hands you are playing against.

Vig Vigorish. The House advantage in a casino game.

Wired A pair dealt down to a player on Third Street.

WSOP World Series of Poker.

Index

About the Author

Ashley Adams was born in 1957 and he began playing poker with his grandfather at age four. Adams has played winning poker in more than 100 venues all over the world, winning tournaments in Connecticut, California, and Las Vegas. He is a regular contributor to the newsgroup rec.gambling.poker and the Internet information site www.thepokerforum.com, providing advice and analysis for poker players. He has also coached several players who have gone on to become consistent winners at low- and medium-stakes casino poker.

By profession he is a union negotiator and representative for teachers as well as an agent for television broadcasters. He has appeared on television and radio to talk about issues affecting teachers, broadcasters, and poker players. He finds that many of the skills that have helped him at the poker table are very useful at the negotiating table and vice versa.

He lives in Boston, is happily married, and is the father of two girls, both of whom play poker.

Printed in the United States
64240LVS00007B/16

9 780818 406355